JOURNAL FOR THE STUDY OF THE NEW TESTAMENT SUPPLEMENT SERIES
143

Executive Editor
Stanley E. Porter

Editorial Board
Richard Bauckham, David Catchpole, R. Alan Culpepper,
Margaret Davies, James D.G. Dunn, Craig A. Evans, Stephen Fowl,
Robert Fowler, Robert Jewett, Elizabeth Struthers Malbon

Sheffield Academic Press

The Cross in Corinth

The Social Significance of the Death of Jesus

Raymond Pickett

Journal for the Study of the New Testament
Supplement Series 143

Copyright © 1997 Sheffield Academic Press

Published by Sheffield Academic Press Ltd
Mansion House
19 Kingfield Road
Sheffield S11 9AS
England

Printed on acid-free paper in Great Britain
by Bookcraft Ltd
Midsomer Norton, Bath

British Library Cataloguing in Publication Data

A catalogue record for this book is available
from the British Library

ISBN 1-85075-663-5

CONTENTS

Acknowledgments	7
Abbreviations	8

Chapter 1
TOWARDS A CONTEXTUAL READING OF PAUL'S REFERENCES
TO THE DEATH OF JESUS — 9
   A Critical Review of Scholarship — 9
   Methodological Considerations: The 'Performance'
      of Paul's References to the Death of Jesus — 24
   Paul as Hermeneutical Theologian — 27
   Social Worlds and Symbolic Universes — 29
   Social Description — 34

Chapter 2
THE CROSS AND CHRISTIAN UNITY: 1 CORINTHIANS 1–4 — 37
   Introduction — 37
   The Social Situation Reflected in 1 Corinthians 1–4 — 39
   The Crucified Christ as the Foundation of the Community:
      1 Corinthians 1.18-31 — 58
   Imitation of the Weak Apostle as the Solution
      to the Problem of Disunity — 74

Chapter 3
THE CROSS AND MORAL DISCOURSE IN 1 CORINTHIANS 5–14 — 85
   Introduction — 85
   The Context of Paul's Ethical Discourse in 1 Corinthians 5–14 — 86
   The Question of Social Identity and the Logic
      of Paul's Moral Exhortation in 1 Corinthians 5–14 — 97
   The Word of the Cross as the Foundation
      of the Ethical Discourse in 1 Corinthians 5–14 — 107

Chapter 4
FUNCTIONS OF PAUL'S REFERENCES TO THE DEATH OF JESUS
IN 2 CORINTHIANS 4.7–5.19 126
  Introduction 126
  2 Corinthians 4.7-12:
    The Death of Jesus and Paul's Apostolic Identity 129
  2 Corinthians 5.14-15:
    The Death of Jesus and Existence for Others 142
  2 Corinthians 5.16-19:
    The Death of Jesus and the New Creation 150

Chapter 5
THE SOCIAL SIGNIFICANCE OF THE DEATH OF JESUS:
2 CORINTHIANS 10–13 160
  The Purpose of Chapters 10–13 160
  The Criticisms of Paul's Apostleship Reflected
    in 2 Corinthians 10–13 163
  The Source of the Criticisms: Paul's Opposition in Corinth 170
  Paul's Reply to the Opposition 176
  The Conflict in Values Underlying Paul's Dispute
    with the Corinthians 183
  The Social Significance of the Weakness and Power of Christ 192
  The Cross as a Symbol for Social Change 208

Epilogue
CHRIST CRUCIFIED AND THE CORINTHIAN COMMUNITY 212

Bibliography 215
Index of References 222
Index of Authors 228

ACKNOWLEDGMENTS

The publication of this revised version of my University of Sheffield dissertation brings to a close a journey that began more than twelve years ago. I have rewritten the introductory chapter and tried to incorporate more recent scholarship into the exegetical discussion. However, there continues to be a steady stream of literature that is pertinent to this topic, and, unfortunately, I have not been able to include it all. If this work contributes anything to the conversation about the nature of early Christianity in Corinth and to the perception of Paul as a pastoral theologian, then I will be gratified.

I would like to express my thanks to all those along the way, too many to name, who have encouraged and supported me in this endeavour. Andrew Lincoln was an exemplary supervisor and has taught me much. His attention to the details of exegesis and his knack for getting to the nub of the matter are but two of the qualities that attest to his erudition. His constant willingness to reflect with me about theological and hermeneutical questions and his friendship have enriched my life more than he will ever know. When I was trying to finish the dissertation while serving an ELCA congregation in Tulsa, Oklahoma, Brandon Scott befriended me and was a constant source of intellectual stimulation. He has been a mentor to me, and much of what I think about the New Testament and early Christianity is the result of his influence. I would also like to thank Stan Porter of Sheffield Academic Press for his interest in my work and for his suggestions on how to improve it.

Most of all I am grateful to my wife Leah for her encouragement and support throughout the years. She supported us financially for the three years we were in England, and has been a partner in this project in every respect for the duration. I could not have completed this work without her constant affirmation and gentle insistence that I see this revision through to its publication. Now that it is done I dedicate it to her and to our children, Benjamin and Sarah.

ABBREVIATIONS

BHT	Beiträge zur historischen Theologie
Bib	*Biblica*
CBQ	*Catholic Biblical Quarterly*
EvT	*Evangelische Theologie*
HNT	Handbuch zum Neuen Testament
HTR	Harvard Theological Review
Int	*Interpretation*
JAAR	*Journal of the American Academy of Religion*
JBL	*Journal of Biblical Literature*
JRH	*Journal of Religious History*
JSNT	*Journal for the Study of the New Testament*
JTS	*Journal of Theological Studies*
NovT	*Novum Testamentum*
NTS	*New Testament Studies*
RB	*Revue biblique*
RevExp	*Review and Expositor*
RSR	*Recherches de science religieuse*
SBLDS	SBL Dissertation Series
SBLSP	SBL Seminar Papers
SBLSS	SBL Semeia Studies
SJT	*Scottish Journal of Theology*
SNTSMS	Society for New Testament Studies Monograph Series
TDNT	G. Kittel and G. Friedrich (eds.), *Theological Dictionary of the New Testament*
TynBul	*Tyndale Bulletin*
ZNW	*Zeitschrift für die neutestamentliche Wissenschaft*
ZTK	*Zeitschrift für Theologie und Kirche*

Chapter 1

TOWARDS A CONTEXTUAL READING OF PAUL'S REFERENCES TO THE DEATH OF JESUS

Paul's interpretation of the death of Jesus figures prominently in all of his authentic letters. In dialectical relationship to his rendering of the resurrection, it is the linchpin of his theology. Even a cursory comparison of references to the death of Jesus in Paul's writings, however, betrays the multivalence of this soteriological symbol. The significance Paul ascribes to the death of Jesus in any given context is always shaped by his rhetorical aims and his perception of issues and concerns in the community at the time he wrote. Hence the death of Jesus was for Paul a symbol with a surplus of meaning. A synchronic reading of the various ways he expounds its significance mitigates attempts to identify the essence of what it represented.

A selective review of some of the scholarly literature on the death of Jesus in Paul attests to the variability of its meaning. Nonetheless, students of Paul have consistently sought to identify what they consider to be the core or most essential aspect(s) of his theology of the cross, and have therefore neglected other nuances of signification. In tracing some of the trajectories of interpretation it is possible to highlight both some of the conceptual categories used to discern the significance of the death of Jesus for Paul, and, more importantly, a number of questions that call for further consideration.

A Critical Review of Scholarship

One of the more predominant conceptual categories in studies of the death of Christ in Paul is that of participation. In his classic work *The Mysticism of Paul the Apostle*, Albert Schweitzer argued that the foundation of Paul's thought was his concept of union with Christ. On this interpretation, the death of Christ was perceived as a cosmic event, which, along with the resurrection, brought to an end the domination of the powers of this age. According to Schweitzer, 'although the outward seeming of their natural existence remains unchanged', the elect are assimilated to Christ and hence become 'beings in whom dying and rising have already begun'.[1] Death and resurrection were thought to be a process at work within the believer whose destiny has been linked with Christ's through mystical union.

Others have followed Schweitzer in regarding participation as the primary conceptual frame of reference in discerning the significance of the death of Jesus in Paul. In his monograph *Dying and Rising with Christ*, Robert Tannehill builds on Schweitzer's work. Like Schweitzer, Tannehill emphasizes that the death of Christ is an eschatological event which provides the basis for life in a new world. For Tannehill, though, the decisive factor in the transition from the old to the new aeon is that human beings are placed under a new Lord.[2] He differentiates between those statements which refer to dying with Christ as past event, and those which refer to it as present experience. Dying with Christ as a present experience is seen to occur primarily through suffering. It is a dying to the old aeon, 'the world of "flesh" and of trust in self'.[3] In this respect, the change of lordships established by the founding events of Christ's death and resurrection is a reality that is apprehended inwardly, and is manifested pre-eminently in the form of a new self-understanding and trust in God.

No one has argued more persuasively that participation in Christ is the central theme in Paul's theology than E.P. Sanders in his *Paul and Palestinian Judaism*.[4] Sanders recognizes that Paul inherited the view that Christ died for trespasses, but in his view those passages that speak of death 'with Christ' reveal its true significance in his thought. Sanders's view of participation in the death of Christ is similar to that of Tannehill inasmuch as it entails being freed from the power of sin to serve a new Lord. However, he claims that an existential interpretation

---

1. A. Schweitzer, *The Mysticism of Paul the Apostle* (London: A. & C. Black, 1931; reprint New York: Seabury Press, 1968), p. 110.

2. R. Tannehill, *Dying and Rising with Christ* (Berlin: Töpelmann, 1967), p. 15.

3. Tannehill affirms that dying and rising with Christ in the present is also manifested as ethical action (see *Dying and Rising with Christ*, pp. 77-80).

4. E.P. Sanders, *Paul and Palestinian Judaism* (Philadelphia: Fortress Press, 1977), p. 146. Sanders asserts that its centrality is substantiated by the fact that 'it is the theme, above all, to which Paul appeals in paraenesis and polemic'.

does not do justice to Paul's conception of participation in Christ's death. So while he agrees with Bultmann against a magical understanding of participation, he does not agree that dying with Christ is ultimately a matter of the elimination of self-reliance so that one can trust in God.

For Sanders, participation in Christ's death involves more than a new self-understanding. He prefers to take Paul 'as saying what he meant and meaning what he said: Christians really are one body and Spirit with Christ...'[5] It is this realism that is the most distinctive feature of Paul's conception of participation in Christ, and yet also poses the greatest challenge for interpreters who have no means of apprehending his conceptual framework. Therefore, having demonstrated the priority of the language of participation in Paul's letters, Sanders can only conclude by conceding that he has no category of perception by which to comprehend real participation in Christ.[6] The practical implications of the death of Christ are inextricably connected with a vision of reality that enabled Paul and other believers to identify themselves with their Lord in his death. The problem is that the ancient symbolic process through which *real* participation may have been apprehended is not easily retrieved by the modern reader.

An important premise of Sanders's study is that for Paul the solution precedes the problem. This means that Paul's evaluation of the human 'plight' was derived from his interpretation of the significance of Christ's death. This presupposition distinguishes Sanders from many scholars who deem Paul's theology of the death of Jesus to have been conceived in response to the soteriological question: how can another procure atonement for my sins? Since Paul was a Jew who lived during a time when the temple cult was operative, his explication of how the death of Jesus dealt with the problem of sin has often been seen to have its antecedents in Jewish theology of sacrifice and atonement. H.J. Schoeps, for example, attempted to show that the 'Aqedath Isaac' was the key to Paul's conception of the soteriological significance of Christ's death.[7] He averred that in rabbinic teaching, the 'Aqedath Isaac' was a sacrificial deed flowing from a divine command that had expiatory efficacy for Israel's sins. Adapting this pattern of thought to explicate

---

5. Sanders, *Paul and Palestinian Judaism*, p. 522.
6. Sanders, *Paul and Palestinian Judaism*, p. 523. He emphasizes, however, that this does not mean that Paul did not have one.
7. H.J. Schoeps, *Paul: The Theology of the Apostle in the Light of Jewish Religious History* (Philadelphia: Westminster Press, 1961), pp. 110-18.

the atoning power of the messianic sacrificial death required only that Paul substitute God for Abraham and Jesus for Isaac.

The difficulty of establishing criteria to validate this sort of history of religions approach to Paul is betrayed by the work of W.D. Davies, who also looks to rabbinic Judaism for the generative ideas of his theology. In *Paul and Rabbinic Judaism* Davies devotes thirty pages to an examination of sacrificial concepts in Paul's rhetoric of the cross only to conclude that these concepts were not native to him because of his rabbinic attitude to the sacrificial system.[8] The late date of extant rabbinic literature makes it inherently problematic as a conceptual frame of reference for Paul's thought, but the more profound deficiency of this approach concerns the superficial nature of the supposed analogies. Mere lexical parallels do not necessarily imply conceptual convergence. There are indeed traces of the language of sacrifice in the letters, but Paul's dependence on the logic of Jewish sacrificial practices is not immediately evident.

In a recent study of Romans, Stan Stowers has made a strong case for the inadequacy of the sacrificial explanation of Rom. 3.24-25, the passage which serves as the primary basis of Paul's supposed doctrine of sacrificial and vicarious substitutionary atonement for human sinfulness.[9] Drawing on anthropological and history of religions study of animal and human sacrifice, Stowers argues that the sacrificing cultures of the Mediterranean attached no special significance to the death of the animal itself. Moreover, he observes that

> The purpose of the sacrificial system both as represented in the priestly sources of the scripture and as instituted in the second temple period was not to atone for personal sin or provide a means for dealing with human alienation from God; these ideas have been projected onto the temple system by Christian and later Jewish theology.[10]

What Stowers's rereading exposes is a tendency to project onto Paul various conceptual frameworks, often erroneously construed, which are presumed to elucidate the logic of his thought. Attempts to reconstruct

---

8. W.D. Davies, *Paul and Rabbinic Judaism* (Philadelphia: Fortress Press, 1948), p. 256. Davies asserts that sacrifice was not the primary factor in Rabbinic thought on sin and atonement, but rather certain moral and spiritual realities. Foremost among these realities was repentance.

9. S. Stowers, *A Rereading of Romans* (New Haven: Yale University Press, 1994), pp. 206-13.

10. Stowers, *A Rereading of Romans*, p. 207.

the structure of Paul's thought on the basis of the constellations of ideas present in the texts are problematic to say the least. These mental constructs are embedded in a larger socio-historical context, and their function in that milieu must serve as the frame of reference for their meaning in the letters. There is no facile way of moving from culture to consciousness. The Pauline letters are artifacts of both, and at best they attest to the dialectical relation between signifier and signified.

Scholarship on the death of Jesus in Paul has largely been preoccupied with questions of consciousness; that is, what Paul *thought* about its significance. The predominant interest in soteriology and how the death of Jesus provides deliverance from sin is a case in point. It is apparent that Paul's theology of the cross does imply an anthropology which presumes the need for the redemption effected by the death and resurrection of Jesus. But when Paul's anthropology is construed exclusively in terms of soteriology, the nexus of interpretation is limited to the mythological scheme of sin and salvation. In other words, his rhetoric of the cross is not decoded in terms of the larger cultural-linguistic context. Davies, for example, says that it was Paul's profound consciousness of sin that revealed to him the depths of meaning in the death of Jesus.[11] Yet Paul's theological language evinces the linguistic conventions and social practices operative in the religious communities to which he belonged as much, if not more, than his own world of thought or emotional state.

The point is that Paul's soteriological terms have connotations for his audience, and do not simply disclose his own theological convictions. So while it is apparent that sin is indeed a theme in certain passages in Paul's writings (e.g. Rom. 1.16-32), there is nothing in these texts themselves that betrays anything of his own sense of sin, so to speak. Whether or not Paul had a 'robust' conscience may be an interesting question from a diachronic point of view, but it has little or nothing to do with the rhetorical aims served by his use of the language of sin and salvation. Even the standard method of deciphering what on the surface appear to be explicitly theological terms in the light of their use in the Old Testament does not pay sufficient attention to how the language is used in a particular context. The semantic domains of much of Paul's theological vocabulary are more extensive than can be adduced by a consideration of morphological derivation.[12] A broader context that

---

11. Davies, *Paul and Rabbinic Judaism*, p. 230.
12. See J. Louw and E. Nida, *Greek–English Lexicon of the New Testament*

defines the range of meanings for Paul's soteriological language is culture, a concept that specifies the global social environment of the speech event.[13]

In his recent book, *Theocracy in Paul's Praxis and Theology*, Dieter Georgi has shown that words such as εὐαγγέλιον, σωτῆρ, πίστις, δικαιοσύνη and εἰρήνη, words that are loaded with soteriological significance in Romans especially, were also important to Roman imperial ideology that ascribed religious significance to the emperor.[14] It is interesting to imagine what kind of images and associations might have been conjured up for Roman Christians who heard this narrative about a 'saviour' other than the emperor whose death exemplified a 'faithfulness' that established 'peace' between God and humanity. It is the narrative structure or framework of Paul's soteriological language that gives it its force, and this one example serves to illustrate that there was more than one option available. On Georgi's reading it is the interplay between the soteriological drama Paul sets forth and the imperial soteriology that is important. The significance of the death of Jesus is defined for Roman Christians in terms of a competing socio-political scheme of salvation that had been imbibed with theological import.

The merit of a study like Georgi's, whether one finds his conclusions compelling or not, is its emphasis on the wider cultural frame of reference. It is not just that Paul's gospel had social implications; its meaning and significance were predicated upon shared cultural values and linguistic conventions of Jews and Gentiles who lived in the Greco-Roman world of the first century. In Gal. 3.1 Paul underlines the importance of the fact that 'Christ was publicly exhibited (προεγράφη) as crucified'. He appeals here to a common public notion of what crucifixion meant in the ancient world. He plays on this further at the end of the letter when he asserts that 'the world has been crucified to me, and I to the world' (6.14). Although Paul begins the letter with an allusion to the soteriological significance of the death Christ as the one 'who gave himself for our sins to set us free from the present evil age', he develops it into a form of cultural criticism of the 'world', or 'the

Based on Semantic Domains (New York: United Bible Societies, 1988), pp. vi-xi.

13. See the discussion of the sociolinguistic model of Halliday in B. Blount, *Cultural Interpretation: Reorienting New Testament Criticism* (Minneapolis: Fortress Press, 1995), pp. 8-16.

14. D. Georgi, *Theocracy in Paul's Praxis and Theology* (Minneapolis: Fortress Press, 1991), pp. 83-88.

present evil age' as he describes it in 1.4.

Despite the presence of the language of soteriology in Galatians, the scheme of salvation which is thought to pervade Romans appears to be conspicuously absent.[15] In this letter Paul develops a theology of the cross over against a rival interpretation of the gospel propounded by his opponents in Galatia. This 'other' gospel betokens not only a different way of construing the significance of the Christ-event, but also contingent circumstances in terms of which Paul developed pertinent connotations of his own understanding of the death of Jesus. If, as Richard Hays argues, a narrative substructure underlies Paul's presentation of the gospel in Galatians, it has been shaped not only by the internal (theo)logic of the narrative itself but also by these external factors.

A preoccupation with soteriological questions in literature on the death of Jesus in Paul has eclipsed interest in circumstantial variables which may have influenced his appropriation of that symbol. From the perspective of soteriology, the primary focus is on the narrative logic of the drama of salvation through Christ. In his article on 'Paul's Understanding of the Death of Jesus', James Dunn appeals to the notion of Christ as representative man to elucidate the plot of the drama of salvation in Christ.[16] According to Dunn, the death and resurrection of Jesus represent the destiny of those who identify with him.[17] Christ dies the death of the disobedient so that the new humanity can emerge in risen life. Dunn weaves together three disparate passages (Rom. 8.3; Phil. 2.7; 1 Cor. 15.27) to depict Jesus as the man who through his obedience unto death fulfilled the destiny God originally intended for all humanity.

Dunn's treatment of Paul's understanding of the death of Jesus falls within the larger spectrum of soteriological approaches. What differentiates his study from other attempts to explain Paul's conception of how the death of Jesus addressed the problem of sin is that for him narrative logic takes precedence over historical antecedents. Typically soteriological explanations of the significance of Jesus' death at least tacitly assume that there is an underlying narrative or mythological substructure that has a certain coherence, but concentrate primarily on

15. Stowers challenges the idea that salvation is the central issue in Romans in *A Rereading of Romans*.
16. J. Dunn, 'Paul's Understanding of the Death of Jesus', in R. Banks (ed.), *Reconciliation and Hope* (Grand Rapids: Eerdmans, 1974), pp. 125-41.
17. Dunn, 'Paul's Understanding of the Death of Jesus', p. 130.

analogous soteriological paradigms that Paul might have drawn on to interpret the death of Jesus. Dunn, on the other hand, intuits some of the problems with the analogy of sacrifice, and proposes instead the idea of representation as a conceptual construct that renders the rationality of the soteriological narrative intelligible.[18]

Dunn begins his analysis of Paul's understanding of the death of Jesus on the history of religions trajectory. However, he does not follow the trajectory very far before he recognizes the impasse to which it leads, and so takes a sharp turn while remaining in the domain of soteriological concerns. In order to make sense of what the death of Jesus meant for Paul, he essentially leaves the world of historical analogy to focus on the internal logic of the drama of salvation. It appears as though Dunn is responding to the dilemma noted by Sanders, that we have no category of thought by which to grasp real participation in Christ's death. On a narrative level his interpretation works, but only because, unlike those who have taken a history of religions approach, he has extricated Paul's interpretation of the death of Jesus from its socio-historical context.

The irony of Dunn's view is that one of his concerns is to show that the Jesus of history played an important role in Paul's soteriology; not so much for what he said or did during his life but for who he was.[19] What he recounts, though, is a mythologization of the historical figure of Jesus, whose historical importance amounts to his representative life of obedience. Morna Hooker has offered a similar interpretation of Paul's understanding of the death of Jesus, and appeals to the Adam myth to ground this mythological rendering of Christ's death in Judaism, thus attempting to provide a historical frame of reference for Paul's soteriological myth. The death of Jesus dealt with the problem of sin and the fallenness of humanity inasmuch as 'Christ became what we are, Adam, in order that we might share in what he is, namely the true image of God'.[20] The premise here is that the story of Adam's transgression is the basis of a typology upon which Paul's view of sinful humanity was predicated. Read in the light of Adam's fall, Jesus' obedience unto death is seen to reverse the disobedience of the

18. For Dunn, the notion of representation clarifies the sacrificial meaning of Jesus' death. This is necessary in his estimation because the narrative or mythological rationale of sacrifice in second temple Judaism is irretrievable if not intractable.
19. 'Paul's Understanding of the Death of Jesus in Paul', p. 126.
20. M. Hooker, 'Interchange in Christ', *JTS* (1971), p. 355.

Adamic state in which all humanity abides.

Although this line of reasoning could help to explain the function of Paul's narrative of salvation through Christ's death and resurrection vis-à-vis other soteriological myths, it is hampered by the fact that Jewish literature before 70 CE shows little interest in the effects of Adam's transgression. Jon Levinson has argued that this exegetical approach is illustrative of the tendency to squeeze Jewish data into the mold of Pauline concepts and motifs. According to Levinson, 'the use of early Jewish texts to provide background material for Paul's letters led to an unwarranted emphasis upon certain dominant Pauline motifs, such as "Adam: the Origin of Sin and Death"... '[21] Levinson has put his finger on a methodological defect of approaches to Paul's understanding of the death of Jesus that have soteriology as their primary focus.

In most instances, the soteriological scheme in terms of which Paul interprets the death and resurrection of Jesus is seen to be derived from Judaism. However, if there is no historical warrant for such a preoccupation with sin in second temple Judaism before 70 CE, then it has been retrojected back onto Paul, and the Judaism that shaped him, from somewhere else. This is probably another reflex of the effective history of the tradition as read by Augustine and Luther which Stendahl unraveled more than thirty years ago.[22] Whatever the source(s) of this way of reading Paul, the conspicuous absence of historical analogies in the Judaism of Paul's day calls into question the emphasis on the scheme of sin and salvation that is presupposed in much Pauline scholarship. Although both concepts can be found in Paul's letters, they are not as central as has often been suggested. Moreover, since an anachronistic definition of these terms has been projected back onto Paul, it is evident that he was using a different lexicon than his modern interpreters.

Any literary text has at least two fields of reference, an internal one and an external one.[23] The internal field of reference is another way of referring to the narrative world itself. The narrative world is virtually a self-contained world of plot and characterization that is usually

---

21. J. Levinson, *Portraits of Adam in Early Judaism: From Sirach to 2 Baruch* (Sheffield: JSOT Press, 1988), p. 13; cited by Stowers, *A Rereading of Romans*, p. 87.

22. K. Stendahl, 'Paul and the Introspective Conscience of the West', reprinted in *idem, Paul among Jews and Gentiles* (Philadelphia: Fortress Press, 1976), pp. 78-96.

23. R. Funk, *The Poetics of Biblical Narrative* (Sonoma, CA: Poleridge Press, 1988), p. 288.

intelligible without appeal to anything outside the text. Dunn's article on the death of Jesus is a good example of a method concerned with internal frame of reference. His explanation of the narrative logic of Paul's story of salvation through the death and resurrection of Christ serves to render it intelligible and more palatable to the modern reader. But apart from an external field of reference, there is no way to ascertain the historical credibility of any given reading, for literary texts are always embedded in the culture in which they are produced. On the other hand, many of the studies that have employed a history of religions approach to locate the antecedents of Paul's understanding of the death of Jesus in second temple Judaism indicate some of the difficulties in attempting to discern the meaning of his statements in relation to a heterogeneous Jewish tradition.

As was already mentioned, a more comprehensive historical frame of reference of Paul's interpretation of the death of Jesus is the Greco-Roman world. In his study *The Atonement: The Origins of the Doctrine in the New Testament*, Martin Hengel shows that a more compelling analogy for the concept of atonement in the New Testament is found in the Greco-Roman ideal of the apotheosis of the dying hero. This ideal was important in a variety of philosophical and religious literary traditions in the Greco-Roman world, and a place where Jewish and Greek conceptions were already fused in the pre-Christian period.[24] Although this theme evolved over time and there are a number of variations, the essential idea is that the hero dies as a martyr for truth and justice on behalf of the common good of the city or the people.[25] This death was seen to be an expiatory sacrifice that had atoning significance. Hengel provides numerous examples of this concept in ancient literature from Homer on, and notes that one fixed ingredient of almost all these traditions is that the voluntary sacrifice was thought to be in response to a divine command.[26]

This idea of heroic, voluntary and vicarious sacrificial death for the common good was familiar to the whole Greco-Roman world, and so would have served as a frame of reference for many of Paul's statements about the significance of Christ's death. This model of vicarious sacrifice also plays on the notion of representation emphasized by

---

24. M. Hengel, *The Atonement: The Origins of the Doctrine in the New Testament* (Philadelphia: Fortress Press, 1981), p. 5.
25. Hengel, *The Atonement*, p. 15.
26. Hengel, *The Atonement*, p. 23.

Dunn. The narrative structure of this version, however, is not based on an idiosyncratic reading of various Old Testament texts, but rather reflects some of the fundamental values and beliefs held by Jews and Gentiles of the Greco-Roman world. Although most of the examples cited by Hengel come from Greco-Roman literature, this ideal also finds expression in the martyr theology of *4 Maccabees*.[27] One of the advantages of reading Paul's commentaries on the death of Jesus through this historical-cultural lens is that it focuses on how his audience might have apprehended what he wrote.

Using this Greco-Roman cultural paradigm of vicarious sacrificial death as a point of departure, Hengel develops a genealogy of Paul's interpretation of the death of Jesus. He rightly observes that the stereotyped form of many of Paul's statements expressing the saving significance of Jesus' death point back to primitive Christian traditions. The most important of these is the 'dying formula' that is found in amplified form in 1 Cor. 15.3b: Χριστὸς ἀπέθανεν ὑπὲρ τῶν ἁμαρτιῶν ἡμῶν. Hengel traces this back to the earliest Hellenistic community, and asserts that it did not undergo any essential metamorphosis when Paul took it over.[28] Paul can cite this traditional interpretation without clarification because he presumes familiarity with it on the part of his readers.

The pre-Pauline tradition about the death of Jesus serves as a rather stable foundation from which to examine the ways Paul adapts and develops it, thus expanding on its meaning. But Hengel is more interested in the origins of the tradition than how it was developed by Paul. Although the first part of the book is devoted to the Greco-Roman background of the saving significance of Jesus' death, the emphasis lies on how the 'Christian message fundamentally broke apart the customary conceptions of atonement in the ancient world and did so at many points'.[29] Hengel attempts to trace the pre-Pauline and Pauline traditions about the death of Jesus back to the earliest Christian community's experience of the risen Christ, and even back to Jesus himself.[30]

There is a tension in Hengel's study between historical method and

---

27. For a compelling interpretation of Paul's references to the death of Jesus in the light of Jewish martyr theology see S. Williams, *Jesus' Death as Saving Event: The Background and Origin of a Concept* (HDR, 2; Missoula, MT: Scholars Press, 1975).

28. Hengel, *The Atonement*, p. 38.

29. Hengel, *The Atonement*, p. 31; see pp. 73-74.

30. Hengel, *The Atonement*, pp. 71-74.

ahistorical theological convictions. Having detailed the historical-cultural landscape in terms of which the saving significance of the death of Jesus would have been rendered intelligible to an ancient reader, he then distinguishes the New Testament interpretation from 'the death of a pure martyr and righteous sufferer' in order to emphasize that ultimately it is an event that 'stemmed from God himself'.[31] Hengel's investigation of the soteriological significance of the death of Jesus is predicated on the idea, intrinsic to the historical-critical method, that insight into the origins and development of a phenomenon contains the key to its understanding.[32] Consequently, while he makes a plausible case for comprehending Paul's theology of the cross in the light of Greco-Roman notions of martyrdom popular at the time, in the end he posits a generative theory that is inscrutable.

For the most part, Hengel's treatment of these texts is self-consciously historicist, and yet even as a first-rate historical critic he cannot transcend a preoccupation with the 'theology of the cross' proper, a characteristic feature of much German New Testament scholarship on the death of Jesus in Paul. Germany has produced a particularly rich corpus of literature on the death of Jesus in recent decades devoted to the 'theology of the cross'.[33] Despite the variety of approaches and judgments reflected in these studies, they share the fundamental Reformation insight that the cross is the starting point and foundation of the whole of New Testament theology. On one level, Paul's writings would seem to corroborate the view that this presupposition is derived from Paul himself. On the other hand, the fact that this shared conviction should produce so many different renderings of the content of Paul's theology of the cross attests to the multivalence of this soteriological symbol. Although a comprehensive review of this important contribution to an understanding of the death of Jesus in Paul is beyond the scope of this brief survey, there are two distinct yet related tendencies that are noteworthy.

Most German exegesis on the death of Jesus in Paul stands unabashedly in the Reformation tradition which understands the 'theology of

---

31. Hengel, *The Atonement*, p. 74.
32. See B. Lategan, 'Hermeneutics', *ABD*, III, p. 151.
33. For a more recent American version of Paul's theology of the cross written primarily in conversation with the German New Testament scholarship of the 1960s and 1970s see C. Cousar, *A Theology of the Cross: The Death of Jesus in the Letters of Paul* (Minneapolis: Fortress Press, 1990).

the cross' to be a theology of revelation and not a specific view of atonement.[34] While some German New Testament scholars have, like Luther, been interested in what the cross discloses about God, Rudolf Bultmann and Ernst Käsemann have, in different ways, focused on the anthropological implications of Jesus' death. For Bultmann, 'every assertion about God is simultaneously an assertion about man and vice versa'. Hence 'Paul's theology is, at the same time, anthropology'.[35] In Bultmann's vocabulary 'anthropology' is used in a philosophical sense to denote the existential hermeneutic in terms of which the cross is in Paul recognizable as salvation-event. Accordingly, the 'word of the cross' has to do with the believer's new self-understanding, and 'whether he will acknowledge the demand to take up the cross by the surrender of his previous understanding of himself, making the cross the determining power of his life... (1 Cor. 1.18-31; Gal. 6.14; cf. 5.24)'.[36]

Paul's theology of the cross has been set forth no more cogently or passionately than by Käsemann in his article 'The Saving Significance of the Death of Jesus'.[37] Käsemann is also interested in the anthropological significance of Jesus' death. For him, this means that 'the cross' consequences for men dominate all Paul's statements to such an extent that the consequences for God simply do not enter his field of vision'.[38] Käsemann argues that Paul's references to the death of Jesus function predominantly as a polemic against human arrogance and self-righteousness, particularly as it found expression in the legalistic piety of Jewish Christians and the enthusiasm of the Hellenistic church. He underlines the fact that this polemic is directed against those within the church.[39] In the light of this perception of the Pauline context, the

34. This theological construct has its origins in Luther, and its classic formulation by him is found in the 'Heidelberg Disputation' of 1518. See Theses 19 and 20 in J. Pelikan and H.T. Lehmann (eds.), *Luther's Works* (Philadelphia: Fortress Press, 1957), XXXI, pp. 52-53.

35. R. Bultmann, *Theology of the New Testament* (New York: Charles Scribner's Sons, 1955), p. 191.

36. Bultmann, *Theology of the New Testament*, p. 303.

37. A translation of 'Die Heilsbedeutung des Todes Jesu nach Paulus', found in *Perspectives on Paul* (Philadelphia: Fortress Press, 1971), pp. 32-59.

38. Käsemann, 'The Saving Significance of the Death of Jesus', p. 43.

39. 'Enmity to the cross does not end where the "Christian" sphere begins. On the contrary: it shows itself there in its most dangerous form... ' ('The Saving Significance of the Death of Jesus', p. 38).

cross serves to disclose and destroy the 'illusion that man can transcend himself, either through his presumption or by his piety'.[40] As an expression of the pivotal Pauline theme of justification by faith, the theology of the cross confronts the believer with a critical and realistic and realistic anthropology which stresses that 'only the creator can be the creature's salvation'.[41]

Although Bultmann and Käsemann have very different conceptions of Paul's theology of the cross, a succinct comparison may prove instructive. Both are existential interpretations, albeit divergent ones, which conceive of how the death of Jesus ought to affect the self-understanding of the believer.[42] Both also claim to be anthropological in their orientation, which is to say that they are concerned with what the cross means for human beings. Without attempting to minimize the profound dissimilarity between their methods and ideas, it is curious that neither of them consider aspects of social and cultural *behaviour* usually included in discussions of anthropology. In other words, despite the fact that Bultmann and Käsemann are exemplary exegetes devoted to the historical-critical method, their respective characterizations of the audiences addressed in Paul's letters are little more than abstract generalizations. Käsemann does at least specify who the implied readers are, but his shorthand descriptions of legalistic Jewish-Christian piety and Hellenistic-Christian enthusiasm are little more than caricatures. In this respect, Nils Dahl's incisive critique of Bultmann's existential hermeneutic applies also to Käsemann. In a critical essay on *Theology of the New Testament*, Dahl observes that Bultmann 'seeks to determine the new possibility of understanding human existence by distilling it out of concrete history'.[43]

There are a number of other German exegetical studies devoted to the theological implications of the cross in Paul.[44] Although methods

---

40. Käsemann, 'The Saving Significance of the Death of Jesus', p. 41.

41. Käsemann, 'The Saving Significance of the Death of Jesus', p. 41.

42. Käsemann asserts that 'In the light of the theology of the cross, demythologizing and an existentialist interpretation are inescapably demanded' ('The Saving Significance of the Death of Jesus', p. 34). Bultmann's existential hermeneutic is concisely explained in the essay 'Is Exegesis without Presuppositions Possible?', in S. Ogden (ed.), *Existence and Faith* (New York: Meridian Books, 1960), p. 295.

43. N. Dahl, 'Rudolf Butmann's *Theology of the New Testament*', in *The Crucified Messiah and Other Essays* (Minneapolis: Augsburg, 1974), p. 96.

44. Among some of the seminal articles dealing with Paul's theology of the cross are G. Delling, 'Der Tod Jesus in der Verkündingung des Paulus', in W. Eltester

vary and judgments diverge, there is general a[greement with the] Reformation insight that Paul's theology of the cross [is an extension] of his doctrine of justification. Some are more intere[sted in what t]he cross intimates about the God who raised Jesus from [the dead;] others, like Luz, are focused on what the cross disclo[ses about the] world, the community, and humanity.⁴⁵ In either case, it [is the inter]play between the traditional interpretation of the death of [Jesus and] Paul's own experience of Christ that is thought to be the ge[nerative] impulse of his theology of the cross.⁴⁶ While it is true that [Paul's] reworking of the tradition would seem to be the most likely pla[ce to] find his creative elaboration of the meaning of the cross, it is imp[ru]dent from an exegetical standpoint to place too much emphasis on h[is] experience because allusions to it in the text are at best opaque. Paul's theology of the cross was undoubtedly shaped by his encounter with Christ, but that is never the subject of his letters. Rather, Paul's references to the cross are an integral part of a rhetorical strategy designed to shape the convictions and conduct of his audience.

In his eighteen theses on Paul's theology of the cross, Stuhlmacher contends that Paul's real contribution to the theology of the cross is more hermeneutical than theological. Moreover, while Stuhlmacher affirms that Paul's own suffering existence provides a living commentary on his theology of the cross, he emphasizes that Christian existence in general is defined as the paradoxical experience of power in weakness. Building on this, it could be said that Paul not only fashions the earliest tradition about the death of Jesus into a hermeneutical lens, but also a model for conduct which he then relates to particular

---

(ed.), *Apophoreta* (Feschrift E. Haenchen; Berlin: Töpelmann, 1964); U. Luz, 'Theologia Crucis als Mitte der Theologie im Nuen Testament', *EvT* 34 (1974), pp. 116-41; H.W. Kuhn, 'Jesus als Gekreuzigter in der Frühchristlichen Verkündingung bis zur Mitte des 2. Jahrhunderts', *ZTK* 72 (1975), pp. 1-46; K. Kertelge, 'Das Verständnis des Todes Jesu bei Paulus', in *idem* (ed.), *Der Tod Jesu: Deutungen im Neuen Testament* (Freiburg: Herder, 1976), pp. 114-36; P. Stuhlmacher, 'Achtzehn Thesen zur paulinischen Kreuztheologie', in J. Friedrich, W. Pöhlmann and P. Stuhlmacher (eds.), *Rechtfertigung* (Tübingen: Mohr, 1976), pp. 509-25.

45. Delling and Kertelge, for example, emphasize that the cross is comprehended by Paul as God's act of love. Luz's method, on the other hand, is a variation on the anthropological hermeneutic of Bultmann and Käsemann.

46. Luz locates the origin of Paul's theology of the cross in his conversion, and Kertelge contends that Paul's authoritative use of the tradition is grounded in his encounter with the living Christ.

24   *The Cross in Corinth*

rhetorical situations. He derives from the symbol of the cross a behavioural paradigm which he expects believers in the community to imitate. This fundamental observation echoes Bultmann's interest in the anthropological implications of Jesus' death, and yet it extends his existential category of 'self-understanding' to include consideration of concomitant values and practices.

Methodological Considerations:
The 'Performance' of Paul's References to the Death of Jesus

All of the studies of the death of Jesus in Paul which have been discussed betray a wide diversity of methods and conclusions, and yet they share a common interest in ascertaining what the death of Jesus meant for Paul. Some scholars have looked to his cultural and religious background as the key to his interpretation of this event. Others have given priority to his experience or his world view (e.g. apocalyptic) as the formative influence. Most interpreters would acknowledge that all of these factors, together with other constituent elements, shaped Paul's conception of this pivotal event. Discrepancies occur when the debate is focused on which aspects are judged to be more prominent. For example, few would dispute the claim that Paul is to some extent dependent on the earliest interpretation of the death of Jesus, but there is much difference of opinion as to the role this tradition played in Paul's own interpretation. Another example would be the question of how much Paul's theology of the death of Jesus was influenced by sacrificial ideas. In certain passages it is explicitly associated with the cultic notion of sacrifice (cf. 1 Cor. 5.6), but there is no agreement on the extent to which Paul thought of the death of Jesus in terms of sacrifice. One of the main problems, it seems, is that research on the death of Jesus in Paul has been almost exclusively concerned with what is 'central' in his thought. Once a particular motif, or a particular cluster of texts, or even a particular letter is regarded as paramount, other motifs and texts are *ipso facto* deemed peripheral.

The lack of consensus about which ideas and texts deserve precedence in these attempts to discern the logic of Paul's statements about the death of Jesus raises questions about method. In *Truth and Method* Hans-Georg Gadamer makes an observation about the problems of historical hermeneutic and criticism which illuminates this divergence of views. Commenting on Heidegger's description of the hermeneutical circle he remarks,

> A person who is trying to understand a text is always performing an act of projecting. He projects before himself a meaning for the text as a whole as soon as some initial meaning emerges in the text. Again, the latter emerges only because he is reading the text with particular expectations in regard to a certain meaning. The working out of this fore-project, which is constantly revised in terms of what emerges as he penetrates into the meaning, is understanding what is there.[47]

No interpreter is exempt from this act of projecting nor, as Gadamer goes on to point out, the prejudices one always brings to the text. What has happened in Pauline studies in general, however, is that meanings which emerge as preeminent, and thereby prescribe the expectations in terms of which the text is read, tend to eclipse other meanings which are also important. The plurality and polysemy of the symbols, metaphors, and concepts in Paul's letters pose a difficult challenge indeed to anyone interested in reading them as an integrated whole. Even if only the corpus of authentic letters is seen as a canvas upon which the interpreter projects, a number of different readings are possible precisely because a whole complex of symbols and ideas compete for preeminence. This is also the case in the interpretation of a given symbol such as the death of Jesus. Although the centrality of this symbol in Paul's theology is beyond dispute, it has a surplus of meaning which is not easily synthesized.

One conceivable way through this methodological impasse would be to suppress the urge to discern which meanings are preeminent, and to focus instead on how each meaning contributes to a particular rhetorical strategy. Instead of asking what a specific theme or symbol meant for Paul, the focus would be on the function of its various expressions within the discourse a given letter(s).[48] The objective of such an approach would be to ascertain how Paul's statements relate to what he is trying to *accomplish* through his written correspondence, which is different from attempts to delineate what his statements disclose about his theology. The method being proposed here seeks to take its cue from Paul's own objectives, so far as they are articulated in or can

---

47. H.-G. Gadamer, *Truth and Method* (New York: Continuum, 1975), p. 236.
48. See the papers written by members of the Pauline Theology Consultation of SBL. The aim of this group is to sketch the theology of each Pauline letter considered individually, and then construct a composite account of Pauline theology by synthesizing the results of the individual sketches (cf. R. Hays, 'Crucified with Christ: A Synthesis of 1 and 2 Thessalonians, Philemon, Philippians, and Galatians' [SBLSP; Atlanta: Scholars Press, 1988], p. 318).

be inferred from the letters. It is more concerned with the performance of his utterances than with what they reveal about his thought.

A method oriented toward the performance of Paul's references to the death of Jesus is predicated on different prejudices than the ones which guide much of the literature dealing with Paul's theology of the cross. Gadamer points out that 'methodologically conscious understanding will be concerned not merely to form anticipatory ideas, but to make them conscious, so as to check them and thus acquire right understanding from the things themselves'.[49] One foundational prejudice which is, in fact, derived from Paul's writings concerns the literary genre which is the vehicle of his communication. His theology is set forth in the form of letters through which he performs his vocation of organizing Christian communities. Understood in the light of his role as an apostle, Paul's letters are, as Helmut Koester has suggested, to be viewed as instruments through which he tried to foster, and if necessary regulate, community life.[50] His exhortations and theological discourse served this larger purpose of community building, and should therefore be construed in terms of how they functioned in this regard.

An analysis of the function of Paul's language about the death of Jesus has as its focus the *grammar* of his utterances. In his examination of some Pauline passages in the light of Wittgenstein's linguistic philosophy, Anthony Thiselton asserts that a concept draws its meaning from its function within a particular language game, and to understand a language game entails knowledge of its grammar.[51] Interpreting Paul's references to the death of Jesus in terms of grammar implies two other methodological prejudices which need to be made explicit. In the first place, the fact that 'grammatical utterances relate not to information but to *understanding*'[52] means that the objective of Paul's statements and exhortations is to expand the horizons of the reader's understanding. In other words, Paul assumes familiarity on the part of the churches with the topics and ideas he discusses and aims to advance their understanding by modifying and adapting notions which were at least familiar to them. It is in this sense that his utterances are

---

49. Gadamer, *Truth and Method*, p. 239.
50. H. Koester, *Introduction to the New Testament* (2 vols.; Philadelphia: Fortress Press, 1982), II, p. 110.
51. A. Thiselton, *The Two Horizons* (Grand Rapids: Eerdmans, 1980), p. 388.
52. Thiselton, *The Two Horizons*, p. 388.

hermeneutical.[53] Secondly, the grammar of a concept is always embedded in a history of events and behaviour,[54] which is to say that Paul's conception of the death of Jesus must be understood with reference to the social context within which it is elaborated.

Paul as Hermeneutical Theologian

It is J.C. Beker who perhaps more than anyone else has emphasized that Paul is a 'hermeneutic theologian', by which he means that his statements and exhortations are always interpretations of a body of traditions or beliefs spoken as 'a word on target' for a particular situation.[55] In *Paul the Apostle* he delineates a method which emphasizes the constant interaction between the coherent centre of Paul's gospel and its contingent interpretation in the letters.[56] Theoretically Beker's method is paradigmatic, but his own reading of Paul does not do justice to the plurality of themes and multivalence of the symbols which comprise his gospel.[57] Although he asserts that Paul's gospel is never an abstraction because of its historical concreteness and contingent specificity, he nonetheless dissociates what he believes to be its coherent core, namely apocalyptic, from its contextual appropriations. Since apocalyptic is the lens through which Beker views the whole of Paul's writings, he does not sufficiently appreciate the extent to which context influenced the form and content of any given exposition of his gospel.

Beker maintains that the coherent centre of Paul's gospel is a symbolic structure 'in which a primordial experience (Paul's call) is brought into language in a particular way', and so for him it is relatively static.[58] For exegetical purposes, however, it is not necessary to look behind the symbolic structure for a 'primordial' experience when it is the symbols themselves that are being explicated. While these

53. Thiselton, *The Two Horizons*, p. 391.
54. Thiselton, *The Two Horizons*, p. 385.
55. J.C. Beker, 'The Faithfulness of God and the Priority of Israel in Paul's Letter to the Romans', *HTR* 79 (1986), p. 10.
56. Beker, *Paul the Apostle*, p. 11.
57. The vulnerability of Beker's reading of Paul is that while he wants to avoid the bifurcation of Paul's thought which is the consequence of the search for one dominant symbol, concept, or 'essence', he himself falls into this trap by equating the coherent centre of Paul's gospel with the apocalyptic texture of his thought (cf. *Paul the Apostle*, p. 16).
58. Beker, *Paul the Apostle*, p. 15.

symbols may reflect something of Paul's own experience, he does not refer to them in order to convey information about his own personal faith. Rather the symbolic structure of Paul's gospel represents a system of convictions he shares with the community, and it is the capacity of these symbols to shape their communal experience which accounts for their rhetorical significance in the letters.

The symbolic structure as a whole does appear to reference a relatively fixed and coherent horizon of meaning which Paul usually does not have to elaborate on. Paul's hermeneutical contribution consisted in reflecting on the interpersonal implications of these soteriological symbols in the light of his perceptions of community life. This is what Robert Funk underscores in his examination of Paul's hermeneutic. Funk affirms that Paul's exposition of the gospel is a 're-presentation' of the kerygma in language which is shaped to a given context.[59] He explains this hermeneutical process by distinguishing between what he calls primordial and reflective discourse. For Funk 'primordial' refers not to some originitive experience underlying the symbolic structure but to the foundational language tradition which comprises it.[60] When Paul recapitulates the gospel in the letters it is in the mode of reflective discourse. He is 'reviewing the destiny of that foundational language in relation to other "worlds", the world of the apostle, the worlds of his readers'.[61]

Funk's description of Paul's interpretive enterprise suggests that his explications of the gospel required that he also interpret the 'world' of his readers. In addition to the 'world' of his readers, there is also a 'world' intended by the symbolic structure of the gospel. His conversation is with the tradition and the community. He infers a vision of the world from the symbolic structure of the gospel and in the texts of his letters this is interfaced with an analysis of the world of his readers. In fact, the problems he confronts can be construed as a discrepancy between his understanding of the world intended by the symbolic structure of the gospel and his perceptions of the real world of his readers.

---

59. R. Funk, 'The Hermeneutical Problem and Historical Criticism', in J. Cobb and J. Robinson (eds.), *New Frontiers in Theology*. II. *The New Hermeneutic* (New York: Harper & Row, 1963), pp. 168-70.

60. R. Funk, *Language, Hermeneutic and Word of God* (New York: Harper & Row, 1966), pp. 232-33. According to Funk, who is following Heidegger, at the level of primordial discourse 'language reflects, without reflecting on the world'.

61. Funk, *Language, Hermeneutic and Word of God*, p. 233.

Paul's rhetorical strategy is to bring the attitudes and conduct of his readers into conformity with patterns of thinking and acting he derives from his gospel.

The aim of this study is to ascertain how one particular symbol, the death of Jesus, served this purpose. In order to achieve this aim it will be necessary to concretize both the world intended by the symbols invoked in the text and the real world of the readers implied therein. As an organizer of Christian communities who wrote letters to sustain and build up those communities, Paul's main concern was with praxis, that is, with how members of the community lived out their faith convictions. The symbols which together comprise the gospel he projects onto the canvas of the community's life[62] serve not so much to amend erroneous theological notions as to validate a vision of community which had been transgressed in some way. This vision of community is implied by the symbolic structure of the gospel and is given concrete expression in the form of exhortations and admonitions. The death of Jesus is one of the foundational symbols upon which that vision is predicated, and the task of this study will be to trace both what it conveys about Paul's ideal of Christian community and how it functions to secure certain kinds of behaviour which comply with it.

Social Worlds and Symbolic Universes

The questions which need to be asked regarding the function of Paul's references to the death of Jesus in the Corinthian letters concern the relationship between a particular soteriological symbol which belongs to a larger complex of symbols, and the behaviour and social arrangements of people who belong to a community that is defined by those symbols. Peter Berger and Thomas Luckmann's *The Social Construction of Reality* is a treatise on the sociology of knowledge which delineates the correlation between symbol systems and social realities. The sociology of knowledge model is capable of elucidating the interaction between the symbolic world of the gospel and the social world of the community by showing how symbols establish and sustain one's relationship to the social worlds they inhabit.

Berger and Luckmann define a symbol as any significative theme that spans spheres of reality, and the linguistic mode by which such

---

62. Cf. Hays, 'Crucified with Christ', p. 319.

transcendence is achieved they call symbolic language.⁶³ The death of Jesus is a symbol inasmuch as it represents a past historical event detached from the reality of everyday life, and yet is capable of shaping the present lives of those for whom it has authority. As a symbol which depicted an event that was unavailable to everyday experience it nonetheless influenced it because, as Berger and Luckmann explain, 'language is capable not only of constructing symbols that are highly abstracted from everyday experience, but also of "bringing back" these symbols and appresenting them as objectively real elements in everyday life'.⁶⁴

Despite their appearance of objectivity, though, symbols are constructed on human subjectivity, and so in addition to a denotative or referential dimension their interpretation also requires consideration of the experience which is symbolized.⁶⁵ As a case in point, the symbol of the cross has no intrinsic meaning, rather what it connotes is defined by what ideas and experiences it references in a given context. The historical event to which it refers has been invested with existential and theological significance as the result of a metaphorical process which involves a re-interpretation of reality through the disclosure of new relationships of meaning.⁶⁶ For example, the meaning of the death of Jesus as atonement or sacrifice is amplified as Paul associated it with his own and others' experience of suffering, weakness and humiliation. As a symbol, the cross served as a lens through which reality was apprehended or redefined in terms of the experiences, ideas, attitudes, values, judgments and beliefs it was thought to encompass.⁶⁷ The interpretive

---

63. P. Berger and T. Luckmann, *The Social Construction of Reality* (New York: Penguin Books, 1967), p. 55.

64. Berger and Luckmann, *The Social Construction of Reality* , p. 55.

65. Cf. H. Boers, 'Interpreting Paul: Demythologizing in Reverse', in P. Opitz and G. Sebba (eds.), *The Philosophy of Order: Essays on History, Consciousness and Politics* (Festschrift Eric Voegelin; Stuttgart: Ernst Klett, 1981), p. 155. Boers distinguishes symbolic from positive thought and language in terms of the sources of their restraints: 'symbolic thought and language from the experience of reality, and positive language and thought from the demands of logical coherence of ideas'.

66. Cf. P. Ricoeur, 'The Metaphorical Process', *Semeia* 4 (1975), pp. 79-84. Ricoeur says that metaphor is 'that strategy of discourse by which language divests itself of its ordinary meaning in order to serve its extraordinary function of redescription' (p. 88).

67. Cf. C. Geertz, *The Interpretation of Cultures* (New York: Basic Books, 1973), p. 91.

1. *Towards a Contextual Reading* 31

task is to ascertain the significations Paul ascibes to this soteriological symbol in a given context by probing the kinds of experiences, behaviour, and social patterns he expects it to engender among those who inhabit the world being formed by it.[68]

The 'world', or vision of community, which Paul wanted to invoke by alluding to the death of Jesus assumed a correlation between this symbol and the entire symbolic structure of the gospel. As Mary Douglas has observed, 'a symbol only has meaning from its relation to other symbols in a pattern'.[69] Accordingly, the death of Jesus derives its meaning from its relationship to the other symbols in the symbolic structure. Together they form a system of sacred symbols which synthesizes a style of life, an ethos, with a world view.[70] In other words, the world to which the sacred symbols give expression is not just a conceptual world. These symbols also serve to define and shape the social world of the community circumscribed by the vision of reality predicated upon them. The aim of this study of the rhetorical function of Paul's references tothe death of Jesus is to move beyond the ideas represented by the symbol of the crucified messiah to a consideration of the social norms and values which it supports. Since it is the Corinthians' conduct that appears to be most problematic for Paul, a working assumption is that he could presuppose a fundamental grasp of the significance of the death of Jesus on the part of the Corinthians, and that he appealed to this mutual understanding in order to promote concomitant social values which either needed some clarification or had been blatantly disregarded.

One reason for the apparent lack of congruity between belief and practice in the Corinthian community was that its ethos was governed by more than one symbol system. Greco-Roman society in the first century was ordered hierarchically and was therefore socially fragmented. Social relations were dictated by social location. It was a

---

68. It is noteworthy that Berger and Luckmann have been greatly influenced by the symbolic-interactionist school of sociology which understands social behaviour to be behaviour in response to symbols (cf. *The Social Construction of Reality*, p. 29). See also G. Vernon, 'The Symbolic Interactionist Approach to the Sociology of Religion', in J. Matthes (ed.), *International Yearbook for the Sociology of Religion. Sociology of Religion: Theoretical Perspectives (I)* (Köln und Opladen: Westdeutscher Verlag, 1966), p.135.

69. M. Douglas, *Natural Symbols* (New York: Penguin Books, 1973), p. 11.

70. Geertz, *The Interpretation of Cultures*, pp. 127-31; cf. also L. Keck, 'On the Ethos of Early Christians', *JAAR* 42 (1974), pp. 435-52.

pluralistic society in which competing 'sub-universes of meaning' caused special problems of legitimation vis-à-vis both outsiders and insiders.[71] According to Berger and Luckmann, there are different types of legitimation, but the ultimate legitimation is that of the symbolic universe because it integrates all provinces of meaning and encompasses the social order in a symbolic totality.[72] The symbolic universe is an all-embracing frame of reference which provides order for the subjective apprehension of biographical experience.

Using the sociology of knowledge as a heuristic model, one way of conceiving of the situations Paul was confronting in Corinth is in terms of discrepant universes of meaning. Paul expected that the symbolic structure of the gospel, a sub-universe of meaning, would have a profound impact on social relations within the community. Reports to the contrary which indicated to him that there was discord and strife provided the occasion for his writing. The fact that he repeatedly contrasts the Corinthians' identity as believers with pagan identity and often draws sharp boundaries between the church and the world betrays a suspicion that certain Greco-Roman ideals and values continued to have a stronghold in the Corinthian congregation. These Greco-Roman ideals and values formed a part of a cultural symbol system which was at odds with ideals and values inferred from gospel symbols. As Geertz observes, like religion, culture is also a symbol system inasmuch as it is a

> historically transmitted pattern of meanings embodied in symbols, a system of inherited conceptions expressed in symbolic forms by means of which men communicate, perpetuate, and develop their knowledge about and attitudes toward life.[73]

While on the one hand Paul's comprehension and communication of the gospel were ineluctably inscribed by Greco-Roman cultural-linguistic codes, at a deep structural level it was inherently subversive of those same cultural-linguistic codes. This symbolic tension appeared to be

---

71. Berger and Luckmann, *The Social Construction of Reality*, pp. 104-105. They describe legitimation as 'a "second order" objectivation of meaning. Legitimation produces new meanings that serve to integrate the meanings already attached to disparate institutional processes. The function of legitimation is to make objectively available and subjectively plausible the 'first-order' objectivations that have been institutionalized' (p. 110)

72. Cf. Berger and Luckmann, *The Social Construction of Reality*, pp. 113-22.

73. Geertz, *The Interpretation of Cultures*, p. 89.

mirrored in the social relations of the communtiy, and is a subtext of the Corinthian correspondence.[74]

According to this sociology of knowledge model, Paul's rhetorical strategy in 1 and 2 Corinthians can be understood in terms of rival universes of meaning. Several sub-universes of meaning were operative in Corinth, and Paul exhorts the members of that community to live in a manner that would reflect their commitment to the 'word of the cross'. From the perspective of the sociology of knowledge, this is largely a matter of socialization. Berger and Luckmann distinguish between primary and secondary socialization, the former being the objective social structures into which a person is born (e.g. culture) and the latter being institution-based 'sub-worlds' which are internalized.[75] To belong to an early Christian community entailed undergoing a process of secondary socialization, or on rare occasions re-socialization,[76] and this was always tenuous because it presupposed a preceding process of primary socialization. This means that the new identity conferred on those who were baptized had to be assimilated into an identity that had already beenshaped by other formative rituals and cultural-linguistic codes.[77] In order to be internalized, the values and patterns of social relations symbolized by the gospel had to be superimposed upon altogether different cultural modes of existence. Consequently, in a heterogeneous congregation like the one in Corinth a variety of different ideologies and practices were legitimated by appealing to the same gospel.

Paul's aim in 1 and 2 Corinthians was to ensure that behaviour within

---

74. L. Keck remarks that the ethos of early Christian communities was not the reflex of the Greco-Roman culture in which they participated but rather 'the result of the ways in which their beliefs interacted with it' ('On the Ethos of Early Christians', *JAAR* 42 [1974], p. 441).

75. Berger and Luckmann, *The Social Construction of Reality*, pp. 149-66.

76. According to Berger and Luckmann, re-socialization is a process of transformation which appears total in comparison with lesser modifications. It involves a radical reinterpretation of the entire biography of the individual (*The Social Construction of Reality*, pp. 176-80). While Paul's own experience can appropriately be described as a re-socialization, the ethical issues he takes up in the letters indicate that many in the community have not undergone such a thorough transformation and on a continuum probably fall somewhere between re-socialization and secondary socialization.

77. Berger and Luckmann emphasize the tendency of primary socialization to persist (*The Social Construction of Reality*, p. 160).

the community was governed by the 'word of the cross' (cf. 1 Cor. 1.18-25). In order to secure the kind of conduct commensurate with the values mediated by the preaching of Christ crucified he called the community's attention to the social significance of this soteriological symbol. The logic of arguing from symbol to social relations is important to Paul's overall rhetorical strategy. In sociology of knowledge parlance, this kind of reasoning is called universe-maintenance. For the purposes of this study, the two main forms of conceptual machinery used to reinforce and develop the symbolic structure of the gospel are theology and mythology.[78] In the context of Paul's letters, theology denotes the act of reflecting upon the symbolic structure of the gospel with reference to specific issues and concerns. The purpose of these reflections, his theologizing, is to relate the symbolic reality of the gospel to the social world of the community in order to bring the two into harmony with one another.[79] This study is concerned with ascertaining how one symbol, the death of Jesus, functions to promote an ethos consistent with the ideals and values it re-presents.

Social Description

The project being proposed here is perhaps best described by what John Elliott has called sociological exegesis. Elliott distinguishes sociological exegesis from the emphasis on social context and *Sitz im Leben* which has been the hallmark of modern biblical interpretation.

---

78. Berger and Luckmann define mythology as 'a conception of reality that posits the ongoing penetration of the world of everyday experience by sacred forces'. In contrast to mythology, which 'entails a high degree of continuity between social and cosmic order', in theological thought sacred forces have been removed to a greater distance. Hence theological thought 'serves to mediate between these two worlds, precisely because their original continuity now appears broken' (*The Social Construction of Reality*, pp. 128-29). In many respects Paul's thought is better described as mythological, but inasmuch as his letters are an attempt to mediate between the eschatological-cosmic order and the social order of the community they are theological. On the mythological character of Paul's thought see Boers, 'Interpreting Paul', pp.153-72.

79. The distinction between Paul's theology and his theologizing comes from N. Petersen who is also using the sociology of knowledge model. Since, as he points out, theology is the *product* of systematic reflection upon a symbolic universe, for our purposes too it is Paul's theologizing that is more important because it 'takes place as a form of social relations between himself and other actors in the sphere of their social universe' (*Rediscovering Paul: Philemon and the Sociology of Paul's Narrative World* [Philadelphia: Fortress Press, 1985], p. 30).

1. *Towards a Contextual Reading* 35

Sociological exegesis is focused on the literary text and seeks 'to discover and explain the interpersonal or social transactions and relationships to which a text points either explicitly or implicitly'.[80] It attempts to move beyond historical and social description of early Christianity to an analysis of the function or social impact a text, or a symbol within the text, was designed to have in the realm of social interaction.[81] It is important to stress, however, that this kind of exegesis builds on, and in fact presupposes, research which describes the historical and social contexts of Pauline Christianity.[82]

The sociology of knowledge may help to explain how Paul employs the symbol of the cross to underwrite certain patterns of interpersonal conduct which correspond to its rhetorically conveyed significations, but as a theoretical model it can only interpret data that must be supplied by historical criticism.[83] Since symbolic universes are always social products with a history,[84] an understanding of how a particular symbol functions requires that that symbol be located within the historical context in which it and the complex of symbols to which it belongs are operative.

Among the various methods available to access the socio-historical context of New Testament documents Theissen delineates three that are pertinent to this study.[85] The constructive method formulates a profile of a group on the basis of statements which directly disclose something about the social situation. There are probably more of these kind of statements in the Corinthian correspondence that any other New Testament writing, and yet it is still necessary to rely on what Theissen

---

80. J. Elliott, *A Home for the Homeless* (London: SCM Press, 1982), pp. 8-9.

81. Elliott, *A Home for the Homeless*, p. 10. Elliott observes that the 'terms "social" and "sociological" have generally been used indiscriminately so that mere social description has been equated—erroneously—with sociological exegesis' (p. 3).

82. Among other works this study is especially indebted to the work of W. Meeks, *The First Urban Christians* (New Haven: Yale University Press, 1983); G. Theissen, *The Social Setting of Pauline Christianity* (Philadelphia: Fortress Press, 1982); and P. Marshall, *Enmity in Corinth: Social Conventions in Paul's Relations with the Corinthians* (Tübingen: Mohr, 1987).

83. See the helpful discussion of social science methodology as it pertains to New Testament study by P. Esler, *Community and Gospel in Luke–Acts* (Cambridge: Cambridge University Press, 1987), pp. 6-12. He identifies three levels of research in the social sciences: description, classification and explanation.

84. Berger and Luckmann, *The Social Construction of Reality*, p. 115.

85. Theissen, *The Social Setting of Pauline Christianity*, pp. 175-200.

refers to as analytic methods, that is, inferences drawn from historical events, social norms or religious symbols. This investigation of the symbol of the crucified messiah is predominantly oriented to the social norms and values reflected in the text, both those which are implied in Paul's allusions to the attitudes and conduct of the Corinthians and those which are idealized in the symbol itself. In trying to ascertain the social norms and values which were influential in the community a comparative method which takes stock of non-Christian sources will be used. In particular, what is inferred from the letters will need to be corroborated as much as possible by knowledge of social norms and values in Greco-Roman society.

Chapter 2

THE CROSS AND CHRISTIAN UNITY: 1 CORINTHIANS 1–4

Introduction

1 Corinthians discloses more about the mundane problems and concerns which Paul encountered in his dealings with Christian communities than any of his other letters. As a window on the life of the Corinthian community, it reveals not so much a climate of theological dispute and debate as one of intense rivalry involving a cross-section of people from different socio-economic and cultural backgrounds. Thus the internal conflict which prompted Paul's dialogue with the Corinthians in this letter is primarily interpersonal rather than theological in nature. To be sure, conduct and belief are interrelated and so Paul addresses the behavioural problems from a theological perspective. But the gospel, the 'word of the cross' which he first preached to the Corinthians, is the point of reference from which he confronts the situation, and he presupposes that they are cognizant of its meaning and importance (cf. 1.17ff.; 2.1-4; 3.10-15).[1] Fundamentally at issue in the community, then, are the attitudes, values and conduct appropriate to this gospel message.

These things are at issue because there are dissensions and disunity in the community, and so Paul expresses his desire that they 'be united in the same mind and the same judgment' (1.10). The terms νοῦς and γνώμη in his exhortation raise the question of what ideas or convictions stand behind these interpersonal problems. Paul gives no indication that any theological conceptions, or misconceptions, are the cause of the dissensions. On the contrary, the discord (ἔρις) has been created by various groups within the community claiming allegiance to different Christian leaders, namely Paul, Apollos and Cephas, not to mention

---

1. See Funk, *Language, Hermeneutic and the Word of God*, pp. 233-34, 244.

Christ (1.11-12).² The one important conceptual category that does emerge in the first two chapters is wisdom, something the Corinthians highly esteemed and probably an important criterion in their evaluation of and commitment to the leaders mentioned in 1.12.

The wisdom motif will be explored in more depth later, but it is worth noting here that Paul never alludes to the content of the Corinthians' notion of wisdom. He does assert that the crucified Christ is the content of God's wisdom (1.18-25; 2.6-10), but it is erroneous to infer from this that he is necessarily countering a rival *understanding* of wisdom in Corinth. Since Paul nowhere directly challenges any particular notion of wisdom or theology as such, there is no reason to assume that a theological misunderstanding is the source of the problems he is dealing with in 1 Corinthians 1–4.³ These chapters of 1 Corinthians have typically been interpreted with reference to the Corinthians' notion of wisdom and concomitant theological ideas.⁴ This

2. Against Schmithals and others who think the slogan 'I am of Christ' is indicative of a 'Christ party' in Corinth, Welborn has emphasized the political connotations of the verb μερίζω and suggested that the rhetorical question 'is Christ divided?' in v. 13 alludes by synecdoche to the notion of the church as the 'body of Christ'. He points out that the word μερίς is the customary term for 'party' in Greek and paraphrases Paul's question thus: 'Has the body of Christ been split into parties?' (L.L. Welborn, 'On the Discord in Corinth: 1 Corinthians 1–4 and Ancient Politics', *JBL* 106 [1987], p. 87; cf. also J.C. Hurd, *The Origin of I Corinthians* [New York: Seabury, 1965], p. 104).

3. Most scholars agree that 1 Cor. 1.10–4.21 is a self-contained section in which Paul deals with the report of Chloe's people concerning divisions in the community. Cf. C.K. Barrett, *The First Epistle to the Corinthians* (New York: Harper & Row, 1968), p. 28; H. Conzelmann, *1 Corinthians* (Philadelphia: Fortress Press, 1975), pp. 30, 93; Hurd, *The Origin of First Corinthians*, p. 77. Dahl observes that the integrity of 1 Corinthians 'is confirmed if it proves possible to understand 1 Cor. 1.10–4.21 as an introductory section with a definite purpose within the letter as a whole' (N. Dahl, 'Paul and the Church at Corinth according to 1 Corinthians 1.10–4.21', in *idem*, *Studies in Paul* [Minneapolis: Augsburg, 1977], p. 44). I will attempt to show the relationship between this section and the rest of the letter in the next chapter.

4. Examples of this approach are U. Wilckens, *Weisheit und Torheit: Eine exegetisch-religionsgeschichtliche Studie zu I Kor 1 und 2* (BHT, 26; Tübingen: Mohr, 1959); B. Pearson, *The Pneumatikos-Psychikos Terminology in I Corinthians* (SBLDS, 12; Missoula, MT: Scholars Press, 1973); J. Davis, *Wisdom and Spirit: An Investigation of 1 Corinthians 1.18–3.20 against the Background of Jewish Sapiential Traditions in the Greco-Roman Period* (Lanham, MD: University Press of America, 1984). Wilckens has altered his views and his method in two recent

study, by contrast, will begin with Paul's assessment of the situation in the community in terms of what he discloses about the attitudes, convictions, values and behaviour of its members. Only then will it be possible to ascertain how he expects his argument to modify or transform them so that they are living in accordance with the gospel.

The Social Situation Reflected in 1 Corinthians 1–4

While there may be a paucity of information in 1 Corinthians 1–4 about the theological antecedents of the position Paul is opposing in Corinth and how it might have deviated from his gospel, there is a substantial amount of data about the σχίσματα which were his main concern (1.10). Paul has received news of the discord from a delegation associated with a woman by the name of Chloe (1.11),[5] and he concisely relates what he has been told in 1.12: 'each one of you says, "I belong to Paul", or "I belong to Apollos", or "I belong to Cephas", or "I belong to Christ"'. Furthermore, his comments in 1.13-16 suggest that baptism was, in part at least, the basis for laying claim to one of these Christian leaders. Two rudimentary factors inferred from these verses form the basis for an inclusive sketch which incorporates the other aspects of the dispute. First, the divisions and strife among members of the community have occurred for non-theological reasons.[6]

---

articles and therefore in interacting with him precedence will be given to his positions as set forth in 'Das Kreuz Christi als die Tiefe der Weisheit Gottes zu I Kor 2.1-16', in L. De Lorenzi (ed.), *Paolo a Una Chiesa Divisa* (Rome: Abbazia di S. Paolo, 1980), pp. 43-81, and 'Zu I Kor 2.1-16', in C. Andersen and G. Klein (eds.), *Theologia crucis—Signum crucis* (Feschrift Dinkler; Tübingen: Mohr, 1979), pp. 501-37. Hurd seems right in his observation that, 'To seek, for example, the nature and source of the superior knowledge and wisdom of the Corinthians leads the scholar away from I Corinthians down various paths of investigation affording a variety of answers' (Hurd, *The Origin of I Corinthians*, p. 107).

5. Nothing else is known about this Chloe and the people associated with her, but Hurd, following Bachmann, is probably right in assuming that these persons were not sent by the Corinthians and therefore their report was unofficial. By contrast, he suggests that the group consisting of Stephanas, Fortunatus and Achaicus, to which Paul refers in 16.17, more than likely brought the letter of the Church from Corinth to Paul and were also the bearers of 1 Corinthians. See Hurd, *The Origin of I Corinthians*, pp. 48-50.

6. Cf. J. Munck, 'The Church without Factions: Studies in I Corinthians 1–4', reprinted in *Paul and the Salvation of Mankind* (London: SCM Press, 1959), p. 138. Many scholars acknowledge that Paul provides almost no information about

In other words, the different cliques seem to be more interested in the characteristic features of the leaders they venerate than the theologies represented by them. Instead of looking *behind* the text for the theological origins of the problem, it may proved instructive to heed Paul's own emphasis on the disposition and behaviour of those involved. Secondly, the existence of a 'Paul-group' indicates that some of the Corinthians were opposed to him and this explains why his own demeanor and behaviour are a major focus of attention throughout this section (cf. 2.1-5; 3.5-15; 4.1-21). There is a correlation between these two factors in that the criticisms of Paul alluded to in this section reflect not only a negative attitude towards him, but also the values and conduct of the people who have instigated the rivalry which has divided the community.

Although Paul does not deal with specific behavioural problems in the community until ch. 5, in 3.3 a rhetorical question serves as a comprehensive and critical appraisal of the Corinthians' conduct: 'For while there is jealousy and strife among you, are you not of the flesh, and behaving like ordinary men?' The σαρκικός designation which Paul ascribes to them contradicts their perception of themselves as πνευματικός (3.1),[7] and its precise meaning is indicated by its contextual link with the party slogans in 3.4. He criticizes the 'jealousy and strife' which were symptomatic of the person-centred rivalry on the grounds that it is behaviour that belongs to the domain of the 'flesh'. Similarly, with no reference to its content, Paul condemns the wisdom they boast of because it is 'the wisdom of the world' (1.20, cf. 1.26; 2.6). In these chapters 'the world' is circumscribed as the realm of existence within which mere human wisdom and effort have failed to obtain a saving knowledge of God (1.18-25), and so those in the community who would have regarded themselves as 'spiritual' would have considered this designation to be an insult. It is the Corinthians'

---

the theological aspects of the controversy, but assume nonetheless that they existed. Cf. Dahl, 'Paul and the Church at Corinth', p. 59.

7. Paul is turning the tables on the self-styled πνευματικόι, also called τέλειοι, who refer to others as ψυχικόι and σαρκικόι. So J. Painter, 'Paul and the πνευματικόι at Corinth', in M.D. Hooker and S.G. Wilson (eds.), *Paul and Paulinism* (Feschrift Barrett; London: SPCK, 1982), p. 237; R. Horsley, 'Pneumatikos vs. Psychikos Distinctions of Spiritual Status among the Corinthians', *HTR* 69 (1976), pp. 269-70.

pneumatic self-consciousness that gives Paul's remarks their force.⁸ By specifying that their behaviour was 'fleshly', or 'worldly', Paul identified them with a mode of existence which they would have disdained, and thereby underlined the inconsistency between their spiritual identity and their fleshly conduct.

It is apparent from the rhetorical question in 3.4 that 'fleshly' behaviour is defined in terms of the Corinthians' misguided views about ministry, specifically the ministries of Paul and Apollos: 'For when one says, "I belong to Paul", and "I belong to Apollos", are you not merely men?' Thiselton has correctly observed that the Corinthians' attitudes toward ministry are the central issue in chs. 1–4, and that questions about wisdom and about divisions which revolve around chosen personalities are discussed within this framework.⁹ From Paul's perspective the interpersonal problems in the community have resulted from an even more fundamental problem concerning perception. In 3.5–4.21 Paul takes up the matter of how he and Apollos are to be regarded as it pertians to the Corinthians' jealousy and strife and the consequent divisions (3.1-4). His judgment that the Corinthians have misconstrued the nature of ministry and the assertion that they were 'behaving like ordinary men' (κατὰ ἄνθρωπον περιπατεῖτε, 3.3) are the two suppositions which constitute his assessment of what had transpired in the community during his absence, but they disclose few concrete details about what actually happened. Nonetheless, there is evidence of specific criticisms of Paul in this section, and these criticisms suggest the character of the attitudes and behaviour of the group which opposed him and thereby aroused rivalry and strife in the community.

That certain charges had been leveled against Paul in Corinth is apparent from his remark in 4.3: 'with me it is a very small thing that I should be judged by you or by any human court'. Dahl has suggested that phrases such as 'not with eloquent wisdom' (1.17), 'not in lofty words of wisdom' (2.1), 'not in persuasiveness of wisdom' (2.4) and 'milk, not solid food' (3.2) betray the content of the criticisms.¹⁰ This leads him to the conclusion that Paul was accused of lacking the

---

8. W.C. Robinson, Jr, rightly remarks that a rhetorical question derives its force from the agreement to which it refers ('Word and Power [I Corinthians 1.17–2.5]', in J. McDowell Richards [ed.], *Soli Deo Gloria: New Testament Studies in Honor of William Childs Robinson* [Richmond: John Knox, 1968], p. 72).

9. A. Thiselton, 'Realized Eschatology at Corinth', *NTS* 24 (1978), p. 513.

10. Dahl, 'Paul and the Church at Corinth', p. 48.

oratorical ability of a Greek rhetor and the gift of pneumatic wisdom. Furthermore, Dahl observes that the catalogue of hardships in 4.11-13 indicates other objections to Paul's apostleship, for example, his instability as one who was 'homeless' (v. 11) and working with his own hands (v. 12).[11] Although Paul does affirm that he has a pneumatic wisdom that he imparts among the 'mature' (2.6-16), he does not contest the verity of any of the other criticisms and even refers to himself, albeit ironically, as 'the refuse of the world, the offscouring of all things' (4.13). That he concedes to these criticisms suggests that they characterize his apostleship with some degree of accuracy and are not just the product of an anti-Pauline sentiment. This being the case, the criticisms explain why some of the Corinthians may have favoured other Christian leaders such as Apollos, but in and of themselves they do not disclose the precise identity of the group that opposed Paul.

What can be inferred from the criticisms is that those who were against Paul valued wisdom and rhetorical skills, and disdained the overall weakness which was characteristic of his apostleship. Although this description could conceivably pertain to any number of a whole spectrum of people, 4.8-10 suggests that Paul had in mind a group which not only esteemed but actually claimed for themselves the qualities he was accused of lacking—wisdom, strength and honour. These verses are couched in the rhetoric of status and hence the contrast in 4.10 is primarily a social one.[12] In the light of the fact that honour and shame were pivotal social values in the Mediterranean world, Peter Marshall asserts that the antitheses of honour and shame and associated ideas here and throughout 1.10–4.21 refer mainly to social status and indicate the attitudes and behaviour of certain upper class Christians toward Paul and toward Corinthians of lowly status.[13] Since it is his own lack of honour and status that Paul emphasizes in the hardship catalogue (4.11-12), and this is obviously meant in a concrete rather than a spiritual sense, it follows that the adjectives he uses to depict the Corinthians he distinguishes himself from also have social connotations.[14]

---

11. Dahl, 'Paul and the Church at Corinth', pp. 48-49.
12. Marshall, *Enmity in Corinth*, p. 210.
13. Marshall, *Enmity in Corinth*, p. 283. On the importance of honour and shame in the Mediterranean world see B. Malina, *The New Testament World: Insights from Cultural Anthropology* (Atlanta: John Knox, 1981), pp. 25-35.
14. For the view that the contrast is between the spiritual wealth of the Corinthians

The term ἔνδοξος and ἄτιμος refer to the social values in terms of which the comparison in 4.10 is made, but they are not the only basis for interpreting the differentiation between Paul and his rivals socially. The ἀσθενής/ἰσχυρός antithesis is likewise a social one inasmuch as it employs language of status rhetoric. Christopher Forbes has shown that these terms, understood in the light of their use in Hellenistic literature contemporary with Paul, usually denote the status or value persons are seen as possessing in their social context.[15] This interpretation, especially with regard to ἀσθενής, is substantiated by Paul's elaboration of the nature of his weakness in 4.11-13 where he presents himself as someone of lowly status. Consequently, the comparison in 4.10 must be between Paul's own debased state and that of certain Corinthians who had honour and status.[16]

Having emphasized the social connotations of the terms used in the context of 4.8-13, it is necessary to consider the relationship of the

and the physical poverty of the apostles, see J.T. Fitzgerald, *Cracks in an Earthen Vessel: An Examination of the Catalogues of Hardships in the Corinthian Correspondence* (SBLDS, 99; Atlanta: Scholars Press, 1988), p. 133-34.

15. C. Forbes, '"Strength" and "Weakness" as Terminology of Status in St Paul: The Historical and Literary Roots of a Metaphor, with Special Reference to 1 and 2 Corinthians' (BA thesis, Macquarie University, 1978). The authors Forbes has focused on are Homer, Diodorus Siculus, Dionysius of Halicarnassus, Josephus, Plutarch and Dio Chrysostom. See also his 'Comparison, Self-Praise and Irony: Paul's Boasting and the Conventions of Hellenistic Rhetoric', *NTS* 32 (1986), p. 19. G. Theissen also sees in these terms a reference to status. See his 'Social Stratification in the Corinthian Community: A Contribution to the Sociology of Early Hellenistic Christianity', in *The Social Setting of Pauline Christianity*, pp. 70-73. Contrast D. Black, *Paul, Apostle of Weakness: Astheneia and its Cognates in the Pauline Literature* (American University Studies, Series 7, Theology and Religion 3; New York: Peter Lang, 1984). Black fails to recognize the social connotations of the weakness terminology in Paul and sees it instead as denoting the powerlessness, transitoriness and bodily frailty of humanity, especially in relation to God (cf. pp. 228-34). K. Plank notes that the ἀσθεν- word group bears both literal and figurative meanings, but the literal sense for him signifies only sickness, disease, or other forms of physical disability (*Paul and the Irony of Affliction* [Atlanta: Scholars Press, 1987], p. 20).

16. Cf. Theissen, *The Social Setting of Pauline Christianity*, pp. 97-98. The μωροί/φρόνιμοι contrast also has social connotations in this context. As Theissen has pointed out, while both Paul and the Corinthians understood wisdom theologically, that does not preclude the prospect that the 'wise' are also educated in the ordinary sense. Hence just as in 1.26, 'wise' here serves in some sense to designate those in the community who belong to the upper strata by virtue of their education and cultural background.

social evaluation expressed by the antitheses to the ironic portrait of the Corinthians Paul is comparing himself with in 4.8. His description of these people as 'filled' (κορέννυμι), 'rich' (πλουτέω), and 'kings' (βασιλεύω) is frequently appealed to as evidence that the problems in Corinth were the result of an over-realized eschatology which led to an 'enthusiastic' view of the Spirit.[17] This appraisal of the situation is largely dependent upon an understanding of 4.8 as illustrative of the Corinthians' exalted spiritual consciousness. According to Thiselton, in the most recent treatment of the matter along these lines, the Corinthian situation is aptly described by A.D. Nock in the following words:

> Many of the converts, convinced that they were on a new plane of life, felt that they could do anything: they were kings (4.8), they were in the Spirit, they were dead to the flesh and emancipated—so that their physical conduct might seem to them a matter of indifference; they were altogether superior to the unchanged men around them.[18]

Thiselton is aware of the fact that in previous scholarship this interpretation of the state of affairs in Corinth has been contingent upon 4.8 as an isolated verse, and he attempts to supply further support for it by showing that 'the eschatological approach pinpoints a single common factor which helps to explain an otherwise utterly diverse array of apparently independent problems at Corinth'.[19] By analyzing the whole series of problems in 1 Corinthians he seeks to demonstrate that an over-realized eschatology provides not a 'necessary' but a 'sufficient' cause for each individual problem.

It is doubtful, however, that one theological misconception could

---

17. E.g. Barrett, *The First Epistle to the Corintians*, pp. 109; Conzelmann, *1 Corinthians*, p. 88; G. Fee, *The First Epistle to the Corinthians* (Grand Rapids: Eerdmans, 1987), p. 172; Dahl, 'Paul and the Church at Corinth', p. 59; E. Käsemann, 'On the Subject of Primitive Christian Apocalyptic', reprinted in *New Testament Questions of Today* (Philadelphia: Fortress Press, 1969), pp. 125-26; Wilckens, *Weisheit und Torheit*, p. 11.

18. A.D. Nock, *St Paul*, p. 174, cited by Thiselton, 'Realized Eschatology at Corinth', p. 512.

19. Thiselton realizes that 'this one verse can hardly stand as the single key to the interpretation and reconstruction of the entire situation behind I Corinthians' and that 'this verse does indeed stand alone', and therefore wants to broaden the basis for understanding the difficulties in Corinth in terms of an over-realized eschatology. But there is no reason even to posit an eschatological interpretation apart from 4.8, so, despite his criticism of scholars who are entirely dependent on 4.8 for this view, Thiselton is himself ultimately dependent on it.

2. *The Cross and Christian Unity*

account for the manifold problems Paul confronts in 1 Corinthians. Moreover, if Paul conceived of the different problems in the letter as having their origin in a misunderstanding or misappropriation of the gospel he first preached to them, then why did he not provide them with a more explicitly theological corrective as he does, for example, in Galatians? Another more serious objection to this view is that an eschatological interpretation of 4.8 does not explain how the dissensions, which are the primary focus of chs. 1–4, are related to the personalities mentioned in 1.12. Since Paul refers only to the interpersonal character of these dissensions, there is no reason to spiritualize 4.8 when it makes perfectly good sense as a description of the social behaviour of some of the Corinthians. It has already been suggested that the labels ἰσχυρός and ἔνδοξος which Paul ascribes to certain Corinthians in 4.10 denote his perception of how they view their social standing, and this would seem to warrant a social rather than an eschatological rendering of 4.8. The implication of such a rendering is that the terms κορέννυμι, πλουτέω and βασιλεύω refer not to a spiritual elitism but rather to the behaviour which was typical of the few in the community who belonged to the upper strata (cf. 1.26).

Peter Marshall has argued that 4.8 does in fact refer to Corinthians whose elitism was predicated on social rather than spiritual status, and he has made a strong case for understanding this verse and the people to whom it refers in terms of the Greek hybristic tradition. He asserts that the ideas of satiety (κόρος), wealth (πλοῦτος), and power (βασιλεύς) present in 4.8 constitute a triad in verbal form of three of the most common terms associated with ὕβρις. As with the terms in 4.10, the nuance of status is also present in κορέννυμι and πλουτέω, so they too betray Paul's estimation of the social standing and disposition of some in the community.[20] More than that, they indicate excessive behaviour of a *hybris* kind. In an article entitled '*Hybris* in Athens', D.M. MacDowell has emphasized the connection between *hybris* and *koros*, 'fullness' or 'satiety', in well-known passages of Greek poetry, and says that 'when the connection was first made the word *koros* referred literally to eating and drinking'. He goes on to point out that 'you cannot eat and drink too much unless you have plenty of food and drink available', and therefore 'it is not surprising that we find *hybris*

---

20. Marshall, *Enmity in Corinth*, p. 209. Marshall's view is also adopted by S. Pogoloff, *LOGOS AND SOPHOS: The Rhetorical Situation of 1 Corinthians* (SBLDS; Atlanta: Scholars Press, 1992), pp. 228-30.

associated with wealth and riches, with having not just plenty of food but plenty of everything'.[21] This correspondence between wealth and excessive conduct which is a feature of the *hybris* tradition is evident in 4.8 and elsewhere in 1 Corinthians, and it provides some perspective on the social causes of the quarreling and strife in the community and the attack on Paul's apostleship.

Hybris is a comprehensive Greek ethical notion which has an extensive vocabulary, but concisely defined 'it represents the self-indulgent arrogant behaviour of the rich and powerful and privileged youth which disregards and oversteps the limits of human and divine authority'.[22] Another important aspect, emphasized by N.R.E. Fisher, is that *hybris* is essentially linked to the ideas of honour and shame.[23] Aristotle's thorough treatment of the concept includes the notion of 'superiority', and involves a breach of status, an insult or dishonour to another.[24] There is a cause and effect relationship between the *hybrist's* efforts to shame and dishonour the victim and the social discord (*stasis*) which is the consequence of this conduct.[25]

While this is a compressed analysis of what must be regarded as a rather fluid category of behaviour, the way in which Paul's analysis of the Corinthian situation coincides with it is striking. He has identified certain Corinthians who consider themselves 'strong', and by this he means that they have social power.[26] That Paul understands the discord in the community to have been effected primarily by this select group's

---

21. D.M. MacDowell, '*Hybris* in Athens', *Greece and Rome* 23 (1976), p. 16.
22. P. Marshall, '*Hybrists* Not Gnostics in Corinth' (SBLSP; Atlanta: Scholars Press, 1984), pp. 276-77.
23. N.R.E. Fisher, '*Hybris* and Dishonour: I', *Greece and Rome* 23 (1976), p. 177. Fisher agrees with MacDowell's definition of *hybris* as 'having energy or power and misusing it self-indulgently', but he goes on to argue that what has been neglected is that *hybris* is 'essentially linked to the ideas of honour and shame'. His account is closely related to Aristotle who finds the core of the concept in 'behaviour intended to produce dishonour or shame to others'.
24. Fisher, '*Hybris* and Dishonour: I', p. 183. For examples see *Rhet.* 2.8.2-3, 6; 16.1-4; Xenophon, *Cry.* 7.2.18; Plutarch, *Mor.* 631 CDF; 634 DEF, cited by Marshall, '*Hybrists* Not Gnostics in Corinth', p. 277.
25. Fisher, '*Hybris* and Dishonour: I', p. 183; Marshall, '*Hybrists* Not Gnostics in Corinth', p. 278. See Aristotle, *Pol.* 5.2.3-4; 5.3.3; 5.6.4-5.
26. According to Forbes, no meaningful distinction in terms of 'status rhetoric' can be drawn between the prime terms for 'strength' or 'power', δύναμις and ἰσχύς. They are used by Paul virtually interchangeably ('"Strength" and "Weakness" as Terminology of Status in St Paul').

2. *The Cross and Christian Unity*

abuse of their social privileges and power has also been espoused recently from a somewhat different yet complementary viewpoint by L.L. Welborn. He proposes that the real problem being addressed in 1 Corinthians 1–4 is one of partisanship, a power struggle which is best understood in the light of classical texts dealing with politics.²⁷ Welborn's thesis is that Paul's goal in this section is what Plutarch describes as the object of the art of politics—the prevention of στάσις. On this interpretation, the slogans in 1.12 are indicative of political parties which according to Greco-Roman political history 'took the form of groups of clients and personal adherents to particular leaders'.²⁸

Especially pertinent to this examination of 1 Corinthians 1–4 is the correlation between στάσις andsocial inequality. According to Welborn, tensions between rich and poor are a constant feature of accounts of στάσις in ancient literature.²⁹ The Corinthians whom Paul accused of being arrogant, that is, 'puffed up in favour of one against another', were powerful according to the prevailing social conventions, and the basis of both their power and the attitude of superiority which Paul criticizes them for in 4.7 was their wealth.³⁰ Paul derides them in 4.8 using terminology which betrays the social inequality which he perceives to lie at the root of the discord. Not only is this verse full of sarcasm, it also combines the two diverse elements of *hybris* noted by Fisher: 'a psychological state of mind (the desire for a particular sort of pleasure) and an activity that both satisfies that desire and has a definite effect on other people'.³¹ This state of mind can be denoted by the verb κορέννυμι and the activity which accompanies it can be described by the verb βασιλεύω. Together with the necessary material means implied by the term πλουτέω, and understood within the context of 4.1-16, all of this would seem to add up to *hybris*.

In addition to Paul's ironic representation of this elite group's disposition and behaviour in 4.6-10, there is also a more covert allusion to them in 1.26 where the social makeup of the community is described: 'For consider your call, brethren; not many of you were wise according

---

27. Welborn, 'On the Discord in Corinth', pp. 85-111.
28. Welborn, 'On the Discord in Corinth', pp. 91-92.
29. Welborn, 'On the Discord in Corinth', pp. 94-95. Welborn cites Aristotle who says: 'Party strife is everywhere due to inequality' (*Pol.* 5.1.6 1301b27).
30. Welborn, 'On the Discord in Corinth', p. 97. According to Welborn, 'the δυνατόι are the πλούσοι throughout Greek literature'.
31. Fisher, '*Hybris* and Dishonour: I', p.184.

to worldly standards, not many were powerful, not many were of noble birth.' Theissen has pointed out that the οὐ πολλοὶ indicates that there were at least some in the community who were wise, powerful and well born, and hence this verse reflects something of the social stratification of the Corinthian community.[32] Here the contrast is between the few influential Corinthian Christians who come from the upper classes and the majority who come from the lower classes.[33] The correlation between this implicit identification of the influential minority in 1.26 and the more explicit portrait of them in 4.6-10 has recently been reinforced by Sänger who suggests that 4.10 is an explication of the sociological categories of 1.26.[34] Since this group stands in the not too distant background of Paul's response to the dissensions in 1 Corinthians 1 and to the fore of his discussion of the character of his own apostolic ministry in 1 Corinthians 4, it is likely that they had a significant part in both the person-centred rivalry which divided the community (1.10-11) and the criticisms Paul responds to in 4.1-16. Moreover, both the attack on Paul's apostleship and the 'quarreling' they were involved in appear to be the result of a preference for leadership that better exemplified the qualities of wisdom, power and honour.

These qualities are the crux of the situation Paul is confronting in 1 Corinthians 1–4, for they represent the social values which determined this group's disposition towards Paul and other Christian leaders. In response to their attack on Paul's apostleship, others in the community evidently professed their loyalty to him (1.12; 3.4) This controversy over allegiance gave rise to the fragmented social intercourse which was uppermost in Paul's mind when he wrote 1 Corinthians. Since the factions were demarcated in terms of associations with the authoritative personalities involved (1.12; 3.3-15), the social values which served as the criteria for evaluating these leaders are in one respect at least the underlying cause of the discord in the community. These values served as standards or norms for establishing what was considered desirable, and because they are concretized in particular

32. Theissen, *The Social Setting of Pauline Christianity*, pp. 73-96.
33. Theissen, *The Social Setting of Pauline Christianity*, pp. 69-73.
34. D. Sänger, 'Die δυνατόι im I Kor 1.26', *ZNW* 76 (1985), p. 288. He correlates the two passages in the following way:

```
            σοφοί      =   φρόνιμοι   μωροί
ὑμεῖς<     δυνατόι    =   ἰσχυροί    ἀσθενής    <ἡμεῖς
            εὐγενεῖς   =   ἔδοξοι     ἄτιμοι
```

behaviours and personal characteristics they can be inferred from the evaluations evident in the first four chapters of 1 Corinthians.[35]

So far, Paul and his antagonists have been identified as the central characters in the situation being dealt with in chs. 1–4, and certain secular values have been shown to serve as the basis of the criticisms of his apostleship. But the mention of Apollos and Cephas (1.12; 3.4-23) and a consideration of the majority of Corinthians who were not wise, powerful, or of noble birth suggests a more complex problem than can be accounted for by the confrontation between Paul and the socially privileged people who opposed him. The dissensions also involved these other leaders and the other members of the community, and so it is necessary to examine in greater depth their part in the controversy and the circumstances surrounding the discordant social relations that existed among the Corinthians themselves and their affiliations with the various leaders mentioned in 1.12.

The references to Cephas and Apollos and the allegation that there were groups within the community attached to them raises the question of the nature of their involvement in the dispute. Paul nowhere implicates either of them so there is no reason to assume that they were in any way responsible for the quarreling that occurred in their names.[36] The splinter groups must have been organized at the initiative of those who comprised them, and their reasons for attaching themselves to either Apollos or Cephas are the key to understanding the central points of contention. The problem is that the paucity of information about the impact of these two important figures on the Corinthian community makes it difficult to ascertain what those reasons were. Nevertheless, as Munck has observed, although we know nothing at all from 1 Corinthians about the Paul faction and the Cephas faction, scholars have treated the Apollos faction differently. Writing more than thirty years ago, he remarked, 'the opinion is that in 1.18ff. Paul is waging a controversy directly with those adherents of Apollos who despised Paul's simple preaching and were striving after wisdom.'[37] There have

---

35. R.M. Williams, 'Values', *International Encyclopedia of the Social Sciences* (New York: Macmillan), XVI, pp. 284-85. Williams asserts that 'by observing which behaviours are praised and otherwise rewarded and which are criticized, condemned, or punished, we gain important data for identifying the socially effective standards that are actually operating in any group or society'.
36. Dahl, 'Paul and the Church at Corinth', p. 50.
37. Munck, 'The Church without Factions', p. 143.

been numerous attempts to elaborate on and modify this view, and despite points of divergence there is widespread agreement that Apollos is the other main authority figure connected with the divisiveness in the community.[38] Hurd, in his survey of opinions about the source of the discord, has noted that the Apollos party has had the advantage with scholars over the other two parties in that both 1 Corinthians and Acts (18.24-28) agree that Apollos actually visited and worked in Corinth.[39] Even more important is the fact that of the three party leaders named in 1.12, it is Apollos who emerges as the central personality in 1 Corinthians 1–4. In addition to the two times Paul mentions him in conjunction with himself and Cephas (1.12; 3.22), he singles Apollos out four times in these chapters (3.4, 5, 6; 4.6).

In 3.3-4 where Paul speaks about the 'jealousy and strife' among the Corinthians he refers only to himself and Apollos. Moreover, he outlines his conception of ministry in 3.5-15 with select mention only of their respective contributions. In v. 6 he employs the metaphors of planting and watering to describe their interdependent forms of service to the church. The complementary tasks they performed are also alluded to in v. 10 where he develops the building metaphor: 'like a skilled master builder I laid a foundation, and another man is building upon it'. Although Paul refrains from identifying his co-worker in this statement, it seems apparent that the unnamed man is Apollos.[40] Why he refers to him here as 'another man' is open to question, but there is no reason to think that his obliqueness betrays a restrained contempt for his co-worker. As Barrett has pointed out, Paul makes it quite clear that building on the foundation he has laid is the proper thing to do and he has no objection to it.[41] However, since the dissensions were the result of certain misconceptions about ministry, it is significant that he and Apollos are together the exclusive focus of his discussion

---

38. Recent scholarship has been more cautious about the extent to which the Apollos party is seen to be the source of the discord, but there is a general consensus that the esteem of wisdom was a dominant factor and these people are regarded as the most likely adherents to the view Paul is arguing against. See Dahl, 'Paul and the Church at Corinth', pp. 45-59; R. Horsley, 'Wisdom of Word and Words of Wisdom', *CBQ* 39.2 (1977), p. 231; Wilckens, 'Zu I Kor 2.1-16', p. 518; E. Best, 'The Power and the Wisdom of God', in *Paolo a Una Chiesa Divisa (1 Co 1–4)* Rome: Abbazia di S. Paolo, 1980), p. 15.

39. Hurd, *The Origin of I Corinthians*, p. 97.
40. Barrett, *The First Epistle to the Corinthians*, p. 87.
41. Barrett, *The First Epistle to the Corinthians*, p. 87.

2. *The Cross and Christian Unity*   51

of this theme. It is evident from what is said in chs. 3–4 that they had the two most influential ministries in Corinth, and it follows from the distinctive functions and character of their respective ministries that they engendered different reactions from the Corinthians. In the light of the predominance of their leadership and Paul's contrast of their individual roles, it seems plausible to affirm that the differences between them were the primary grounds for the divided loyalties of the two groups professing allegiance to them. If, as has been suggested, the criticisms of Paul most likely stemmed from those who claimed to belong to Apollos, it is reasonable to assume that in some respect they viewed themselves and Apollos as superior, and that this superiority complex accounts for the internal strife in the community.

Attempts by scholars to ascertain the distinguishing characteristics of the Corinthians who committed themselves in some sense to Apollos have concentrated primarily on the wisdom motif in 1 Corinthians 1–2. The reason for this is that Paul's initial reply to the problem of discord in the community is an extended discourse on how 'the wisdom of the world' has been undermined and superseded by 'the wisdom of God' as revealed in the crucified Christ (1.18–2.16), and this is seen to imply the theological complexion of the dissensions and the priority of a particular notion of wisdom which Paul deems incompatible with the gospel he preached. In accordance with this view, Apollos is believed to be the person responsible for the problematic view of wisdom which Paul challenges with 'the word of the cross'. For example, R. Horsley asserts that in Apollos there is a possible historical link between the Hellenistic-Jewish wisdom tradition represented by Philo and the Corinthian situation.[42] Although the prominence of the wisdom theme in this section warrants this type of tradition-history analysis, Horsley and the many others who have approached the passage from this angle, invariably arriving at different conclusions, hastily abandon the immediate context for a more conjectural history of religions context hoping to identify the source of the presumed theological error.[43] This

---

42. Horsley, 'Wisdom of Word and Words of Wisdom', p. 231.
43. The view that Gnosticism provides the background to the wisdom theme in 1 Cor. 1–2 has been undermined (cf. R. McWilson, 'Gnosis at Corinth', in *Paul and Paulinism* and Robin Scroggs' criticisms of Wilckens' view in 'Paul: ΣοφοΣ and ΠΝΕΥΜΑΤΙΚΟΣ', *NTS* 14 [1967], pp.33-35), but Hellenistic Judaism is such a vast sea that there is no consensus as to its precise *Sitz im Leben*. The majority of scholars follow Horsley in finding the most striking parallels in Philo, but the grounds for this

examination of the situation as it is disclosed by the criticisms of Paul, references to other authority figures and comments about the sociological structure of the community has emphasized the interpersonal aspects of the conflict. While this does not necessarily negate or neglect the theological dimension or the importance of the wisdom motif, it does require that they be integrated into the coherent picture of the social dynamics of the dispute that has so far been constructed.

What has been adduced from the sociological data gleaned from the text is that Paul was criticized for being socially inferior by a wealthy and powerful minority whose behaviour was reported to be arrogant. If Paul and Apollos were the two most influential leaders in the community and unwittingly represented the two main competing groups, then Paul's opponents and the group belonging to Apollos are one and the same. Furthermore, there is a correlation between the content of their criticisms of Paul and the basis of their commitment to Apollos in that the social values in terms of which they rejected Paul served at the same time as the criteria in terms of which they revered Apollos. In other words, they found in Apollos the very qualities they accused Paul of lacking.

In ch. 3 where Paul turns his attention to the topic of ministry he restricts his discussion to the two party slogans pertaining to himself and Apollos (3.4). This appears to be in keeping with the situation in Corinth.[44] Thus the subsequent rhetorical questions in 3.5 ('What then

---

connection are questionable. There is no historical evidence which indicates that Philo was as influential a theologian as this view suggests or that his ideas about wisdom were that pervasive. A. Culpepper observes that recent scholarship has steadily diminished earlier estimates of Philo's influence, and he himself thinks Philo exerted little influence even on his own community (*The Johannine School* [SBLDS; Missoula, MT: Scholars Press, 1975], p. 213). J. Davis, in *Wisdom and Spirit*, has recently argued that Paul is responding to a 'Torah-centric' wisdom at Corinth, but, in addition to the fact that Paul speaks of a wisdom which Greeks seek (1.22), it is unlikely that he would be so discreet in reacting to an esoteric form of Judaizing. The history of religions method common to all of these studies is ultimately of no value for our purposes because the paucity of historical data renders any linguistic or conceptual correspondences of no consequence in explaining the socio-historical context of wisdom in Corinth.

44. Conzelmann, *1 Corinthians*, p. 72. Conzelmann says that he does not know how, meaning in what sense, this is the case, but it seems reasonable to assume that the mention of only the two party slogans which pertain to Paul and Apollos indicates that they represent the two main rivaling groups.

is Apollos? What is Paul?') are probably indicative of comparisons that have actually occurred in the community. Paul offers his own constructive comparison when he uses the imagery of planting and cultivation to differentiate his work in Corinth from Apollos's, but some of the Corinthians were apparently more interested in the style rather than the function of their respective ministries. Despite the fact that Paul conveys no direct information about the character of Apollos's ministry and the features which endeared him to his followers, it is likely that Paul was discredited for his weakness and shame. Conversely, Apollos was credited with possessing honour and power, the operative values of the privileged elite in the community. Constitutive of the social criteria which were the basis of this group's evaluations of Paul and Apollos was their notion of wisdom. A closer examination of the wisdom motif in the first two chapters not only reinforces the connection between Apollos and wisdom in Corinth, but it also shows that this connection is based primarily on the perception that Apollos, in contrast to Paul, measured up to the ideal of a cultivated person current in Greco-Roman society. Although the wisdom Paul denounces as being opposed to 'the wisdom of God' is comprehensively termed 'the wisdom of the world' (1.20-21), it is telling that he singles out σοφία λόγου as the particular manifestation of wisdom which threatens to empty the cross of Christ of its power (1.17; cf. 2.1, 4). This phrase is the only sure guide to the kind of wisdom Paul rejects in 1 Corinthians 1–2, and in both verses it denotes not content but a form of speech, that is, wisdom as a rhetorical device.[45] It is specifically rhetorical eloquence that he condemns, and it is evident, especially from 2.1-5, that this has something to do with the charge that his own preaching lacked eloquence. Moreover, 2.3-4 suggests that this rhetorical deficiency was the main characteristic of his avowed weakness. In v. 4 Paul asserts that instead of being delivered in 'plausible (πειθοῖ[ς]) words of wisdom' his proclamation of Christ crucified was attended by a 'demonstration of the Spirit and of power (δυνάμεως)', and in v. 5 he sets the δύναμις θεοῦ over against the σοφία ἀνθρώπων.

Marshall observes that in the Hellenistic literature the word δύναμις

---

45. Barrett, *The First Epistle to the Corinthians*, p. 49. Barrett notes that Paul uses the word wisdom in other senses, both good and bad, but goes on to say that 'wisdom as a formal characteristic of skilful speech is not far from describing also the content of a preaching in which the cross may come to look like a foolish error'.

is commonly associated with rhetoric and that it is used interchangeably with ἰσχύς to denote strength, power and influence, their primary meaning having to do with importance or worth.[46] The wisdom terminology also has these connotations in the context of 1 Corinthians 1–2 where it is precisely Paul's worth, judged especially with reference to wisdom in the sense of rhetorical eloquence, that is being questioned by his opponents. This means that wisdom here has more to do with social status and influence than it does a particular theological position, and Paul raises his own questions about the validity of this 'wisdom of the world' by emphasizing that his weakness and rhetorical inferiority occasioned the display of God's power.

God's power stands in direct opposition to the Greco-Roman comprehension of rhetoric implied in the phrases καθ' ὑπεροχὴν λόγου ἢ σοφίας and ἐν πειθοῖς σοφίας λόγοις (1 Cor. 2.1, 4).[47] Since in these passages and in 1.17 σοφία signifies 'a kind of eloquence, a technique for persuading the hearer', it seems plausible to follow Barrett who says that 'it is not an unreasonable guess that it was Apollos who popularized the wisdom method of preaching'.[48] According to Acts 18.24 Apollos was reputed to be 'an eloquent man', and it must have been in the light of his rhetorical proficiency that his following in Corinth criticized Paul.[49] The identification of Paul's opponents as members of a social elite further clarifies how Apollos, whose rhetorical eloquence qualified him as a cultivated person in Greco-Roman society, served as

---

46. Marshall, *Enmity in Corinth*, p. 387.
47. Marshall, *Enmity in Corinth*, p. 600.
48. C.K. Barrett, 'Christianity at Corinth', in *Essays on Paul* (Philadelphia: Westminster Press, 1982), pp. 8, 11. Based on an analysis of Alexandrian rhetoric, Pogoloff argues the opposite, that is, that 'Paul's rhetoric might have been more appealing to more sophisticated tastes, Apollos to the less cultured'. The problem with this view is that it does not sufficiently account for the criticisms of Paul implied in the letter (*LOGOS AND SOPHIA*, pp. 187-89).
49. A. Robertson and A. Plummer, *A Critical and Exegetical Commentary on the First Epistle of St Paul to the Corinthians* (ICC; Edinburgh: T. & T. Clark, 1914), pp. 15-16; Barrett, 'Christianity at Corinth', p. 11; F. Watson, *Paul, Judaism and the Gentiles* (SNTSMS, 56; Cambridge: Cambridge University Press, 1986), p. 83. Watson argues that there was tension between Paul and Apollos and that 1.17–2.5 is a personal attack on Apollos. But the fact that in 4.6 Paul points to Apollos and himself as positive examples militates against this view and supports our earlier claim that Apollos was not necessarily responsible for the behaviour of those who professed allegiance to him.

2. *The Cross and Christian Unity*

the yardstick of Christian leadership for them. With the social values of honour and power as their criteria, this dominant minority determined that Apollos more aptly exemplified an ideal of apostleship which was constructed on these values.[50]

This group, then, compared Paul and Apollos in terms of external strengths and weaknesses, and yet its own claims to superiority seem to have been of a 'spiritual' nature. The πνευματικός–ψυχικός contrast in 1 Cor. 2.6-16 is usually taken as deriving from Paul's opponents and designating 'a qualitative distinction between people of two different levels of religious-ethical ability and achievement'.[51] On this interpretation the term πνευματικός is seen to reflect the exalted spiritual status attained by this elite circle of people by virtue of their possession and cultivation of wisdom.[52] While it does seem apparent that in 2.13-16. Paul has taken up his opponents' terminology in order to radically reinterpret it, there is nothing in the text which suggests that their pneumatic self-consciousness is the product of privileged access to an esoteric or 'deeper' wisdom, such as is associated with Philo, or that what is being contrasted are two different theological conceptions of wisdom. Nowhere in this section does Paul counter, or even allude to, the *content* of a rival understanding of wisdom. He identifies 'Christ crucified' as the content of the 'wisdom of God' (1.21-24) and in 2.6-16 he again turns his attention to this 'secret and hidden wisdom' (2.7), but there is no reason to infer from this that he is arguing against a contrary 'revelation' of wisdom. What is at issue is the form of wisdom. Even when Paul changes the subject from form to content, he does so only to emphasize that the content of God's wisdom is cruciform.[53]

Once it is realized that Paul's discussion of wisdom is not oriented to content as such, then the view that his argument is aimed at his opponents' theology is undermined and the theological aspect of their

---

50. Robertson and Plummer, *First Epistle of St Paul to the Corinthians*, pp. 15-16. Robertson and Plummer do not identify these criteria, but they rightly observe that the Corinthians 'were judging by externals' and that this 'fault would conspicuously apply, no doubt, to those who "ran after" Apollos'.

51. Horsley, 'Pneumatikos vs. Psychikos', p. 278; cf. Pearson, *The Pneumatikos-Psychikos Terminology in I Corinthians*, p. 38.

52. Horsley, 'Pneumatikos vs. Psychikos', p. 269; Pearson, *The Pneumatikos-Psychikos Terminology in I Corinthians*, p. 39.

53. Contra R. Barbour, 'Wisdom and the Cross in I Cor 1 and 2', in C. Andersen and G. Klein (eds.), *Theologia crucis—Signum crucis* (Tübingen: Mohr, 1979), p. 60.

exalted spiritual status is minimized. Hence there must be another explanation for the πνευματικός–ψυχικός designations. The theological explanation can explain neither the party strife nor the criticisms of Paul, for both clearly revolve around the social values implied by the other antitheses in the passage, namely weakness–strength/power, honour–shame, and wisdom–foolishness. Each of these antitheses is defined by the Greco-Roman social system and together they are indicative of a conflict that is preeminently social, though the secular criteria which are at the centre of the dispute seem to have been invested with theological import. In fact, it is conceivable that it was the personification of these values that was spiritualized in Corinth.

H.D. Betz has shown that in Greco-Roman society rhetorical skill could be regarded as proof of the speaker's possession of the Spirit,[54] and the contextual link between σοφία λόγου and πνευματικός suggests that it was precisely this sort of connection that was being made by the Apollos party. That σοφία λόγου was the pivotal criterion in terms of which Paul was criticized and Apollos esteemed makes it likely that it was also a decisive mark of spirituality for these people. Hence it is not necessary to posit that in addition to rhetorical eloquence the Apollos party also thought of wisdom as a claim to revelation. Barrett, for example, delineates two good senses and two bad senses of Paul's use of the word in 1.17-25, but it is preferable to limit the distinction to a positive and negative sense.[55] Generally speaking, God's wisdom is distinguished from the wisdom of the world, but in those instances where σοφία is modified by λόγος this broadly conceived negative category is given more precise definition.

This monolithic interpretation of wisdom accords with what Paul's remarks imply about what actually transpired in the community with respect to his own preaching and that of Apollos. His description of the work he and Apollos did in Corinth as planting and watering, respectively (3.6-9), suggests that the contribution of Apollos may have been a version of Christianity more advanced in its presentation even if no more advanced in its content.[56] Correspondingly, Theissen avers that 2.6-16 presupposes an oral type of pneumatic speech form and that the

54. H.D. Betz, *Der Apostel Paulus und die sokratische Tradition: Eine exegetische Untersuchung zu seiner 'Apologie' 2 Korinther 10–13* (BHT, 45; Tübingen: Mohr, 1972), pp. 58-59.
55. Barrett, *The First Epistle to the Corinthians*, p. 53.
56. Barrett, 'Christianity at Corinth', pp. 11-12.

Sitz im Leben of wisdom was an inner circle in the community in which higher wisdom was perceived as inspired speech.[57] Even if this inner circle did advance claims to higher religious knowledge as well, it is the divisive effect and not the content of this knowledge that concerns Paul.[58] Together these observations lead me to conclude that wisdom was regarded primarily as rhetorical eloquence by the followers of Apollos in Corinth, and that wisdom construed in this way was the basis not only of their attack on Paul but also of an exalted self-consciousness which gave a semblance of spirituality to their avowed superiority.

In working toward a synthesis of the various aspects of the multi-dimensional situation that existed in Corinth, the unifying factor and the main target of Paul's response is the Apollos party's conviction that it was superior. The social discord which heads his agenda in chs. 1–4 was the result of rival groups being 'puffed up in favour of one against another' (4.6; 3.21-22), and I have attempted to show that those who professed to belong to Apollos comprised the influential minority that was largely responsible for evaluations of Paul and Apollos that divided the community. The qualities which attracted these people to Apollos served also as criteria according to which Paul was judged inferior, and hence they sought to shame and discredit him. What is most significant about this group, however, is that both their commitment to Apollos and their criticisms of Paul betray an arrogant disposition which was inseparable from their social standing (cf. 4.8, 10). This disposition is reflected throughout in words such as καυχάομαι (1.29, 31; 3.21; 4.7; cf. 5.6) and φυσίοω (4.6, 18, 19; cf. 5.2; 8.1; 13.4), and is associated with excessive conduct of the *hybris* kind.

The injunction in 4.6 'not to go beyond what is written' is aimed at these individuals who have overstepped the limits of self-knowledge and wisdom as they were defined by the concept of *sophrosyne*, the

---

57. G. Theissen, *Psychologische Aspekte paulinischer Theologie* (Göttingen: Vandenhoeck & Ruprecht, 1983), p. 344. He points out that the predominance of examples of λαλεῖν shows that an oral form of communication is at issue.

58. Cf. Welborn, 'On the Discord in Corinth', pp. 105-106. Welborn points out that the history of civil strife at Rome shows that 'religious knowledge was constantly manipulated by the ruling elite... for the benefit of one faction in rivalry with another'. In accordance with this, he suggests that the leaders of the rival faction in Corinth made claims to higher religious knowledge in order to gain control of the church.

very antithesis of *hybris*.⁵⁹ In 4.7 Paul uses two different words to designate the arrogance which characterized the excessive social conduct of these Corinthians when he explicitly asks: 'Who concedes you any superiority (διακρίνω)? What do you have that you did not receive? If then you received it, why do you boast (καυχάομαι) as if it were not a gift?'⁶⁰ The same arrogant disposition also explains the need for the exhortation in 3.21: 'So let no one boast of men. For all things are yours...' and the citation from Jer. 9.22 in 1.31: 'Let him who boasts, boast of the Lord'. This attitude of arrogant superiority and the conduct which attended it are common to every aspect of the situation Paul confronts in 1 Corinthians 1–4. Moreover, this disposition had its origins in certain social values that were prized and in some instances personified by a minority in Corinth who either belonged or aspired to belong to the upper strata of Greco-Roman society.

The Crucified Christ as the Foundation of the Community:
1 Corinthians 1.18-31

The circumstances described above constitute the socio-historical context within which Paul's exposition of the 'word of the cross' in 1.18-31 is to be interpreted. Of primary concern to Paul was the person-centred rivalry which threatened the unity of the community, and the fact that his extended discourse on Christ crucified as the wisdom of God in 1.18ff. is immediately preceded by his account of the existing dissensions indicates that it is directed toward this problem. Nevertheless, Paul's endeavour to resolve the conflict theologically by drawing attention to the significance of 'Christ crucified' does not, as has been argued, imply that it was caused by erroneous theological ideas. Rather, as Munck has put it, 'the Corinthians' shortcomings in respect of their bickerings are regarded in this section as primarily ethical failures'.⁶¹

---

59. Marshall, *Enmity in Corinth*, pp. 190-95. *Hybris* is 'behaviour which oversteps the bounds or limits or which exceeds the mean' and *sophrosyne* is its traditional antithesis and is translated variously as 'moderation', 'self-control', 'restraint', 'sanity', or 'prudence'. Marshall asserts that 'the association of *sophrosyne* with self-knowledge and *sophia* contrasts clearly with *hybris* as ignorance of one's true self and thus foolishness'. See the major study by H. North, *Sophrosyne: Self-Knowledge and Self-Restraint in Greek Literature* (Ithaca, NY: Cornell University Press, 1996). I will offer a more detailed exegesis of 4.6 in a subsequent section.

60. This is the translation of τίς γάρ σε διακρίνει; given in BAGD, p. 185.

61. Munck, 'The Church Without Factions', p. 152; cf. also E. Ellis, 'Christ

2. *The Cross and Christian Unity* 59

Paul's contingent application of the theology of the cross to the interpersonal dispute in the community must, therefore, be understood as an attempt to elicit behaviour which, unlike that reported to him by Chloe's people, would be congruous with the gospel of 'Jesus Christ and him crucified'. Paul claims that this gospel was the exclusive focus of his first preaching in Corinth (cf. 2.1-2) and he aims to reestablish it as the basis of communal life.

That Paul's objective in 1 Corinthians 1–4 is to reform the Corinthians' conduct so that it is governed by 'the word of the cross' is confirmed by his use of the verb παρακαλέω. According to Dahl, this verb is employed by Paul when setting forth the main purpose of his letters; 'expressing what he wants the addressees to do'.[62] There are two passages where Paul uses this verb to recommend the course of action he wants his readers to take.[63] In 1.10 he 'urges' (παρακαλῶ) that 'all of you agree (τὸ αὐτὸ λέγητε)[64] and that there be no dissensions (σχίσματα) among you, but that you be united in the same mind and the same judgment'. The παρακαλω construct, which in 1.10 opens this section of the letter (1.10–4.21), is used in 4.16 to bring it to a close: 'I urge you, then, be imitators of me'. Following this exhortation is the statement in v. 17 in which Paul explains that the reason he sent Timothy was to remind them of his 'ways in Christ'. If the exhortations in 1.10 and 4.16 convey both Paul's purpose in writing and how to accomplish it, then the unity he desires is somehow connected with, even contingent upon, imitation of him, namely his 'ways in Christ'. Paul considers his life worthy of imitation because it is defined by the 'word of the cross'. But before pointing to the example of his own life of weakness and dishonour (4.10), he first delineates the gospel of 'Christ crucified' with a view to affirming both its power and its contrariety to the 'wisdom of the world' (1.18-25).

The Corinthian community had been fragmented into competing groups with the most influential one claiming to belong to Apollos. Although identification with different authority figures was one of the

Crucified', in *Prophecy and Hermeneutic in Early Christianity* (Grand Rapids: Eerdmans, 1980), p. 75

62. Dahl, 'Paul and the Church at Corinth', p. 46.
63. Cf. Dahl, 'Paul and the Church at Corinth', p. 46.
64. Cf. Robertson and Plummer, *First Epistle of St Paul to the Corinthians*, p. 10. They suggest assert that the expression is taken from Greek political life and means to 'be at peace' or 'make up differences'.

main causes of the divisiveness, it is clear from Paul's criticisms of the Corinthians' behaviour (cf. 3.3) and his admonition for them to conduct themselves in accordance with his example (4.6, 16-17) that the dispute involved more than mere personal loyalties. He describes the behaviour of those involved in the dispute as being 'puffed up in favour of one against another' (4.6), but the disposition denoted by the word φυσιόω here is symptomatic of a more pervasive arrogance that manifested itself in other ethical problems which are dealt with elsewhere in the letter (cf. 5.2; 8.1-13; 13.4). This arrogance is inextricably connected with the social values which were the basis of the Apollos people's commitment to Apollos and their criticisms of Paul.

Throughout these chapters Paul challenges the status system which forms the basis of the Corinthians' arrogant behaviour, but as Judge observes, he does not analyse human affairs in institutional terms but rather attacks the problems at a personal level.[65] In this instance he broaches the problem by focusing on the ground and origin of the Christian's identity. He introduces the subject of Christian identity with the rhetorical questions which immediately follow his reference to the different parties: 'Is Christ divided? Was Paul crucified for you? Or were you baptized into the name of Paul?' (1.13). The first of these questions serves to confront the Corinthians with the most serious implication of the dissensions, and the other two questions raise a more fundamental question about whether their calling as saints (cf. 1.2) was the result of identification with Paul or Apollos, or the consequence of Christ's death on their behalf.[66]

Although the earliest Christian communities understood baptism as a rite of initiation carried out in 'the name of the Lord Jesus Christ' (1 Cor. 6.11), in the Corinthian community it may have been a means of identifying with the one who was baptizing (e.g. Paul, Apollos or possibly Cephas). That is probably why Paul is reluctant to admit that he baptized anyone in Corinth (1.14-17).[67] Instead he draws attention

---

65. E.A. Judge, 'Cultural Conformity and Innovation in Paul: Some Clues from Contemporary Documents', *TynBul* 35 (1984), p. 5.

66. Since Christians understood baptism as participation in Christ's death (Rom. 6.3-11), the second rhetorical question in 1.13 parallels the first in that it also challenges the reader to consider their relationship to the Christ who was indeed crucified for them.

67. Meeks, *The First Urban Christians*, p. 117; cf. Conzelmann, *1 Corinthians*, p. 35.

to the fact that Christ did not send him to baptize but to preach the gospel (1.17). As a rule Paul did regard baptism as the decisive point of entry into new life in Christ (cf. Rom. 6.1-11), but in this instance he takes the community back to its origins in the cross.[68] He affirms that the content of the gospel he preaches is 'the word of the cross' and then reminds the Corinthians that it was by virtue of their response to that word that they had been included among those who are 'being saved' (σῳζομένοις) as opposed to those who are 'perishing' (ἀπολλυμένοις, 1.18). By using present participles in drawing the distinction between these two categories of people Paul contemporizes the initial effect of his preaching of the cross in order to stress its continued significance for the life of the community.[69]

Paul rehearses the origins of the Corinthians' incorporation into the church and formulates their ecclesial identity in terms of their response to the 'word of the cross' because his argument in 1.10–4.21 is dependent on their recognition that the event of Christ's death is, so to speak, the very ground of their being. Best rightly observes that Paul does not argue for the centrality of the cross but assumes that if he recalls his readers to this they will accept his argument.[70] Thus he makes a strong emotional appeal by referring to the Corinthians' common experience of the gospel (1.18, cf. 1.9) and thereby establishes the foundation from which he argues.[71] This experiential foundation corresponds to the foundational reality upon which he himself began to build the community (cf. 3.10-14). According to Berger and Luckmann, 'theories about identity are always embedded in a more general interpretation of reality; they are "built into" the symbolic universe....'[72] In effect, what Paul does is locate the identity of the Corinthian community in

---

68. J. Schütz, *Paul and the Anatomy of Apostolic Authority* (SNTSMS, 26; Cambridge: Cambridge University Press, 1975), p. 191. Meeks points out that baptism is the usual point of reference when Paul tries to get his addressees to recall what happened when they first became Christians (*The First Urban Christians*, p. 154), but here he diverts the Corinthians' attention away from baptism and focuses it on the cross.

69. On the force of the present participles see Barrett, *The First Epistle to the Corinthians*, p. 51.

70. Best, 'The Power and the Wisdom of God', p. 11.

71. Cf. R. Humphries, 'Paul's Rhetoric of Argumentation in I Corinthians 1–4' (unpublished PhD dissertation, Berkeley, The Graduate Theological Union, 1979), p. 40.

72. Berger and Luckmann, *The Social Construction of Reality*, p. 195.

their shared understanding of Christian reality,[73] but in this context reality is defined exclusively in terms of the symbol of the cross: 'For I decided to know nothing among you except Jesus Christ and him crucified' (2.2).

Paul takes it for granted that the Corinthians will acknowledge that God has called the community into existence through his preaching of the crucified Christ, and so from this given he proceeds to draw out the implications of the content of the message they first received. Humphries observes that Paul's argumentative strategy is to show the Corinthians in what respects their behaviour is inconsistent with what they and Paul believe.[74] More constructively, his aim is to create a symmetry between the objective reality symbolized and mediated by the 'word of the cross' and the subjective reality of the Corinthians, including both their identity and their lifestyle, and this is largely a matter of socialization.[75] One way the interpersonal problems in the church can be explained is as an identity crisis which was the result of belonging to two discrepant universes of meaning. Membership in the Christian community entailed embracing a definition of reality and corresponding identity which ran counter to the everyday realities of the Greco-Roman world into which the Corinthian believers had been socialized. Hence the incongruity between faith and conduct reflected in 1 Corinthians 1–4 can be described as an existential tension which resulted in part from living in two polarized social worlds.[76] This tension must have been especially acute for those Corinthian Christians of high social standing, that is, the few who were wise, powerful and well born according to worldly standards (1.26; 4.8, 10).

While these Corinthian Christians laid claim to a Christian identity, the values according to which they denigrated Paul and distinguished

---

73. Cf. Berger and Luckmann, *The Social Construction of Reality*, p. 195. Berger and Luckmann assert that 'identity remains unintelligible unless it is located in a world'.

74. Humphries, 'Paul's Rhetoric', p. 62.

75. Cf. Berger and Luckmann, *The Social Construction of Reality*, p. 183. This is their definition of 'successful socialization'.

76. Cf. Berger and Luckmann, *The Social Construction of Reality*, p. 194; V. Hasler, 'Das Evangelium des Paulus in Korinth. Erwägungen zur Hermeneutik', *NTS* 30 (1984), p. 109. B. Bernstein asserts that 'the identity of the individual will be refracted to him by the concrete symbols of the group...' ('Social Class and Psycho-therapy', *British Journal of Sociology* 15 [1964], pp. 59-60, cited by Douglas, *Natural Symbols*, p. 46).

2. The Cross and Christian Unity

themselves as superior were the same values by which an individual was considered either weak or strong, honoured or dishonoured in Greco-Roman society. Paul elucidates this discrepancy between their baptismal identity and their adherence to secular values in 3.1-3 where he says that, despite their pneumatic self-consciousness, he could not address them 'as spiritual people (πνευματικοί)', but as 'people of the flesh (σαρκικοί)'. And they 'are still people of the flesh (σαρκικοί)' because they are 'behaving like ordinary people (κατὰ ἄνθρωπον περιπατεῖτε)'. In this context σαρκικός denotes 'natural' rather than sinful humanity (cf. ψυχικὸς ἄνθρωπος in 2.14).[77] Barrett remarks that 'fleshly people' are 'those whose existence is determined not by God but by considerations internal to themselves',[78] but this is to over-estimate human autonomy and to underestimate the influence of social worlds. Paul himself suggests as much in his description of the Christian as one who has 'received not the spirit of the world, but the Spirit which is from God' (2.12). The opposite of a life guided by the Spirit of God is one that is determined by the 'spirit of the world'. This phrase designates an external force which influences the behaviour of those in the κόσμος who are subject to it.

The word κόσμος has a comprehensive significance for Paul and therefore has a wide range of meanings. In this section of 1 Corinthians the phrase τὸ πνεῦμα τοῦ κόσμου is virtually synonymous with, and therefore is given more precise definition by, the corresponding phrase ἡ σοφία τοῦ κόσμου (3.19; cf. 1.21; 2.6).[79] The latter phrase demystifies the former in that it shows that to be under the influence of the 'spirit of the world' is to be guided by the values which constitute its wisdom (e.g. σοφία λόγου). Paul's remark in 2.12, understood within the context of 2.6-16, further clarifies what is at issue in the antithesis between God and the world. It reveals that there is an epistemological difference between σαρκικός and πνευματικός existence. The person who has received the Spirit of God 'understands' what she/he has received from God and, more importantly for Paul's purposes, 'judges (ἀνακρίνει) all things, but is himself judged by no one' (2.15). Conversely, the 'natural' (ψυχικὸς) person does not understand (οὐ

---

77. Barrett, *The First Epistle to the Corinthians*, p. 80; Conzelmann, *1 Corinthians*, p. 71; Fee, *The First Epistle to the Corinthians*, p. 124.

78. Barrett, *The First Epistle to the Corinthians*, p.80.

79. Barrett, *The First Epistle to the Corinthians*, p. 75; Sasse, 'κόσμος', *TDNT*, III, p. 892.

δύναται γνῶναι) the things of the Spirit of God 'for they are folly (μωρία) to him' (2.14).

These verses recall Paul's comment in 1.21: 'since, in the wisdom of God, the world did not know God through wisdom, it pleased God through the folly of what we preach to save those who believe'. In all of these passages Paul emphasizes the distinction between God and the world in order to distinguish between two incompatible ways of perceiving and judging: one which is the result of having received the 'Spirit of God' and one which is dictated by the 'spirit of the world'. It is important to note, however, that perception and judgment always presuppose values (i.e. criteria) in terms of which the perceptions and judgments are made, and these values are always, to some extent anyway, socially determined.[80] Thus the world which stands in opposition to God is a real social world, and the 'spirit of the world' refers, in some sense at least, to the values which govern the attitudes, judgments and behaviour of the people in that world.[81]

The interpersonal problems which are the primary focus of Paul's attention in 1 Corinthians 1–4, as well as the criticisms levelled against him, are construed in terms of an opposition between the God and 'the world'. Within the Corinthian community this opposition was manifested in the form of discordant values which are here denoted primarily by the power–weakness antithesis. The social connotations the power–weakness contrast had in the Greco-Roman world were established in the previous section. However, in 1.18-25 Paul also ascribes

---

80. Cf. Sasse, 'κόσμος', p. 892. He also points out the connection between epistemology and values in his commentary on 1 Cor. 2.12: 'According to 1 Cor. 2.12 the πνεῦμα τοῦ κόσμου and the πνεῦμα τὸ ἐκ τοῦ θεοῦ are mutually exclusive opposites. The σοφία τοῦ κόσμου is μωρία παρὰ τῷ θεῷ, 1 Cor. 1.20ff.; 3.19, cf. 1.27, and the θεοῦ σοφία is not understood by the wise of the world, 1 Cor. 2.6ff., 14. God's standards for assessing men are different from those of the world, 1 Cor. 1.26ff.'

81. It is interesting that although Bultmann's approach is existential rather than sociological, his definition of this phrase echoes Berger and Luckmann's explanation of the character of the social world. According to Bultmann, '"the spirit of the world" is the atmosphere to whose compelling influence every man contributes but to which he is also always subject' (*Theology of the New Testament*, p. 257). Correspondingly, Berger and Luckmann assert that 'the relationship between man, the producer, and the social world, his product, is and remains a dialectic one. That is, man and his social world interact with each other. The product acts back upon the producer' (*The Social Construction of Reality*, p. 78).

2. *The Cross and Christian Unity* 65

positive theological significance to both terms by using them to delineate the paradoxical revelation of God's power in the weakness of the cross. He transforms this antithesis signifying diametrically opposed social values into a theological dialectic by affirming that though the cross denotes foolishness and weakness, it is rightly conceived as power because of its efficacy for those who apprehend its import: 'the word of the cross is folly to those who are perishing, but to us who are being saved it is the power of God' (1.18).

In this verse Paul reminds the Corinthians that God's power was demonstrated in the call they received through his preaching of the cross (cf. 1.26-31).[82] This affirmation must be understood in relation to the preceding statement in 1.17 in which he suggests that it is possible to nullify this paradoxical power of the cross by the manner in which it is verbalized.[83] In view of the criticism that his own 'speech and message were not in plausible words of wisdom' (2.4), Paul asserts that such rhetorical eloquence threatens to empty or undermine the cross of Christ. In these two passages (1.17; 2.1-4) he counterbalances references to the power which attended his proclamation of Christ crucified with an emphasis on the conspicuous absence of σοφία λόγου in his presentation of that message because for him rhetorical eloquence represented an exhibition of power that was incongruous with the power of God as exemplified in the cross of Christ. While the phrase 'power of God' refers to eschatological salvation (cf. Rom. 1.16), in the Greco-Roman world rhetoric had connotations of power in the sense of importance or worth. This constituted a social definition of power rooted in the values cultivated by those in society who had wealth, status and honour, that is, who were socially powerful; Paul's theological understanding of power, on the other hand, was rooted in the conviction that God's power has been manifested through the weakness of the crucified Christ inasmuch as he has been made 'wisdom', 'righteousness', 'sanctification' and 'redemption' for the believer (1.30).

The difference between these two notions of power is relevant to the actual situation in Corinth because it applied to the social elite in the community whose understanding of power was determined by the secular values which for Paul invalidated God's power as it was mediated through the 'word of the cross'. Paul further develops

82. Schütz, *Paul and the Anatomy of Apostolic Authority*, p. 202.
83. Humphries, 'Paul's Rhetoric', p. 63.

66   *The Cross in Corinth*

this distinction between secular and theological power in 1.18–2.5. Corresponding to these two types of power are two groups of people who are characterized in terms of their eschatological destiny, and Paul distinguishes between them on the basis of their respective attitudes to the cross: 'the word of the cross is folly to those who are perishing, but to those who are being saved it is the power of God' (1.18).[84] Although the only explicit mention of power in this verse and in 1.19–2.5 pertains to the apprehension of Christ crucified as the power and the wisdom of God (1.24), the judgment that the cross is folly implies a contrary perception of power associated with those Greco-Roman social values in terms of which strength and honour were esteemed and weakness and shame disdained. Paul asserts that the 'word of the cross' separates 'those who are perishing' from 'we who are being saved' first in order to emphasize that the Corinthians belong to the latter group, and secondly to underline the definition and experience of power appropriate to participation in the eschatological destiny of that group.

The eschatological contrast in 1.18 is critical to Paul's argument in this context not because the Corinthians' salvation is in question, but rather because it serves to set up his discussion of the opposition between God and the world, or, more precisely, between 'the wisdom of God' and 'the wisdom of the world' (1.20-24). By using the participle ἀπολλυμένοις to designate those who stand outside the realm of God's saving activity because they reject the cross as foolishness, Paul is able to discredit the world and its wisdom at the outset. The reason he discredits it is that despite the inclusion of the Corinthians among those who 'are being saved', some of them act as though they still belong to the world (3.1-4). Moreover, their criticisms of Paul reflect the fact that they have judged him according to worldly standards (2.1-4; 4.10). The conduct and disposition of these Corinthian Christians betrayed an ambivalence which must have been caused by the convergence of an identity embedded in the values and social structure of Greco-Roman society, and the new consciousness mediated by the Christian symbol system.[85] The community of those who were 'being saved' was counter-

---

84.   Cf. Barrett, *The First Epistle to the Corinthians*, p. 51, who, following Lietzmann and Kümmel, *An die Korinther I/II* (HNT, 9; Tübingen: Mohr, 1969), rightly observes that ἀπόλλυμι and σῴζω are eschatological terms and thus the distinction between the groups they describe is an eschatological one.

85.   On the question of social identity and the confrontation of discrepant

2. *The Cross and Christian Unity*

cultural inasmuch as its comprehension of reality and concomitant norms and values were expected to be at variance with those of the larger society. The values of that society were the basis of their criticisms of Paul and the discord and strife in the community, and yet they were inextricably bound to a secular social identity. Paul reminds the Corinthians of the eschatological destiny of those who from a temporal standpoint perceive the cross to be foolishness. Then he submits a full-scale repudiation of the wisdom upon which this judgment is founded, namely the 'wisdom of the world' (1.19-25).

The word κόσμος here signifies not only 'the sphere of earthly life's conditions'; it also implies opposition to the sphere of God.[86] Accordingly, the σοφία τοῦ κόσμου is the way of looking at things which is characteristic of this particular sphere of 'ethical and social conditions'.[87] As Conzelmann points out, wisdom in this context 'is not primarily a piece of knowledge, but an attitude'.[88] Paul discounts this attitude or mode of perception on the grounds that 'the world did not know God through wisdom' (1.21). But in v. 22 he divides the 'world' into Jews and Greeks and it becomes evident that wisdom consists of standards or values pertaining only to Greek perception: 'Jews demand signs and Greeks seek wisdom'. According to Conzelmann, both groups demand a proof of the divine truth, and thus what makes their attitude 'worldly' is that they expect God to submit to their criteria.[89] The problem, however, is not just that these criteria are imposed on God, but that the criteria are themselves *worldly*. It is with respect to these criteria that Paul's remark is addressed to the Corinthian situation, for the Corinthians are among the 'called' and therefore are not implicated in the negative comments about the 'world' and its failure to know the God who is revealed in the cross of Christ (1.19-21). Nevertheless, since some of them are still 'men of the flesh' (3.1, 3) and are 'behaving like ordinary men' (3.3) they continued to

---

realities see Berger and Luckmann, *The Social Construction of Reality*, pp. 183-93.

86. Bultmann, *Theology of the New Testament*, pp. 255-56. Bultmann correctly notes that in this context κόσμος is not a cosmological term but an historical one.

87. Cf. Plummer, *First Epistle of St Paul to the Corinthians*, p. 20. This is his definition of τοῦ αἰῶνος τούτου, which he asserts is practically synonymous with τοῦ κόσμου.

88. Conzelmann, *1 Corinthians*, pp. 43-44.

89. Conzelmann, *1 Corinthians*, p. 47.

be guided by the 'wisdom of the world'.⁹⁰ In other words, despite their apprehension of Christ crucified as the power of God, the behaviour and judgments of these Corinthian believers betray the influence of the Greco-Roman values according to which the cross is deemed weakness and foolishness.

A rhetorical analysis of 1.18-25 discloses the import of Paul's general discussion of the conflict between the wisdom of God and the wisdom of the world for the issues he is confronting in 1 Corinthians 1–4. Wilhelm Wuellner has made a case for understanding this passage as epideictic rhetoric as it is defined in the following way:

> the argumentation in epideictic discourse sets out to increase the intensity of adherence to certain values, which might not be contested when considered on their own but may nevertheless prevail against other values that might come into conflict with them. The speaker tries to establish a sense of communion centred around particular values recognized by the audience, and to this end the whole range of means available to the rhetorician for purposes of amplification and enhancement.⁹¹

The purpose of increasing adherence to the values lauded is to strengthen the disposition toward action,⁹² and the desired action expressed in 1 Corinthians is, as Wuellner affirms, 'the one stated in 1.10, and restated in the *recapitulatio* in 16.13-14, namely that they all be of 'one mind'.⁹³ Paul reckons this unity of mind to be the ground of the social harmony that he seeks to obtain, and it is dependent on a

---

90. Cf. R. Jewett, *Paul's Anthropological Terms* (Leiden: Brill, 1971), p. 122; Fee, *The First Epistle to the Corinthians*, p. 124. Both Jewett and Fee note the subtle difference in meaning between σάρκινος and σαρκικός. They point out that the word σάρκινος emphasizes the Corinthians' humanness and the physical side of their existence over against the spiritual while the word σαρκικός has ethical overtones and indicates that 'their behaviour belongs to the present age, with its fallen, twisted values' (Fee, *The First Epistle to the Corinthians*, p. 127).

91. C. Perelman and L. Olbrechts-Tyteca, *The New Rhetoric: A Treatise on Argumentation* (Notre Dame, IN: University of Notre Dame Press, 1969), p. 51, cited by W. Wuellner, 'Greek Rhetoric and Pauline Argumentation', in W. Schoedel and R. Wilken (eds.), *Early Christian Literature and the Classical Intellectual Tradition* (Paris: Editions Beauchesne, 1979), p. 184. Cf. also Humphries, 'Paul's Rhetoric', p. 110.

92. Perelman and Olbrechts-Tyteca, *The New Rhetoric*, p. 9. On p. 54 they observe that 'epideictic discourse is less directed toward changing beliefs than to strengthening the adherence to what is already accepted'.

93. Wuellner, 'Greek Rhetoric and Pauline Argumentation', p. 183.

unanimous commitment to values which befit a community that has been called into existence through the 'word of the cross' (cf. 1.26-28).

The Corinthian church was founded upon the preaching of 'Christ crucified' (2.1-2; cf. 3.10-11), and in 1.18-25 Paul not only re-establishes the content of that preaching as the foundation but also delineates the values which correspond to it.[94] The point of departure for his explication of these values is the conviction which he supports with a quotation from Isa. 29.14 (1.19) that God has turned the world's values on their head, that is, has 'made foolish the wisdom of the world' (1.20). The constructive corollary to this verdict is the declaration that God's wisdom and power have been revealed in the cross of Christ (1.23-24). These assertions express the positive and negative aspects of Paul's inversion of the temporal claim that the cross is foolishness (1.18, 23). In the negative assessment of 1.19 the cross represents God's judgment of the world and its wisdom (1.19-21),[95] and in the positive appraisal of 1.23-24 'Christ crucified' is the embodiment of God's wisdom and power. Wisdom and power as they have been re-defined by the 'word of the cross' are the fundamental values which Paul reinforces here, but it is the element of negation which predominates in this particular passage.[96] In this context the critical function of Paul's theology of the cross comes to the fore inasmuch as it serves as the basis for denouncing those cultural values according to which the cross is rejected as foolishness.[97]

94. The phrase 'Christ crucified' is an elaboration of the phrase 'the word of the cross', and the use of the perfect participle ἐσταυρωμένον is a way of emphasizing the continued significance of the cross. As Ellis puts it, 'the term expresses the perspective from which the risen Christ presently works and, thus, the perspective from which "God's wisdom" is presently manifested' ('Christ Crucified', pp. 73-74; cf. Robinson, 'Word and Power', p. 71).

95. The quotation in 1.19 states the main theme of the passage, which is the divine judgment on human wisdom. So Conzelmann, *1 Corinthians*, pp. 42-43; W. Wuellner, 'Haggadic Homily Genre in I Corinthians 1–3', *JBL* 89 (1970), pp. 201-202.

96. Beker, *Paul the Apostle*, p. 204. Beker asserts that 'wisdom and the law are both structures of this age, normative powers for Greeks and Jews respectively. They are symbolic abbreviations of what "the civilized and religious world" considers its highest values... The world of the law is leveled, along with that of wisdom, because both fall impartially and equally under the judgement on the cross'.

97. It was Käsemann who revived the Reformation emphasis on the critical function of the theology of the cross. While his exegesis is sometimes too influenced by contemporary theological reflection, he has a knack for penetrating to the nub of

It is necessary to highlight the cultural antecedents of the Greek attitude to the cross conveyed by the term μωρία in order to appreciate the full force of Paul's critique. Martin Hengel has emphasized the shame associated with crucifixion in the Greco-Roman world. With respect to the offence of 'the word of the cross' he remarks that it 'ran counter not only to Roman political thinking, but to the whole ethos of religion in ancient times and in particular to the ideas of God held by educated people'.[98] In the light of the fact that Paul makes an effort to preserve the scandal of the cross (cf. Gal. 5.11), it is not difficult to imagine the cognitive dissonance experienced by the social elite in the Corinthian community. Despite their membership in the community of saints, they were also counted among the socially powerful in a society where belief in a messiah who, as Celsus put it was 'executed in a shameful way', was a contradiction in terms and therefore considered foolish.[99] Although these people are not singled out in Paul's unequivocal indictment of the 'wisdom of the world', they are inculpated by virtue of their adherence to the secular values symbolized by the phrase. Paul's argument in 1.18-25 is in substance a criticism of culture and, as Bertram observes, this criticism is clearly displayed in the transvaluation of wisdom and folly, but finds its most pertinent expression in the contrasting of strength and weakness.[100]

the matter, as the following passage shows: 'Thus Pauline theology significantly avoids directing its attack primarily against religious outsiders and the morally unstable. Hate taught Nietzsche to see, not without a degree of truth, that the apostle almost exclusively attacks the strong and the devout. This is to shift the line of demarcation between the church and the world. We generally understand by the world the sphere in which the name of Christ is not acknowledged. Paul, on the other hand, is aware of a world which penetrates and gains ground within Christianity itself, dividing it into two camps. According to him there are actual enemies of Christ in the Christian communities in Galatia and Corinth, in Philippi and Rome; and they are not to be found so much among the waverers as among the keenest and most devout church members. The fact that Jesus is proclaimed and believed in as Lord is not the point. Everything depends on whether Christian devotion, in Kähler's words, finds its foundation and its criterion in the cross, right down to everyday life' ('The Saving Significance of the Death of Jesus in Paul', pp. 38-39).

98. M. Hengel, *Crucifixion* (Philadelphia: Fortress Press, 1977), p. 5. Hengel provides an extensive survey of the Greek-speaking world's attitude to this 'particularly cruel and shameful death, which as a rule was reserved for hardened criminals, rebellious slaves and rebels against the Roman state' (p. 83).

99. Cf. Hengel, *Crucifixion*, pp. 1-10.

100. G. Bertram, 'μωρός', *TDNT*, IV, p. 847.

It is apparent from the way μωρία is set over against the δύναμις θεοῦ in 1.18 that the comparison of wisdom and folly is fundamentally related to the power–weakness antithesis,[101] and this is further substantiated by the conclusion Paul draws in v. 25: 'For the foolishness of God is wiser than men, and the weakness of God is stronger than men'. Since honour and strength were qualities highly esteemed in the Greco-Roman world, the cross is perceived to be foolish precisely because it symbolizes weakness and shame. Paul's discussion of these antithetical values with reference to the identification of God's power with the crucified Christ (1.23-24) culminates in their reversal.[102] He concedes that the cross is indeed foolishness and weakness by the world's standards only to affirm that it is also the wisdom and power of God. The paradox is that the 'weakness of God' (1.25) and the 'power of God' (1.18) are synonymous in that they are both defined in terms of the cross.[103] However, this only means that although the cross represents weakness according to worldly values, it is nonetheless a manifestation of power insofar as the 'power of God' is defined eschatologically (1.18) rather that socially. The upshot of this line of reasoning is that the social values denoted by the folly–wisdom and weakness–strength antitheses have been superseded by an alternative set of values which are centred in the cross. These values are established without regard to human assessment, and their authority resides in the fact that the crucified Christ is none other than the 'Lord of glory' (2.8).[104] Consequently, in contradistinction to the Greco-Roman standpoint, weakness is given positive significance because it is in the cross, a symbol of weakness and shame, that God has disclosed divine wisdom and power (1.23-24), and it is through the preaching of 'Christ crucified' that the Corinthian community has been called into existence.

Although in 1.18-25 Paul does not elaborate on the opposition

---

101. Bertram, 'μωρός', p. 847; cf. F.F. Bruce, *I & II Corinthians* (London: Marshall, Morgan & Scott, 1971), p. 34.

102. H. Lietzmann, *An die Korinther I/II* (ed. W.G. Kümmel; HNT, 9; Tübingen: Mohr, 1969), p. 10, remarks that v. 25 is 'Prägnante Ausdrucksweise für die Umkehrung der Werte im neuen Äon'.

103. Cf. B.A. Babcock, *The Reversible World* (Ithaca, NY: Cornell University Press, 1978), pp. 14-17. Paul's argument in 1.18-25 fits Babcock's definition of symbolic inversion as a form of cultural negation which always employs paradox to challenge some form of orthodoxy or convention.

104. Cf. H. Weder, *Das Kreuz Jesu bei Paulus* (Göttingen: Vandenhoeck & Ruprecht, 1981), pp. 167-68.

between God's wisdom and the world's wisdom with reference to the particular problems he is confronting in Corinth, in 1.26-31 he shows that the effects of God's overturning of the world's values are evident in the community. There is a correlation between the cruciform display of God's wisdom and power, or the 'foolishness' and 'weakness' of God (1.25), and the social structure of the Corinthian church: 'not many of you were wise according to worldly standards, not many were powerful, not many were of noble birth' (1.26). On the one hand, then, the social standing of the majority of Corinthian Christians verifies Paul's exposition of the 'word of the cross' in 1.18-25.[105] On the other hand, since the social stratification of the community was a contributing factor in the interpersonal disputes which are Paul's primary concern in chs. 1–4, it seems likely that the main purpose of 1.18-25 is to provide a theological legitimation of a community comprised of a majority of people who were socially inferior to the few Corinthian Christians of high social status. Paul's point is that those whom society and the world regard as nothing (1.28) are in reality representatives of that true wisdom made known in the crucified Christ.[106]

The legitimating function of this passage (1.18-25) is corroborated by the purpose clauses in 1.27-29.[107] Having narrowed the scope of the discussion from the distinction between those who are perishing and those who are being saved (1.18) to the specific calling of the Corinthians in 1.26,[108] Paul explains that 'God chose what is foolish in the world to shame the wise, God chose what is weak in the world to shame the strong, God chose what is low and despised in the world, even things that are not, to bring to nothing things that are' (vv. 27-28). With the social tensions in the community in view, Paul asserts that God has chosen the 'foolish' and the 'weak' not just to save them (1.18, 21), but 'to shame' the 'wise' and the 'strong' (1.27).[109] Here

105. Weder, *Das Kreuz Jesu bei Paulus*, p. 159; Schütz, *Paul and the Anatomy of Apostolic Authority*, p. 197; Barrett, *The First Epistle to the Corinthians*, p. 56.

106. Theissen, *The Social Setting of Pauline Christianity*, p. 71.

107. Each of the clauses begins with ἵνα thus indicating God's purpose with the final ἵνα clause expressing God's ultimate aim (Conzelmann, *1 Corinthians*, p. 50).

108. Barrett, *The First Epistle to the Corinthians*, p. 57, observes that the term κλῆσις here 'means "the circumstances in which you were called", and thus points forward to the kind of person called and the nature of the community brought into being by the call'.

109. The irony is perhaps also accentuated by the rhetorical skill reflected in the construction of 1.26-29. Cf. BDF, p. 490: 'From any Greek orator the artistry of

2. The Cross and Christian Unity

the critical function of the theology of the cross is directly relevant to the problems in the community. On the surface, the string of clauses in vv. 27-28 seems to be a general conclusion of the kind voiced in the preceding passage (1.18-25), but the specificity of the social description in 1.26 suggests that they contained a more incisive message for those few Corinthians who were included among the 'wise' and 'strong', and there can be little doubt that they felt the full force of these pointed remarks. Moreover, the twofold use of κατὰ σάρκα suggests that Paul drives his point home by the use of irony. If we are correct in thinking of these people as *hybrists* and therefore as engaged in shaming and dishonouring those members of the community that they considered socially inferior (behaviour which is attested by their criticisms of Paul), then he has turned the tables on them by averring that as wise and strong according to worldly standards (κατὰ σάρκα) they have been shamed by God. The irony is further heightened when the reader grasps that the cross, the epitome of shame and dishonour in Greco-Roman culture, is the vehicle of their shame.[110]

Paul has argued in 1.18-25 that God has annulled all conventional canons of wisdom, power, reputation and value, and, as Bruce puts it, 'nothing could be more subversive of these canons in the first century Greco-Roman world than the proclamation of a crucified man exalted as Lord'.[111] In 1.26ff. he brings this argument to bear on the Corinthian situation. First he reminds the Corinthians that the community has been shaped by the 'word of the cross' and hence that its social structure reflects God's displacement of worldly wisdom and power, and then he concludes that as a result God has shamed the 'wise' and the 'strong' of the world.[112] Both deductions serve to confront the 'wise' and 'strong' Corinthian Christians who continued to behave and judge fellow believers κατὰ σάρκα (cf. 3.1-4) with the social implications of the cross. This minority from the upper strata of society thought of themselves as superior according to the values cultivated by those of

---

this passage... would have called forth the utmost admiration...'
  110. Schütz, *The Anatomy of Apostolic Authority*, p. 198.
  111. Bruce, *I & II Corinthians*, p. 36.
  112. Although Paul's use of καταισχύνω here is primarily determined by the LXX usage where it denotes experience of the judgment of God, it could also denote the cultural shame which was the antithesis of honour for the few Corinthians who were 'wise', 'powerful' and 'of noble birth'. For the use of καταισχύνω in the LXX see Bultmann, 'αἰσχύνω', *TDNT*, I, p.189.

high status in Greco-Roman society, and in Paul's estimation their pretentious attitudes and actions were the main cause of discord in the community.[113] Paul's explication of the theology of the cross pertains to the arrogant disposition of this elite group, and its intended effect is made explicit in the final purpose clause in v. 29: 'so that no human being might boast in the presence of God'. This statement expresses the ultimate consequence of God's activity as set out in vv. 27-28, and it is reiterated in 1.31 in the form of an admonition which alludes to Jer. 9.22-23: 'Let him who boasts, boast of the Lord'. By disclosing the divine wisdom and power in the cross of Christ and choosing the weak and foolish of the world, God has undermined all grounds of human boasting, especially the secular values which were the basis of the Corinthians' arrogance.

Imitation of the Weak Apostle as the Solution to the Problem of Disunity

In 2.1-5 Paul continues his consideration of the implications of the 'word of the cross', but the centre of gravity is shifted from the preaching to the preacher. Wilckens rightly points out that 1.26-31 and 2.1-5 are parallel arguments because in both Paul follows up what he has basically set out in 1.18-25.[114] Just as there is a correspondence between the content of preaching and the social structure of the Corinthian church, so also is there a correspondence between the content and form of the preaching, and this includes the demeanor of the apostle.[115] Paul again identifies the content of his initial preaching in Corinth as 'Jesus Christ and him crucified' (2.2), and then affirms that 'I was with you in weakness and in much fear and trembling; and my speech and my message were not in plausible words of wisdom, but in demonstration of the Spirit and of power' (2.3-4). The purpose clause in v. 5 suggests that, from a retrospective viewpoint in any case, Paul intentionally adopted the posture of someone who was weak

---

113. Marshall, *Enmity in Corinth*, p. 187, observes that one of the most common characteristics of ὕβρις is that denoted by στάσις, 'discord', and similar notions of divisions and disorder. He remarks that 'ὕβρις results in either political or social factions and together with κέρδος, "gain", is the most obvious cause of faction between the dominating classes and the disadvantaged'.

114. Wilckens, 'Zu I Kor 2.1-16', p. 502.

115. Conzelmann, *1 Corinthians*, pp. 53-54.

and deliberately failed to measure up to standards of rhetorical excellence (v. 4), and that he did this so that the Corinthians' faith 'might not rest in the wisdom of men but in the power of God'. The contrasts between ἐν πειθοῖς σοφίας λόγοις and ἐν ἀποδείξει πνεύματος καὶ δυνάμεως (2.4), and ἐν σοφίᾳ ἀνθρώπων and ἐν δυνάμει θεου (2.5) recall the more fundamental antithesis between the 'wisdom of God' and the 'wisdom of the world' in all that it entails in 1.18-25. In this context first hand experience of God's power is set directly over against rhetorical eloquence, an opposition which discloses what Paul perceives to be the critical issue in the interpersonal problems he is dealing with in 1 Corinthians 1–4.

Although I have followed Dahl's suggestion that Paul's comments in 2.1-4 reflect certain criticisms of his apostolate, there is nothing in this passage or anywhere else in chs. 1–4 to support his claim that the entire section contains an apology for Paul.[116] Paul here endorses the very weakness and rhetorical deficiency for which he has been criticized, and he seems to be guided as much by theological conviction as a need to defend himself. The sense of purpose with which he embraces these characteristic features of a socially inferior person by Greco-Roman standards is confirmed by the fact that, despite his disavowal of eloquent speech (2.1, 4), his writing (which according to Barrett always reads like speech) 'has genuine eloquence, and for all its common touch and occasional Semitic structure rises to the heights of Greek prose'.[117] While eloquence in writing and eloquence in speaking are not necessarily the same, it is significant that Paul cleverly employs terminology which traditionally belongs to rhetoric in order to discount preaching which was too heavily dependent on the art of persuasive speech, that is, 'persuasive words of wisdom' (2.4).[118] More fundamentally though, his denunciation of the devices and strategies of

116. Dahl, 'Church at Corinth', p. 49. In a concluding footnote Dahl concedes that his characterization of 1 Cor. 1.10–4.21 as an apologetic section is one-sided, but he still maintains that it contains apologetic elements and serves to reestablish Paul's authority (p. 61 n. 50). This will be discussed in more detail below.

117. Barrett, *The First Epistle to the Corinthians*, p. 64.

118. T. Lim, 'Not in Persuasive Words of Wisdom, but in the Demonstration of the Spirit and Power', *NovT* 29.2 (1987), p. 147, points out that ἀποδείξεις occurs frequently as a technical term in rhetoric which means a demonstration or cogent proof of argument from commonly agreed premises. He says that 'by employing it with πνεύματος and δυνάμεως, Paul uses ἀποδείξεις in a way which is different from and counter to the rhetorical meaning of the term'.

rhetoric in preaching, taken together with his affirmation of his own weakness (4.10-12; cf. 2 Cor. 12.9-10), has the appearance of an outright repudiation of the social conventions in terms of which the 'strong' (1.27) were considered superior in Greco-Roman society. The decisive point at issue is that the social prestige associated with rhetorical eloquence and the 'demonstration of the Spirit and power' which attended a style of preaching which was conformed to the content of its message, namely 'Jesus Christ and him crucified', are mutually exclusive phenomena (2.5; cf. 1.17).

There is a theological rationale for Paul's position here, but he appears to be guided largely by practical concerns. On a personal level Paul understood his own apostolic existence, which was characterized by weakness, in the light of the cross and could even refer to it as a 'carrying in the body the death of Jesus' (2 Cor. 4.10).[119] However, in 1 Corinthians 1–4 he is not preoccupied with the character of his apostolic ministry *per se* but with its significance as it pertains to the discord in the community. Since this discord was the result of a boasting of men (i.e. Paul, Apollos and Peter, 3.21), Paul's attempt to invalidate the grounds of boasting in the preceding verses (1.29-31) is more pointed than the general tenor of his remarks might suggest. More precisely, these statements allude to those few 'wise', 'powerful' and 'well-born' Corinthian Christians (1.26) who gauged their own worth and that of other Christian leaders in terms of the accepted standards of people of high social rank, and consequently they considered themselves and Apollos to be superior. It is in response to the arrogance of these people (cf. 4.18) that Paul draws attention to his weakness and unimpressive speech, both of which signified a lack of status in Greco-Roman society. The conscious reversal of socio-cultural expectations connoted by this depiction of the character of his apostleship and the style of his preaching is in conformity with the subversion of human expectations and judgments wrought by God in the cross of Christ (1.18-29).[120]

Paul's apostolic existence personified God's negation of the world's wisdom, but for a definite reason which he makes clear in 2.5: 'that your faith might not rest in the wisdom of men but in the power of God'. The social elite in the Corinthian community evidently equated the experienceof God's power with the display of social power,

119. Cf. Conzelmann, *1 Corinthians*, p. 54.
120. Judge, 'Cultural Conformity and Innovation in Paul', p. 14.

especially as it found expression in rhetorical eloquence. They probably conceived of the qualities of a cultivated person as evidence of spiritual superiority. Someone like Apollos was perceived to be πευματικός because of his rhetorical skill and perhaps his physical appearance, while Paul's failure to comply with the prevailing status system was taken to be indicative of an inferior spiritual status.[121] Paul attempts to render this way of thinking null and void by reminding the Corinthians that his abasement and unimpressive style of preaching occasioned the manifestation of God's power (2.4-5).

The eschatological power of God mediated by the cross is for Paul the crux of the dispute. In 1.18-25 the power and wisdom of God, defined as 'Christ crucified', is set in relief to the world's wisdom, and the opposition between them is more sharply delineated in 2.4 where the demonstration of this power is contrasted with rhetorical eloquence. The conflict between the two different types of power at issue here is shown by the firm warning with which Paul concludes this section: 'But I will come to you soon, if the Lord wills, and I will find out not the talk of these arrogant people but their power. For the kingdom of God does not consist in talk but in power' (4.19-20).[122] Throughout chs. 1–2 Paul consistently drives a wedge between the revelation of God's power in the cross and the display of social power associated with σοφία λόγου.[123] But he is interested primarily in the effect which respective manifestations of divine and secular power have had on the community. The Corinthians had experienced God's power in their

---

121. Whatever the origin of the πευματικός-ψυχικός terminology, it seems apparent that Paul has taken it over from the Corinthians in order to redefine it. He is being more than a little ironic when he says that he could not address as 'spiritual' those who thought of themselves as such because they were 'still of the flesh' and 'behaving like ordinary men' (3.3). He makes this statement with reference to their claiming to belong to Apollos and to himself. The irony of his remarks and the fact that he and Apollos are the exclusive focus of the subsequent discussion of ministry which provides the immediate context for the interpretation of these terms (3.5-15) suggests the possibility that Paul's opponents have applied these designations in such a way as to subordinate him to Apollos.

122. Paul uses the word λόγος which he used earlier in conjunction with σοφία to denote rhetorical eloquence (1.17; 2.1, 4). Barrett, *The First Epistle to the Corinthians*, p. 118, appropriately translates it as 'eloquence' here.

123. S. Pogoloff observes that σοφία and λόγος, when combined in ancient usage, frequently imply far more than technical skill at language. They 'imply a whole world of social status related to speech' (*LOGOS AND SOPHIA*, p. 113).

incorporation into the community of saints (1.27-28), but their orientation to power in the sense of status as it was determined by worldly standards had a destructive impact. While the social structure of the community attested to the creative character of God's power (1.26), the dissensions attested to the detrimental effect of the secular values in terms of which social power was defined.

Paul's self-effacing remarks in 2.1-4 are a continuation of his argument in 1.18-31 and therefore they are also relevant to the interpersonal problems he is addressing. The message of 1.18-25 is that God's power is exercised through the 'word of the cross' and thereby subverts the world's wisdom, which in this instance is represented by the values according to which the cross is designated foolishness and weakness (1.25). Correspondingly, the social makeup of the community and Paul's preaching prove God's disregard for worldly distinctions of status associated with these values because even though both are characterized by weakness, God's power is at work in and through them. These are two cases in point of God's *modus operandi* and what Paul infers from them is that boasting (1.29-31) and confidence in the 'wisdom of men' (2.5) are precluded. Although his deductions are formulated as generalizations, they reflect his understanding of the cause of the jealousy and strife among the Corinthians (3.3; cf. 3.21). The human boasting which has resulted in dissensions has to do with what Judge calls the fundamental features of Greek ethical thought, namely self-cultivation and the importance of status. By accentuating his weakness and rhetorical deficiency, Paul in effect was rejecting the status system which provided the foundation for distinctions of class and rank in the established order as well as a pseudo-spiritual hierarchy in the Corinthian church.[124] Paul's self-denigration was significant as far as the situation in the community was concerned because it constituted a negation of the yardstick used in the comparisons and the boasting at the centre of the dispute. However, it is not until ch. 4 that he straightforwardly presents the example of his own apostolate as the solution to the problem of disunity.[125]

In 4.6-7 Paul makes explicit the paradigmatic importance of his own apostleship when he responds directly to the arrogant pride which has generated the disunity by pointing to himself and Apollos as counter-

---

124. E. Judge, 'St Paul as a Radical Critic of Society', *Interchange* 16 (1974), p. 193.

125. Cf. Humphries, 'Paul's Rhetoric', p. 13.

examples of harmony and humility. With reference to his preceding discussion of the nature of ministry (3.5–4.5) in which he emphasized that he and Apollos occupy the role of 'servants' (3.5, διάκονοι; 4.1, ὑπηρέται) he asserts: 'I have applied all of this to myself and Apollos for your benefit, brethren, so that you may learn not to go beyond what is written, that none of you may be puffed up in favour of one against another' (4.6).[126] The force of this admonition is dependent on the meaning of the enigmatic phrase τὸ μὴ ὑπὲρ ἃ γέγραπται. Among the numerous interpretations that have been proposed, the majority of those which do not consider it to be unintelligible or dismiss it as a gloss suggest that the phrase refers to the Old Testament allusions in 3.19-20 and ch. 1.[127] But, as Fee points out, it is not clear how the Corinthians would have understood the cited texts as something they were 'not to go beyond'.[128]

Another possibility is that the expression was a popular proverb which both he and the Corinthians knew. In this case the saying would mean something like 'keep within the rules' (NEB). Again, though, the problem is that if the saying is in fact a proverb the context provides no further clarification of its origin or significance. Recently Fitzgerald has suggested that the maxim in 4.6 has as its background the instruction given young children in how to write, and the merit of his explanation of this saying is that it relates 4.6 to the imitation theme of 4.16. In view of Paul's remark that 'not to go beyond what is written' is something the Corinthians are to 'learn' from him and Apollos, the idea of the exemplar seems to be central to both the verse and the argument as a whole in this section.

Fitzgerald interprets the saying in 4.6 in the light of Plato, *Prt.* 326D, where Protagoras remarks that 'writing-masters first draw letters in faint outline with the pen for their less advanced pupils, and then give them the copy-book and make them write according to the guidance of their lines'. He notes that in this way children were given a model by

---

126. The ταῦτα refers to the whole of the preceding discussion from 3.5 onwards. So Plummer, *First Epistle of St Paul to the Corinthians*, p. 80; Barrett, *The First Epistle to the Corinthians*, p. 106.

127. For the view that 'what is written' refers to the Old Testament passages cited in chs. 1–3 see M. Hooker, '"Beyond the Things which are Written": An Examination of I Cor. IV.6', *NTS* 10 (1963–64), pp. 127-32.

128. Fee, *The First Epistle to the Corinthians*, p. 169.

which they could learn how to draw or write correctly.[129] This background is significant in light of the fact that Paul presents the Corinthians as children (3.1-3) and uses a rhetorical term to characterize his own teaching.[130] The parallel is even more striking when the Protagoras quotation is read in its larger context. The predominant theme of *Prt.* 320C–28D is moral education, and the imagery of children learning to draw by means of a model serves as an illustration of moral guidance.[131] The virtues are learned by imitating those whose lives exemplify them. Since the Corinthians are still immature, Paul provides them with a model to imitate.[132] Boykin Sanders has pointed out that imitation implies the notion of transfer of character or personality from one person to another, for example, from parents to children, from teacher to pupil and from God to human beings. By listening and observing one should learn to imitate the personality and spirituality of one's model.[133]

---

129. Fitzgerald, *Cracks in an Earthen Vessel*, p. 124. It is noteworthy that although Marshall understands γέγραπται to denote a scriptural quotation or Scripture in general, he nonetheless emphasizes the Hellenistic character of the phrase. He points out that Greek authors frequently used ὑπέρ to express hybristic behaviour, or behaviour that is beyond moderation, and he compares it with Rom. 12.3 where Paul talks about excessive or moderate behaviour in a manner which recalls the traditional Hellenistic commonplaces of self-knowledge (*Enmity in Corinth*, pp. 197-99).

130. Fitzgerald, *Cracks in an Earthen Vessel*, p. 124.

131. Fitzgerald, *Cracks in an Earthen Vessel*, p. 125. Fitgerald points out that the reference to schoolboys copying their ABCs serves as an analogy to the moral model provided by the laws of the city:

> And when they are released from their schooling the city next compels them to learn the laws and to live according to them as after a pattern, that their conduct may not be swayed by their own light fancies, but just as writing-masters first draw letters in faint outline with the pen for their less advanced pupils, and then give them the copy-book and make them write according to the guidance of their lines, so the city sketches out for them the laws devised by good lawgivers of yore, and constrains them to govern and be governed according to these (326D).

Fitzgerald then points out that immediately following this analogy is the important statement: ὅσ δ' ἄν ἐχτὸς βαίνη τούτων χολάζει: 'And whoever goes beyond these (laws), (the city) punishes' (Fitzgerald's translation).

132. Fitzgerald paraphrases 4.6 in this way: 'By our example in attitude and action Apollos and I provide you with a model for your imitation. Copy us, learn how to write "not over the lines"...' (*Cracks in an Earthen Vessel*, p. 127).

133. B. Sanders, 'Imitating Paul: I Cor 4.16', *HTR* 74.4 (1981), p. 358.

2. *The Cross and Christian Unity* 81

Paul's intention is to instruct or admonish the Corinthians, an aim which he expressly states in 4.14 and which is also conveyed by the παρακαλέω constructs in 1.10 and 4.16. This is the objective of the whole of 1.10–4.21, and it is necessitated by the claims to superiority alluded to throughout and clearly stated in the three questions in v. 7.[134] According to Fitzgerald, 'admonition is the instilling of sense in the person who is being admonished, and teaching him what should and should not be done'. Moreover, it is 'the proper response to insolence and arrogance (ὕβρις)'.[135] The chief means through which Paul pursues this goal is the catalogue of hardships in 4.9-13 where he reminds the Corinthians of his 'ways in Christ' in order that they might imitate him (4.16-17).[136]

Paul introduces the hardship catalogue with a sarcastic remark about the social status of those whose behaviour he has just characterized as arrogant: 'Already you are filled! Already you have become rich! Without us you have become kings! And would that you did reign, so that we might share in the rule with you!'[137] He then proceeds with an antithetical comparison of the privileged social position of these people and his own position as someone who was socially disadvantaged. Paul begins the *synkrisis* in v. 9 by asserting that, unlike those described in v. 8, the apostles 'have become a spectacle to the world' and he concludes in v. 13 with a similar affirmation of how from the world's point of view they have been disparaged: 'we have become, and are now, as the refuse of the world, the offscouring of all things'. Both of these statements recall his exposition of the opposition between the wisdom of God and the wisdom of the world in 1.18-25 and suggest that the world's attitude to apostolic existence is analogous to its apprehension of the 'word of the cross' as foolishness. Thus the irony which pervades this passage is given even more of an edge, for the implication is that the portrait of the 'arrogant' Corinthians is in keeping with the secular values to which they adhere but which God has nullified by revealing his power through the cross. Paul's own self-denigration,

---

134. Marshall, *Enmity in Corinth*, p. 205. Marshall remarks that although the term ὕβρις does not appear in 1 Cor. 4.6-13, the vocabulary and the ideas associated with it suggests that the idea of ὕβρις underlies the whole passage (pp. 194-95).
135. Fitzgerald, *Cracks in an Earthen Vessel*, pp. 117-18.
136. Fitzgerald, *Cracks in an Earthen Vessel*, p. 122.
137. Cf. Marshall, *Enmity in Corinth*, pp. 209-11.

on the other hand, identifies him with the crucified Christ, the agent of God's activity in the world.[138]

The progression of Paul's argument in 4.9-13 is the same as in ch. 1 in that he makes a transition from 'the world's' general antipathy to weakness and foolishness, as is evidenced in its response to the cross of Christ and the apostles respectively (1.18-25; 4.9), to a social contrast which highlights the exemplification of these very qualities. The weakness, foolishness and dishonour symbolized by the cross and disdained by the world are in 1.26-28 illustrated by the social makeup of the community and in 4.10 by the life of the apostle. The only other difference between the two passages is that whereas in the former Paul only tacitly refers to the few Corinthians who were wise, strong and held in honour, in 4.10 they are the ones with whom he compares himself. In the hardship catalogue that follows Paul continues in this vein by identifying poverty and labouring with his hands as things which demonstrate his lack of status and honour (4.11-12a).[139]

Up to this point the emphasis has been on his social inferiority in contrast with the social superiority of the Corinthians who belong to the upper strata, but in vv. 12b-13 attention is shifted to the way in which the apostles respond to abuse: 'when persecuted, we endure; when slandered, we try to conciliate'. Given the fact that Paul has been slandered in Corinth, precisely because he was socially inferior, and that his purpose in writing was to conciliate or admonish, this statement seems to be directed toward the privileged people who are the focus of the comparisons. There is an implicit contrast between the apostles' conduct, which is concomitant with their disadvantaged social and economic state, and the arrogant behaviour of this elite group of Corinthian Christians. In their self-indulgent arrogance they powerfully assert their rights against their fellow believers (cf. 1 Cor. 6.1-6; 8.1-13; 10.23–11.1), while the apostles, who are shamed and dishonoured and therefore the victims of *hybris*, refuse to retaliate and are willing

---

138. On the importance of the idea of agency for Paul's understanding of the significance of Christ's death see C.A. Wanamaker, 'Christ as Divine Agent in Paul', *SJT* 39 (1986), pp. 517-28.

139. Marshall, *Enmity in Corinth*, p. 212. On the social stigma attached to work and the implications for Paul's ministry see R. Hock, *The Social Context of Paul's Ministry: Tentmaking and Apostleship* (Philadelphia: Fortress Press, 1980).

2. *The Cross and Christian Unity*   83

to forego their rights (1 Cor. 9), suffer wrong, and be defrauded (1 Cor. 6.7).[140]

In the peristasis catalogue in 4.11-13 Paul singularly develops the notion of shame with reference to apostolic existence, but the ironic tone of the entire passage (4.8-13) suggests that he has accentuated his own social inferiority in order to shame the Corinthians whom he has implicated.[141] Although he writes in v. 14 that the purpose of the preceding verses was not to make them ashamed (ἐντρέπω), but to admonish (νουθετέω) them, it would not have been necessary to make this clarification unless he was aware that the comparisons did indeed have this effect. If Paul had ended on this ironic note then the thesis that he is defending himself in an effort to re-establish his apostolic authority would be more compelling. But this is not the case, for he closes the section with an exhortation for the Corinthians to imitate him (4.15-17).

Paul has presented himself in 4.9-13 as someone who in his own weakness embodies the weakness of the crucified Christ, and in accordance with the theology of the cross as set out in 1.18-25 his example has both a critical and hortatory function.[142] The hardship catalogue does serve to reprove those in the community who were arrogant, but Paul's main objective in these verses is to offer his apostolic existence as the praiseworthy paradigm for Christian existence.[143] His comment in v. 14 is transitional and, as Sanders observes, signals a change in mood from the reproof to which the 'these things' refers to a tone of paternal concern.[144] Having referred to the Corinthians as 'my beloved children' (v. 14), Paul reminds them that he became their 'father in

---

140. Fitzgerald, *Cracks in an Earthen Vessel*, p. 139. It is Marshall who suggests that in this passage Paul appears to be placing himself in the position of one who is the victim of ὕβρις. He notes that the viewpoint he expresses here is the traditional one in Greek authors of the sufferer whose status or rank has been violated (*Enmity in Corinth*, p. 210).

141. Marshall, *Enmity in Corinth*, p. 216. Plank's study, *Paul and the Irony of Affliction*, shows how Paul uses ironic language, especially in 1 Cor. 4.9-13, to challenge the Corinthian system of value and assert the force of his own fundamental convictions. He affirms that the system of value expressed through 1 Cor. 1–4 is a thoroughly paradoxical one, predicated on God's scandalous activity in the cross (see pp. 55, 64, 74).

142. Fitzgerald, *Cracks in an Earthen Vessel*, p. 122.
143. Sanders, 'Imitating Paul', p. 353.
144. Sanders, 'Imitating Paul', p. 356.

Christ Jesus through the gospel' (v. 15), and then urges them to 'be imitators' of him (v. 16). He qualifies the term 'father' by the phrase 'through the gospel' because he conceives of imitation in terms of the gospel in which Christ is proclaimed as crucified (1.23-24; 2.2).[145]

Paul's apostolic existence as it is characterized in 2.1-4 and especially in 4.9-13 conforms to this gospel. Since he is their spiritual father, the Corinthians should pattern their lives after him.[146] However, it is not the things which denote his inferior social standing (e.g. weakness, dishonour, lack of rhetorical eloquence, poverty and work) that constitute his 'ways in Christ' as such (4.17), but rather the self-disregard implied in his abasement.[147] In assuming the position of a socially disadvantaged person Paul is exemplifying the disposition which is epitomized by the Christ who gives himself in death for all humankind (cf. 2 Cor. 5.14-15). The imitation of Paul, then, requires that the Corinthians renounce the self-indulgent and arrogant behaviour which has led some of them to exalt themselves and Apollos over against other members of the community. If they would follow Paul's example of setting aside self-interest, the interpersonal problems in the community would resolve themselves and Paul could come 'in a spirit of gentleness' instead of 'with a rod' (4.21).

---

145. Sanders notes that in the Hellenistic period the classical notion of mimicking was transformed into an ethical concept ('Imitating Paul', p. 358). Whereas in 4.6 Paul uses the teacher-pupil imagery, in 4.14-21 he appeals to familial imagery.

146. Cf. Hasler, 'Das Evangelium des Paulus', p. 114.

147. E. Castelli has recently appealed to the work of M. Foucault to argue that the notion of mimesis functions in Paul's letters as a strategy of power. She claims that in exhorting those in the community to imitate him, Paul was constructing a hierarchical 'economy of sameness'. However, if Paul was invoking his own weakness, humility and self-disregard to subvert what he percieved to be abuses of power by a cultivated elite within the community, then mimesis in this context does not function primarily to erase difference (E. Castelli, *Imitating Paul: A Discourse of Power* [Lousville: Westminster/John Knox Press, 1991], pp. 15-17, 98-111).

Chapter 3

THE CROSS AND MORAL DISCOURSE IN 1 CORINTHIANS 5–14

Introduction

In 1 Corinthians 1–4 Paul is preoccupied with the quarreling and strife reported to him by Chloe's people (1.11), and his exposition of 'the word of the cross' in these chapters is expressly directed toward this problem. In view of the scholarly consensus that 1 Corinthians 1–4 comprises a self-contained section dealing primarily with internal conflict within the community, it is necessary to establish the relationship between the content of chs. 1–4 and the various ethical issues to which Paul responds in subsequent chapters. Although the death of Christ is mentioned or alluded to elsewhere in the letter (cf. 5.7; 8.11; 11.26; 15.3), it is in these opening chapters that Paul spells out the significance of his initial preaching of the crucified Christ (1.18ff.) in relation to the problem of dissensions among the Corinthians. The question, then, is does his discussion of the cross in 1 Corinthians 1–4 have any intended applicability to the ethical quandaries discussed in 1 Corinthians 5–14, or is its relevance limited only to the subject matter of these first four chapters?

One obstacle to affirming a certain continuity between chs. 1–4 and chs. 5–14 is the increasing number of scholars who doubt the integrity of the letter and assume that it is a composition of a number of fragments.[1] If any one of these partition theories proved to be the most plausible explanation for 1 Corinthians in its present canonical form, then it would be unlikely that there is a connection between what Paul says about the cross in chs. 1–4 and the ethical discourse in ensuing

1. Cf. G.W. Kümmel, *Introduction to the New Testament* (trans. H.C. Kee; Nashville and New York: Abingdon Press, 1975), pp. 202-205; Hurd, *The Origin of First Corinthians*, pp. 43-47, 69-71, 86-89, 131-42; and more recently R. Jewett, 'The Redaction of 1 Corinthians and the Trajectory of the Pauline School', *JAAR* 44.4 (1978), pp. 389-444.

chapters. But the question of integrity can also be approached from the opposite direction, as Dahl has done. He sets out the conditions in this way: 'The integrity of 1 Corinthians may be assumed as a working hypothesis which is confirmed if it proves possible to understand 1 Cor. 1.10–4.21 as an introductory section with a definite purpose within the letter as a whole'.[2] According to Dahl the main function of 1 Cor. 1.10–4.21 is to re-establish Paul's authority, but he also emphasizes that it provides the theological basis for the answers which Paul gives to the questions raised in the remainder of the letter.[3]

In the preceding chapter the view that the purpose of 1 Corinthians 1–4 was apologetic was challenged, and it was proposed instead that Paul's primary objective was to put forward his own embodiment of the weakness of the cross as the solution to the problem of disunity in the community. A closer examination of Paul's reply to the ethical questions raised in 1 Corinthians 5–14 suggests that, as in 1 Corinthians 1–4, he is still concerned first and foremost with the disunifying effect the conduct of certain Corinthians is having on the community, and if this is the case then it would follow that the theology of the cross set out in chs. 1–4 is in some sense pertinent to the discussion of ethical behaviour in succeeding chapters. Therefore, rather than enter into the complex and highly theoretical debate about the integrity of 1 Corinthians, I will, with Dahl, assume its integrity and then attempt to substantiate this assumption by showing the correlation between the introductory section (1 Corinthians 1–4) and the rest of the letter.

The Context of Paul's Ethical Discourse in 1 Corinthians 5–14

In 1 Corinthians 5–14 Paul critiques the behaviour of certain Corinthians in terms of its adverse effect on the life of the community. He makes no attempt to analyse the underlying causes of the conduct of which he disapproves because he is more concerned with its interpersonal consequences. Instead he draws attention to how the actions of certain Corinthians are incongruous with the gospel he first preached to them. Paul does not here delineate the content of the gospel of the cross as he did in chs. 1–4. Rather his moral exhortations have their foundation in a vision of community which is predicated on his understanding of the social implications of that same gospel. There are a few

2. Dahl, 'Paul and the Church at Corinth', p. 44.
3. Dahl, 'Paul and the Church at Corinth', p. 60.

important themes in the letter which provide insight into his conception of Christian community, and it is only against the backdrop of the coherent picture which emerges from an examination and integration of these themes that we can adduce what Paul conceived to be the proper theological ground and motivation for authentic Christian behaviour.[4]

A consideration of the relationship between the gospel of the cross set out in chs. 1–4 and the ethical discourse in chs. 5–14 raises the question of how Paul's vision of community was shaped by his conception of the significance of Christ's death. However, before this question can be addressed it is first necessary to ascertain why and in what sense Paul considers the various incidents he deals with in the paraenetic section to be in violation of his ideal of Christian community. Focusing on this discrepancy between his views about how the Corinthians should be living as a community and his perception of their moral quandaries serves as a means of moving beyond an abstraction of Paul's ethic to an appreciation of the intended function of his theology.

Furnish has rightly pointed out that Paul does not himself deliberate on the ways the ethical concerns in the letters are related to his basic theological convictions, and it could be added that neither does he deliberate on how the Corinthians' conduct is related to their theological convictions.[5] He simply takes it for granted that he and the Corinthians are committed to the same gospel. But in order to grasp the force of Paul's moral exhortations in their socio-historical context something of the dialectic between the cognitive and the behavioural aspects of the Corinthians' practice must be discerned. Ethics is never just a matter of what people do, but a question of the interplay between their identity, attitudes and beliefs, and behaviour. Alastair MacIntyre asserts that 'every action is the bearer and expression of more or less

---

4. For an explanation of how Paul's exhortations function to promote ethical conduct within the community see A. Malherbe, 'Exhortation in First Thessalonians', *NovT* 15.3 (1983), p. 251.

5. For this reason we would expect the message of the cross to be more implicit than explicit in the paraenetic section of 1 Corinthians. Furnish rightly remarks that 'the apostle himself seems not to have conceived of any special "ethical" side to his message or mission and certainly never attempts appraisal or even presentation of ethical principles, norms or theories'. But he also correctly points out that 'while it is true that Paul does not reflect critically and systematically upon the problems of ethics... his concern for the practical conduct of Christians is inseparably related to the central themes of his preaching' (V. Furnish, *Theology and Ethics in Paul* [Nashville: Abingdon Press, 1968], pp. 210-11).

theory-laden beliefs and concepts; every piece of theorising and every expression of belief is a political and moral action'.[6] Although Paul does not engage the Corinthians on a theoretical level about how their theology is misguided, his ethical discourse does operate on a cognitive level. His efforts to reform the Corinthians' conduct are informed by an interpretation of the attitudes and beliefs which undergird it. The exhortations in 1 Corinthians 5–14 are an attempt to modify their mind-set by having them reconsider the significance of what God has done in Christ.

MacIntyre's observation about the reciprocity between theory and praxis suggests that the Corinthians' attitudes and beliefs can be inferred from their behaviour. This correspondence between the Corinthians' behaviour and their theorizing can be illuminated by anthropological models. Both the theory and praxis of the Corinthians need to be described rather than categorized, and for this purpose anthropological constructs and explanations are more useful than are theological ones because they tend to be more descriptive and have the advantage of allowing one to perceive the situation from a distance. Furthermore, attitudes and beliefs, even if couched in theological language, are not necessarily synonymous with theological ideas, rather, they refer to a person's deepest convictions about life and the world.[7] Although the situation in Corinth is necessarily being viewed from Paul's perspective, an equitable description of the Corinthians' conduct is still possible. But both the theory and praxis of the Christians in Corinth will have to be understood in terms of the interpretive categories Paul uses.

The context for moral concern in 1 Corinthians is the Christian community, and, as Meeks observes, 'the complementary terms which define what the community's character ought to be are its "holiness" and unity'.[8] The idea of purity is closely related to the theme of 'holiness',

6. A. MacIntyre, *After Virtue: A Study in Moral Theory* (Notre Dame, IN: University of Notre Dame Press, 1981), p. 58.

7. See Patte's discussion of the distinction between convictions and ideas. He avers that believing (convictions) and knowing (ideas) are different types of cognitive activities which can have the same subject matter. The difference is in the way they function. He notes that 'we have power over ideas, but they merely have indirect power over us. By contrast, convictions have direct power over us... they impose themselves on us... They transcend us' (D. Patte, *Paul's Faith and the Power of the Gospel* [Philadelphia: Fortress Press, 1983], pp. 10-25).

8. W. Meeks, *The Moral World of the First Christians* (Philadelphia: Westminster Press, 1986), p. 130.

3. *The Cross and Moral Discourse* 89

and they both pertain to the theme of unity which is sustained throughout the whole of 1 Corinthians. The image which predominates in chs. 5–14, and which Paul invests with theological import, is that of the body. The term body here denotes both the individual body and the metaphorical 'body of Christ',[9] with Paul frequently trying to get the Corinthians to view the activity of the former, the individual body, with reference to its effect on the latter, the corporate body. Since the individual's relationship to the community seems to be largely what is at issue in Paul's dealings with the ethical problems in 1 Corinthians 5–14, his use of the imagery of the body here is a hermeneutical key to understanding both the nature of problems he is confronting and also what he conceives of as a proper theological foundation of ethics.

Mary Douglas has made a persuasive case for understanding the human body in all its activity as a microcosm of the social body. She describes the relationship in this way:

> The social body constrains the way the physical body is perceived. The physical experience of the body, always modified by the social categories through which it is known, sustains a particular view of society. There is a continual exchange of meanings between the two kinds of bodily experience so that each reinforces the categories of the other. As a result the body itself is a highly restricted medium of expression. The forms it adopts in movement and repose express social pressures in manifold ways.[10]

Douglas argues that the character of the social body, especially the extent to which the group influences individuals, but also its values and ideology, is evidenced in the bodily control exhibited by the members of the body.[11] Her thesis, simply stated, is that strong social control demands strong bodily control, and conversely, that weak bodily control reflects weak social control. This insight is relevant to a consideration of the ethical issues in 1 Corinthians 5–14 because it elucidates the correlation between the disunity which is of paramount importance to Paul, and the ethical disputes, all of which involve the physical body. In the light of Douglas's anthropological model, Paul's concern for the lack of bodily control among some of the Corinthians in matters

---

9. Cf. W. Meeks, '"Since then you Would Need to Go out of the World": Group Boundaries in Pauline Christianity', in T.J. Ryan (ed.), *Critical History and Biblical Faith: New Testament Perspectives* (The Annual Publication of the College Theology Society; Villanova, PA: The College Theology Society, 1979), p. 18.

10. Douglas, *Natural Symbols*, p. 93.

11. Douglas, *Natural Symbols*, p. 99.

sexual (1 Cor. 5–7), related to eating (1 Cor. 8; 10–11), and of speaking (1 Cor. 12–14) may betray his desire to maintain the unity of the body of Christ.[12] More than that, it suggests that he emphasizes strong bodily control in these matters precisely because of the corporate body's lack of social cohesion.

Part and parcel of concern for bodily control is a concern to preserve social boundaries.[13] It is with reference to social boundaries that purity and the concomitant theme of holiness become an issue. These boundaries serve to circumscribe the community in order to keep it 'pure' from outsiders and in so doing they facilitate group cohesion, that is their function. As Neyrey points out, in Douglas's model of purity and pollution, purity refers not only to what conforms to the classification of boundaries whereby a social group is structured, but also to its 'wholeness'. Any division within the social body is a violent threat.[14] On this model, Paul emphasizes the purity and holiness of the Corinthian community in order to distinguish it from 'outside' society, and the reason he needs to do this is that the unity or 'wholeness' of the body of Christ is in jeopardy.[15]

Throughout 1 Corinthians Paul stresses the distinction between the Corinthians, who have been 'washed', 'sanctified', and 'justified in the name of the Lord Jesus Christ and in the Spirit of God' (1 Cor. 6.11), and 'the outsiders' (5.12, 13; cf. 1 Thess. 4.12; Col. 4.5). The outsiders are stigmatized not only matter-of-factly as 'nonbelievers' (1 Cor. 6.6; 7.12-15; 10.27; 14.22-24), but also as 'unrighteous' (1 Cor. 6.1, 9), and 'those despised in the church' (1 Cor. 6.4).[16] Even the neutral designation 'Gentiles' is used pejoratively to refer to outsiders (1 Cor. 5.1; 12.2).[17] And yet over against this emphasis on the separateness of the

---

12. Cf. J. Neyrey, 'Body Language in 1 Corinthians: The Use of Anthropological Models for Understanding Paul and his Opponents', *Semeia* 35 (1986), pp. 129-70.

13. Douglas, *Natural Symbols*, p. 98.

14. Neyrey, 'Body Language in 1 Corinthians', p. 144. Neyrey notes that holiness in this context is perceived in terms of the wholeness or unity of the body (p. 157).

15. M. Newton, *The Concept of Purity at Qumran and in the Letters of Paul* (SNTSMS, 53; Cambridge: Cambridge University Press, 1985), p. 101, remarks that 'Paul's concern is with the unity of the Church and it is to that end, within the Church, that he makes use of the concept of purity'.

16. Meeks, *The First Urban Christians*, p. 94.

17. Meeks, *The First Urban Christians*, p. 95. Meeks observes that pagan society as a whole is, as in Jewish apologetic traditions, characterized by catalogues of vices (cf. 1 Cor. 5.10; 6.9-11).

3. *The Cross and Moral Discourse* 91

Christian community are statements in which Paul asserts that all social distinctions, especially between Jew and Gentile (1 Cor. 12.13; cf. also Gal. 3.28), have been relativized by the gospel, and that Jewish rules of purity have been abandoned because as boundary markers they impede his mission to the Gentiles. Moreover, Paul's express comment about social boundaries in 1 Cor. 5.9-10 indicates that something he had said earlier had been misunderstood by the Corinthians, and so with tongue in cheek he clarifies what he meant by telling them that if they were to avoid interacting with 'the immoral of this world' they 'would need to go out of this world'.

What appears to be a paradox, if not a contradiction, namely that sometimes Paul draws sharp boundary lines between Christians and 'the world' and other times radically rejects anything which even smacks of being a line of demarcation, is explained by the way social boundaries function to promote the solidarity of a group by reminding it of its distinctiveness, that is, its purity and holiness. In his discussion of purity and boundaries, Meeks highlights the ambiguity of Paul's affirmation of social intercourse with outsiders while at the same time maintaining the exclusivity of the community. But he also points out that the emphasis in his paraenesis 'is not upon the maintenance of boundaries, but upon internal cohesion: the mutual responsibility of members, especially that of strong for weak, and the undiluted loyalty of all to the One God and One Lord'.[18] In contrast to the Jewish practice of ritual purity, which for him had become dysfunctional, Paul defines the purity of the community more directly in social terms.[19]

Paul brings together the themes of purity and unity in 1 Corinthians because of certain fundamental theological convictions, and it is these theological convictions that reveal what is ultimately at stake for him. That in the introduction to the letter he refers to the church of God in Corinth as those 'sanctified in Christ Jesus, called to be saints' (1.2) signifies that the concept of purity which includes ἅγιος and its cognates conveys his understanding of the identity and character of the Christian community. In accordance with this understanding, he construes the divisive behaviour of the Corinthians to be a betrayal of the new identity they have been given in Christ (cf. 6.11). This identity is conceived of in corporate as well as individual terms as belonging to the holy People of God, a People whose existence is defined by God's

---

18. Meeks, *The First Urban Christians*, p. 100.
19. Meeks, *The First Urban Christians*, p. 103.

action in Christ.[20] Therefore Newton is right when he says that Paul uses cultic language to elucidate the community's self-understanding.[21] However, identity is always social, and so Paul also employs cultic language in order to emphasize that only certain patterns of behaviour are congruous with the identity conferred by this language.[22]

One of the images which best symbolizes the ontological reality on which this identity and the corresponding typifications are predicated is that of the temple of God (1 Cor. 3.16-17). Newton asserts that 'much of Paul's use of purity terminology centres upon his view that the believers constitute the temple of God and as such enjoy the presence of God in their midst'.[23] The temple must remain pure if God is to remain present, and this means that its members must preserve strict standards of behaviour.[24] Both the manifestation of God's presence in the community and the holiness of the people who belong to it are attested to by the indwelling of God's 'Holy' Spirit (cf. 1 Cor. 3.16-17). It was the church's experience of the Holy Spirit which was the basis for understanding itself as the holy people of God 'upon whom the end of the ages has come' (1 Cor. 10.11).[25] There are, then, a number of themes which converge on this theme of purity, an idea which seems to underlie much of the moral exhortation in 1 Corinthians, and these themes reflect not only what was important to Paul, but also in what sense he thought the Corinthians had gone astray.

It is noteworthy that Paul's use of the temple imagery to describe the

---

20. Cf. T.J. Deidun, *New Covenant Morality in Paul* (Rome: Biblical Institute Press, 1981), p. 12. Deidun emphasizes the continuity with the Old Testament theme of election, which he says entails separation and consecration, the twofold constituent of cult-holiness (p. 16).

21. Newton, *The Concept of Purity*, p. 53.

22. This is what Berger and Luckman call 'reification'. In *The Social Construction of Reality*, p. 108 they say that reification is 'a total identification of the individual with his socially assigned typifications'. It involves bestowing an ontological status on these typifications, but as these typifications are internalized only a segment of the self is objectified.

23. Newton, *The Concept of Purity*, p. 52. Newton asserts that

> by saying that 'God's Spirit dwells within you' (1 Cor. 3.16), 'your body is a temple of the Holy Spirit within you' (1 Cor. 6.19) and, in the context of the Church as Temple, 'I will live in them' (2 Cor. 6.16), Paul is transferring the idea of God's presence from the physical Temple to the believers and the community to which they belong (p. 55).

24. Newton, *The Concept of Purity*, p. 52.

25. Deidun, *New Covenant Morality in Paul*, p. 39.

3. *The Cross and Moral Discourse* 93

character of the Corinthian church occurs in chs. 1–4 where he focuses on the problem of disunity. This reinforces what was said earlier about the correlation between boundaries, purity and Paul's concern for unity in the community. Moreover, in view of the fact that purity, holiness and the social boundaries that define them denote distinction from society, it can be inferred that something from outside the community has contributed to the discord in the church and this is why he stresses the idea of holiness. That this is indeed the case is confirmed by the way Paul sets the message of the cross over against the world and its wisdom in 1.18-25. As was argued in the preceding chapter, 'the wisdom of the world' (3.19) is not just an abstract designation, it refers to the Greco-Roman social values which are the basis of the attitude of superiority exhibited by a select group of Corinthians. Their arrogance and claims to power are the primary cause of the dissensions, and so the gospel is presented in a way that challenges the very source of the mimetic rivalry. It is significant that Paul picks up the themes of 'the wisdom of the world' and 'boasting' immediately after issuing the strongest of warnings to anyone who would destroy God's holy temple (3.16-23).[26] The world's wisdom has influenced some of the Corinthians to the extent that they may destroy the holy temple of God which they themselves embody.

That the holiness of the community and the boundaries which distinguish it from the world and its wisdom are important features of Paul's response to the report of dissensions provides support for the claim that there is continuity between 1 Corinthians 1–4 and 1 Corinthians 5–14. In chs. 5–14 he confronts what is essentially the same problem from basically the same perspective, the main difference is that here he critically examines the specific behaviours that are fragmenting the community. The reason the discord, rivalry and strife in the community are incompatible with its being the holy people of God set apart from the world is elucidated by the use of the temple imagery in 3.16-17. The holiness of the community consists in its being indwelt by the Holy Spirit, and so it is God's continued presence through the Spirit that will be nullified by conduct which is not consistent with the holiness with which the church is imbued.[27] The presence of the Holy Spirit in

26. Cf. E. Käsemann, 'Sentences of Holy Law in the New Testament', reprinted in *New Testament Questions of Today* (Philadelphia: Fortress Press, 1969), pp. 66ff.

27. Newton, *The Concept of Purity*, p. 56; Neyrey, 'Body Language in 1 Corinthians', p. 157.

the church is what makes it holy, and it is the Holy Spirit which is offended by the failure of some of the Corinthians to live up to the standards of holiness. What needs to be remembered, however, is that for Paul the holiness of the community is perceived primarily in terms of its wholeness or unity.

What appears to have happened in the community is that some of the practices which were dividing it into splinter-groups were being passed off as alternative forms of spirituality. These forms of spirituality were probably not so much the result of a developed doctrine of the Spirit as they were the consequence of a particular attitude to the spiritual. The irony of the situation is that while for Paul the church is distinguished from the world by virtue of its self-understanding as God's temple in which the Holy Spirit resides (1 Cor. 3.16), some of the Corinthians were distinguishing themselves from other members of the community, and in at least one instance manifestations of the Spirit were the basis for the distinction (1 Cor. 12; 14). Their attempts to set themselves apart are antithetical to the activity of the Holy Spirit who is responsible for creating unity (cf. 1 Cor. 12). All conduct which counteracts the unifying work of the Spirit is, from Paul's standpoint, an offence to the holiness of the community. But with the exception of the problem concerning the gift of tongues, nothing in the paraenetic section suggests that the divisive behaviour he is opposed to is done in the name of the Spirit.

If Paul is not emphasizing the sanctifying and unifying work of the Holy Spirit in response to contrary interpretations of the Spirit's activity, then the question is how did the various cliques in the community legitimate, theologically or otherwise, their respective elitist positions? Some of the Corinthians seem to be promoting a novel spirituality, and every one of the incidents in question, whether intentionally or not, represents a spirituality different from the model Paul advocates in 1 Corinthians. Spirituality is a useful category of interpretation here because it embraces more than just the cognitive dimensions of Christian existence and is therefore a more comprehensive category of description than theology. An examination of aspects of the spirituality implied by the Corinthians' conduct will disclose the dynamics of the situation rather than suggesting ideas which might have caused it.

The one characteristic which seems to be common to all of those who were trying to distinguish themselves from other members of the commmunity was a sense of freedom. The most explicit evidence of

3. *The Cross and Moral Discourse*

an orientation to freedom is the phrase πάντα μοι ἔξεστιν, generally acknowledged to be a Corinthian slogan. This slogan occurs in the context of Paul's discussion of sexual immorality (6.12) and the problem of eating food offered to idols (10.23; cf. 8.9), and those in the community who engaged in these activities probably made recourse to it in order to provide some sort of theological legitimation for them.[28] Although Paul does not cite this slogan in conjunction with the other ethical issues he addresses in this section, all of the conduct in question can be characterized as indulgent by his standards and as such reflects an emphasis on personal freedom. In the other matter which concerns eating, the wealthier members of the community feel they have a right to eat a meal which they have provided even though it excludes others who have come to partake of the Lord's Supper (11.17-34). The ethical norm of those who insisted on their personal rights was that of individualistic freedom, and this same disposition also appears to be the crux of the episode involving lawsuits among believers (6.1-8) and the case involving ascetics who are resolute about their prerogative to abstain from sexual intercourse (7.1-16).

The controversy surrounding speaking in tongues is more categorically spiritual in character, but in terms of behavioural norms freedom is also the operative theme. Neyrey has examined what Paul has to say about speaking in tongues in 1 Corinthians 12–14 in the light of Douglas's anthropological model, and has shown that freedom is the underlying value of the spiritual enthusiasm of those who esteemed this manifestation of the Spirit. He notes that for these people the gift of tongues is highly valued as a symbol of effervescent spirit possession (cf. 14.2).[29] According to Douglas, spirit possession indicates a lower degree of social structure and control as well as strong individualism,

---

28. Conzelmann, *1 Corinthians*, p. 108 translates this slogan 'I am free to do anything', and remarks with reference to Paul's citation of it in 6.12 that πορνεία in Corinth is not merely a remnant of pagan customs. It is provided with an active/ speculative justification on the ground of this basic principle'. As far as those who were eating idol meat were concerned, this slogan was correlated with the complementary slogan 'πάντες γνῶσιν ἔχομεν' (8.1) to justify the eating of idol meat.

29. Neyrey suggests that Douglas would classify speaking in tongues as a form of trance and thus quotes the following pertinent statement from *Natural Symbols* (p. 109): 'Where trance is not regarded as at all dangerous, but as a benign source of power and guidance for the community at large, I would expect to find a very loosely structured community, group boundaries unimportant, social categories undefined' (cited in 'Body Language in 1 Corinthians', p. 149).

and this leads Neyrey to the conclusion that 'the cosmology of those who prized speaking in tongues is highly individualistic and freedom-oriented; no rules are appropriate to this uncontrolled body'.[30] That this explanation coincides with Paul's interpretation of the situation is indicated by the fact that he establishes 'building up the church' as the criterion for the manifestation of spiritual gifts (14.12; cf. 14.5, 26). In response to those for whom 'spiritual' freedom is the absolute value, Paul emphasizes the need to exercise spiritual gifts which edify and thus contribute to the unity of the body of Christ.

Although spiritual phenomena as such are not constituent of the other ethical issues in 1 Corinthians 5–14, they are characterized by claims to freedom which are symptomatic of a certain type of spirituality. The correlation between this orientation to freedom, spirituality, and social experience is, again, aptly described by Douglas:

> To insist on the superiority of spiritual over material elements is to insist on the liberties of the individual and to imply a political program for freeing him from social constraints. . . Put crudely, those who are on the side of spontaneity, freedom and the elevation of spiritual values, reject society in its established form.[31]

For the Corinthians who placed a high premium on speaking in tongues, and probably also for those who represented the two extremes in sexual matters—the libertines (1 Cor. 5–6) and the ascetics (1 Cor. 7.1-16)—the spiritual did take priority over the material. What Douglas's analysis shows is that this tendency is directly related to the individualistic expressions of freedom which were, in part anyhow, the reflex of their experience of Greco-Roman society. While it would be reductionist to account for the enthusiasm of these so-called pneumatics solely in terms of their lack of integration into the larger social world, the fact that 'not many' of the Corinthians were 'powerful' or 'wise according to worldly standards' (1.26) suggests that some of them may have found opportunities for individual expressions of freedom in the church that were not available to them in the larger society.[32]

---

30. Neyrey, 'Body Language in 1 Corinthians', p. 149.

31. M. Douglas, 'Social Preconditions of Enthusiasm and Heterodoxy', in R. Spencer (ed.), *Forms of Symbolic Action: Proceedings of the 1969 Annual Spring Meetings of the American Ethnological Society* (Seattle: University of Washington Press, 1969), p. 69.

32. See Meeks's discussion of manifestations of the Spirit as a means of gaining and using prestige and influence in the Corinthian church (*The First Urban*

3. *The Cross and Moral Discourse*

Douglas's explanation is not pertinent to the two eating controversies addressed in chs. 8–10 and 11.17-34 because the claims to freedom of those who wanted to maintain certain practices at community meals have a more political character inasmuch as they seem to be based on rights and privileges associated with higher socio-economic status. Social standing probably influenced their orientation to freedom differently than those who emphasized the priority of the spiritual because they lived in conformity with the norms and values adhered to by people of the upper strata in Greco-Roman society.[33] Just as there is a social dimension to the controveries involving the pnuematics, it is also possible that those involved in the conflicts concerning meals conceived of their rights in spiritual terms. The problems Paul deals with in 1 Corinthians 5–14 are, of course, toocomplex to be accounted for solely by social or theological explanations. The point, however, is that the Corinthian community was comprised of a cross-section of people whose social identities influenced their spiritual activities in the church. The result was a community that was as diverse spiritually as it was socially, and yet all of the problems Paul confronts in this section are construed as an abuse of freedom, which is both a social and a spiritual value.

The Question of Social Identity and the Logic of Paul's Moral Exhortation in 1 Corinthians 5–14

While Paul may have been distressed by the way some of the Corinthians were exercising their freedom in a manner which was inconsiderate of others, it is unlikely that he was surprised that freedom had become the main feature of their spirituality, for it was a major theme of his own gospel. The basic idea seems to be the one stated in 2 Cor. 3.17:

Christians, pp. 119-22). He remarks that 'a person who could visibly demonstrate, in the assembly of Christians, that the Spirit of God was speaking through him or her certainly held some currency of social power' (p. 119). Furthermore, he points out that 'the social distance between the poorer and wealthier members of the community leads us to expect the more articulated forms of power to be exercised by the latter and the less articulate by the former', but he notes that the prominent Corinthians who showed signs of status inconsistency may also have been 'candidates for the more dissociative experiences of the Spirit' (pp. 120-21).

33. That does not mean, however, that they were totally integrated into the upper strata of Greco-Roman society. See Meeks's discussion of the social status of the Corinthians in *The First Urban Christians* (chapter 2).

'where the Spirit of the Lord is, there is freedom'. Taken to its logical conclusion in an individualistic vein this came to have the connotation that where freedom is, 'everything is permitted' (1 Cor. 6.12; 10.23).[34] Paul is concerned to show the Corinthians that this attitude, and the consequent behaviour, are inconsistent with their 'calling' (1 Cor. 1.1-9) and his vision of community (cf. 1 Cor. 12.12-26). Since the individual and corporate identity conferred on them by God through Christ serves as a constant point of reference in the moral exhortation in 1 Corinthians 5–14, Paul's perception of the repercussions of the various expressions of a spirituality which regarded freedom as an absolute value will be examined. In addition to this, the extent to which social circumstances have influenced the way the different groups in Corinth have conceptualized and embodied the freedom of the gospel will also be considered.

In the first four chapters of the letter Paul highlights some of the socio-economic factors which lay behind the quarreling and strife in the community (1.26; 4.8-10) and he also seems to be aware of the socio-economic dimension of the eating controversies in chs. 8–11. This aspect of the problems in Corinth is critical because the various socio-economic statuses represented in the community reflect a different basis for self-understanding than the gospel. While embracing the gospel meant receiving a new identity and participation in a new social reality, all as a consequence of being baptized into Christ, it also brought into sharp relief the question of the efficacy of the believer's previous historical identity and the social forces which shaped it. Meeks explains the significance of baptism for Pauline converts in terms of the process of resocialization and says that 'the sect was intended to become virtually the primary group for its members, supplanting all other loyalties'.[35] Nonetheless, while the goal may have been resocialization, secondary socialization better describes conversion experiences because it denotes a process of socialization which is always partial in comparison with primary socialization.[36] According to Berger and Luckmann,

---

34. H.D. Betz, 'The Problem of Rhetoric and Theology according to the Apostle Paul', in A. Vanhoye (ed.), *L'Apôtre Paul: Personalité, style et conception du ministère* (Leuven: Leuven University Press, 1986), p. 25.

35. Meeks, *The First Urban Christians*, p. 78.

36. See the reference to Berger and Luckmann's explanation of re-socialization, *The Social Construction of Reality*, p. 68 n. 32. They elaborate further on this phenomenon in a way that pertains to religious conversion:

3. *The Cross and Moral Discourse*

in primary socialization the world mediated by the child's significant others is internalized, and this 'base-world' is always presupposed in secondary socialization. They contend that secondary socialization causes a problem of consistency between the original and new internalizations, and hence whatever new contents are now to be internalized must somehow be superimposed upon the already present reality.[37]

Paul's perennial underlining of the distinctiveness of the Christian's new identity in Christ and the theological reality on which it is founded betray his awareness of the enduring effects of the Corinthians' respective social identities in their attempts to live out their Christian calling. Although they understood themselves to be 'in Christ' and belonging to the holy people of God, the Corinthians continued to be influenced by the social norms and values of the larger society into which they were socialized. That is why Paul makes an unconditional distinction between 'those who are perishing' and those 'who are being saved', between the 'world' and the church (1.18-31).[38] Yet, even though these distinctions are carried over into his discussion of immorality (cf. 5.1, 12; 6.1-6, 9-11), they are not crucial to his subsequent moral exhortation. On the contrary, much of Paul's ethical instruction is characterized by a realistic affirmation of the fluidity of the social

> The old reality, as well as the collectivities and significant others that previously mediated it to the individual, must be reinterpreted *within* the legitimating apparatus of the new reality. This reinterpretation brings about a rupture in the subjective biography of the individual in terms of 'B.C.' and 'A.D.', 'pre-Damascus' and 'post-Damascus'... This involves a reinterpretation of past biography *in toto*, following the formula, 'Then I *thought*... now I *know*' (p. 179).

They go on to differentiate between re-socialization and secondary socialization in this way:

> In re-socialization the past is reinterpreted to conform to the present reality, with the tendency to retroject into the past various elements that were subjectively unavailable at the time. In secondary socialization the present is interpreted so as to stand in a continuous relationship with the past, with the tendency to minimize such transformations as have actually taken place (p. 182).

I propose that the difference between these two types of socialization suggests the difference between Paul's expectation of the Corinthians, which is based on his own Damascus experience and consequent thoroughgoing reinterpretation of reality, and the Corinthians' experience in which there seems to be substantial continuity between who they were in the world and who they have become in Christ.

37. Berger and Luckmann, *The Social Construction of Reality*, p. 128.
38. See the discussion of 1 Cor. 1–4 in Chapter 2.

boundaries separating believers from unbelievers (cf. 5.9-10; 7.12-16, 17-24; 10.25-27).

It was pointed out above that Paul's seemingly inconsistent attitude toward social boundaries reflects his own struggle with a fundamental ambiguity in his conception of the social character of the church.[39] If Paul was himself unclear about these lines of demarcation, then the ambiguity which he felt must have been intensified for the Corinthian believers who were living simultaneously in two social worlds. Although Paul does affirm the mutual interpenetration of the sacred and profane and hence does not draw sharp lines dividing them, he nevertheless sought to instill in the Corinthians a sense of separateness from pagan society because their continued identification with it had a decisive influence on interpersonal relations in the community.

It has already been noted that all of the ethical problems in 1 Corinthians 5–14 are interpersonal problems as far as Paul is concerned; even the incidents of sexual immorality are construed in relational terms. In considering these interpersonal problems in the community, social identity is an important factor because how people relate to one another is determined primarily by social location. Greco-Roman society was structured in terms of a ranking system which governed peoples' expectations of themselves and others' expectations of them.[40] According to Meeks, the close stratification of the society also affected the moral perceptions and moral choices of its members.[41] Despite Paul's vision of a community in which social, sexual and racial distinctions were relativized, it is apparent that this social ranking system continued to be operative to some extent in the Corinthian community, itself a microcosm of the social stratification of the macro-society (cf. 1.26).

The dissonance between the status ascribed by society and the status conferred by God through Christ was an important factor in the ethical issues Paul deals with in 1 Corinthians 5–14. If Paul's attempt to build a community shaped by the reality of what God had done in Christ is understood in terms of the process of re-socialization, then this dissonance between social and religious identity can be described as unsuccessful socialization. In view of the individualistic orientation to freedom which seems to be the common denominator of the various

---

39. Cf. Meeks, '"Since then you Would Need to Go out of the World"', p. 18.
40. Cf. Meeks, *The Moral World of the First Christians*, pp. 32-38.
41. Meeks, *The Moral World of the First Christians*, p. 35.

3. *The Cross and Moral Discourse*

behaviours Paul seeks to reform, it is noteworthy that Berger and Luckmann see a direct link between unsuccessful socialization and 'individualism', which they define as 'individual choice between discrepant realities and identities'.[42] They argue that unsuccessful socialization opens up the question of 'Who am I?', which in turn opens up a Pandora's box of individualistic choices:

> The 'individualist' emerges as a specific social type who has at least the potential to migrate between a number of available worlds and who has deliberately and awarely constructed a self out of the 'material' provided by a number of available identities.[43]

The insight that the possibility of individualism is contingent upon the availability of options in formulating an identity further illuminates the relationship between the ideology of freedom which predominated in Corinth and the diverse behaviours which, when measured against the ideal for which Paul was arguing, seemed self-indulgent. To put it concisely, membership in the community of saints and Paul's theological interpretation of the self supplied the Corinthians with a basis for a new social identity, but, as is always the case in secondary socialization, the new was superimposed on an already existing identity. Hence, in many of the moral crises dealt with in 1 Corinthians 5–14, the Corinthians' excessive conduct could have been a matter of them expressing their new identity in Christ in terms of the values, norms and typifications of the world of primary socialization. If freedom was one of the more popular theological themes in the community, it may well have been conceived of and personified differently by the slave or the freed person than it was by the few who were socially powerful.

The psycho-social forces at work in the ethical quandaries Paul is confronting are too complicated to be explained exclusively in terms of the interplay between social rank, including the values, roles and norms it implies, and a theology of the Spirit which emphasizes freedom; and yet what can be inferred from the letter about the social stratification of the community and the character of its spiritual expression suggests that it was an important aspect of the situation in Corinth. The two main blocks of ethical material deal with eating (1 Cor. 8–11) and spiritual gifts (1 Cor. 12–14). The controversies over idol meat and

---

42. Berger and Luckmann, *The Social Construction of Reality*, p. 190.
43. Berger and Luckmann, *The Social Construction of Reality*, p. 191.

the meal before the Lord's Supper both have a socio-economic dimension, and it seems likely that the individualistic freedom exhibited by those who ate idol meat and their own meal before the Lord's Supper is directly related to their social rank. Likewise, the activity of those who so highly prized the gift of tongues is probably also at least indirectly related to social standing, only at the opposite end of the spectrum. Whereas the wealthier Corinthians must have previously known the options which make individualism possible, many of the slaves, freedmen and women in the community were perhaps for the first time provided with the 'material' to construct an identity, and so it is not surprising that the freedom of the Spirit enabled them to transcend the social ranking system.

The point of these observations is not to identify one basic cause for all of the behavioural problems in the community, for the situation Paul is addressing eludes any monolithic interpretation.[44] Rather, the point is that the moral crisis in the Corinthian church was, from Paul's perspective, fundamentally a crisis of identity—that is to say, at issue was a discrepancy between social and baptismal identity. Although Paul does not take up the subject of Christian identity as a theme in itself, that it is indeed a major focus of his attention in 1 Corinthians is shown by the way he employs what Meeks calls the language of belonging. This language pervades 1 Corinthians and includes the designation ἅγιος and its cognates (1.2; 6.1-2; 14.33; 16.1, 15; cf. 1.30; 3.17; 7.14, 34), the term 'called' (1.9, 26; 7.17, 24) and the corresponding verb for being 'elect' (1.27), and language which speaks of the members of the community as if they were a family (especially the words 'brother' and 'sister' in 1 Cor. 1.10, 11, 26; 2.1; 3.1; 4.6; 5.11; 6.5-8; 7.12, 15, 24, 29; 8.11-13; 10.1; 11.33; 12.1; 14.6, 20, 26, 39). Paul's theological description of the community (6.11), the metaphor of the body of Christ (12.12-27), the idea of 'being known by God' (8.3), the language of the baptismal ritual (12.13), and even the words of institution (11.23-26) can also be added to this list. Meeks remarks that the repetitive use of this language serves the process of resocializa-

---

44. It is doubtful that the problem of sexual immorality has anything to do with identification with the norms and values of society, for, as Furnish points out, Paul's ideas of 'good' and 'bad' in such matters are in accord with contemporary ethical writers. However, it may be connected in some way with a theological conception of freedom (V. Furnish, *Theology and Ethics in Paul* [Nashville: Abingdon Press, 1968], p. 71).

tion 'by which an individual's identity is revised and knit together with the identity of the group, especially when it is accompanied by special terms for "the outsiders", "the world"'.[45] Designations for those outside the fold also pervade 1 Corinthians, and they were perhaps an even more poignant reminder of the believer's break with the past. All of these terms and phrases are theologically loaded and are constituent of a language game which functioned to reinforce the discontinuity between the 'old' self and the 'new' self created in Christ which should now be determinative for how the Christian lives.

The priority of the question of identity in any consideration of ethics has been confirmed by contemporary moral theorists. Stanley Hauerwas, following Alasdair MacIntyre, asserts that the question 'what ought I to be?' precedes the question 'what ought I to do?'[46] In other words, how a person behaves is largely a matter of which aspect(s) of identity prevail. While Paul does speak to this question of Christian identity, he is even more oriented toward the reality upon which this identity is grounded. In this sense his approach in this section is continuous with the way he handled the problem of disunity in 1 Corinthians 1–4. In the preceding discussion of chs. 1–4 I cited Berger and Luckmann's maxim that 'theories of identity are always embedded in a more general interpretation of reality' and suggested that in that context Paul locates the Corinthians' identity in Christ in a theological conception of reality defined exclusively by the 'word of the cross'. In chs. 5–14 he uses different symbols and metaphors to convey the theological definition of reality to which he and the Corinthians are committed, but the symbol of the cross is still foundational here. In fact, the significance of the cross is further elucidated by these other symbols and metaphors.

In order to ascertain how these symbols and metaphors function, though, the horizons of our interpretation of Paul's moral exhortation need to be expanded by taking into account the correlation between the theological representation of reality in which identity in Christ is embedded and the ideal of Christian conduct and community he is espousing. Geertz's model of religion as a system of symbols illuminates

---

45. Meeks, *The First Urban Christians*, pp.85-86.
46. S. Hauerwas, 'Casuistry as a Narrative Art', *Int* 37 (1983), p. 378. MacIntyre's version is 'I can only answer the question "What am I to do?" if I can answer the prior question "Of what story or stories do I find myself a part?"' (*After Virtue*, p. 201).

this dynamic inasmuch as it explains how the religious symbols through which reality is mediated serve to synthesize a people's ethos (i.e. 'the approved style of life') and their world view (i.e. 'the assumed structure of reality').[47] He asserts that religion is never merely metaphysics or ethics, rather 'the source of its moral vitality is conceived to lie in the fidelity with which it expresses the fundamental nature of reality'.[48] Understood in terms of Geertz's model, Paul's moral discourse in 1 Corinthians 5–14 is an attempt to establish a counterpoint between the community's 'moral and aesthetic style and mood' (ethos) and the theological conception of reality on which it is founded.

Throughout 1 Corinthians 5–14 Paul's moral exhortations are supported by statements describing the theological reality which he hopes will motivate the Corinthians to reform their conduct.[49] Malherbe has noted that Paul often stresses the motivation for the actions rather than the actions themselves, and, following A.D. Nock, he suggests that it is this theological motivation, and not so much the content, that distinguishes his ethical injunctions from those in pagan moral tradition.[50] With reference to this difference between Paul and contemporary ethical writers Furnish remarks that 'he does not seek to distinguish between the content of his ethical advice and theirs, but supports his own exhortations by relating them to what, on other grounds, his readers are already willing to acknowledge'.[51] Paul presupposes that the Corinthians have a general comprehension of reality as it is mediated by the Christian symbol system, and on that basis he re-presents the Christian definition of reality with a view to getting them to bring their lifestyles into conformity with it. In trying to accomplish this objective Paul's theological representations of reality are informed both by his diagnosis of how the Corinthians are in fact behaving and by his expectations of them as believers. Consequently, he uses a variety

47. Geertz, *The Interpretation of Cultures*, pp. 127-29.
48. Geertz, *The Interpretation of Cultures*, p. 128.
49. It is noteworthy that Berger and Luckmann conceive of theology as a type of 'conceptual machinery' whose primary function is to legitimate the definition of reality which is called into question by an alternative definition or a problematic situation (cf. *The Social Construction of Reality*, pp. 122-34). Similarly, Petersen says that 'theology is a form of systematic reflection upon prior knowledge' (*Rediscovering Paul*, p. 202). In 1 Corinthians Paul invites the Corinthians to reflect with him on the theological knowledge which is the basis of their shared faith.
50. Malherbe, 'Exhortation in First Thessalonians', pp. 250-51.
51. Furnish, *Theology and Ethics in Paul*, p. 71.

of motivations, and, as Deidun points out, often his choice of motivations is determined more by the moral and psychological dispositions of his readers than by the intrinsic importance of the motivations themselves.[52]

The most obvious indication that Paul appeals to the fundamental theological convictions that he shares with the Corinthians to motivate them to behave in a manner consistent with the gospel is his frequent use of the rhetorical question 'do you not know?' (3.16; 5.6; 6.2, 3, 9, 15, 16, 19; 9.13, 24). According to Wuellner, these rhetorical questions function to increase adherence to what is already accepted.[53] The one characteristic which most of them have in common is that they describe the community and its members in theological terms (cf. 3.16; 5.6; 6.2, 15). But in addition to emphasizing the theological character of the church, many of them also stress its corporate nature. Paul's intention is to get the Corinthians to consider their behaviour in the light of what they know to be true, that is, that they belong to God and to one another by virtue of what God has done in Christ. His method is one of intrinsic rather than extrinsic motivation.

While Paul's use of rhetorical questions is an indirect approach to motivating the Corinthians to live in accordance with what he knows they already believe, there are other passages in which he defines the reality which is the ground of Christian existence in ways that are more specifically directed to the problems he is addressing. A brief catalogue of some of these passages will demonstrate how Paul recalls the theological world view he shares with the Corinthians in ways which promote the ethos he envisions.

In his discussion of immorality among the Corinthians, the theological rationale for Paul's exhortation to 'cleanse out the old leaven that you may be a new lump' is that 'Christ, our paschal lamb, has been sacrificed' (5.7). Continuing with the same topic, Paul asserts that 'the body is not meant for immorality, but for the Lord', and he supports this claim by reminding the Corinthians that 'God raised the Lord and will also raise us up by his power' (6.13-14). To those who wish to change their status Paul tries to convince them to 'remain with God' instead of becoming 'slaves of men' by telling them that they 'were bought with a price' (7.23-24). In his treatment of the dispute over

---

52. Deidun, *New Covenant Morality in Paul*, pp. 51-52.
53. W. Wuellner, 'Paul as Pastor: The Function of Rhetorical Questions in First Corinthians', in Vanhoye (ed.), *L'Apôtre Paul*, p. 60.

idol meat Paul sympathizes with those who would eat by acknowledging that 'there is one God' (8.4, 6), but this knowledge is to be qualified by another reality, namely that Christ died for the person whose conscience is weak (8.11). In addressing the abuses at the Lord's Supper he need only cite the words of institution for they convey the significance of the meal: 'you proclaim the Lord's death until he comes' (11.26). Awareness of what is being proclaimed should determine how people behave. Finally, in response to an elitism based on a preference for the gift of tongues (cf. ch. 14), Paul points to the Spirit as the ground of Christian unity and reminds the Corinthians that 'by one Spirit we were all baptized into one body' (12.13; cf. all of ch. 12).

These passages disclose Paul's attempts to synthesize ethos and world view. It is the ethos of the community, its 'approved style of life', that is in question. He apparently had no reason to question the Corinthians' fidelity to the religious symbol system which they acquired when they were baptized into Christ. Some of them may have interpreted the tradition differently than Paul, but he still had a foundation upon which he could establish or re-establish norms for community life (cf. 3.10). The symbols of the tradition mediated the vision of reality that was authoritative for the community, and Paul was able to elaborate on particular aspects of this vision in ways which lent authority to his moral exhortations. Geertz's explanation of how religious symbols function to legitimate social norms and values illuminates the underlying dynamic of Paul's approach and is worth quoting at length:

> The force of a religion in supporting social values rests, then, on the ability of its symbols to formulate a world in which those values, as well as the forces opposing their realization, are fundamental ingredients. It represents the power of the human imagination to construct an image of reality in which, to quote Max Weber, 'events are not just there and happen, but they have a meaning and happen because of that meaning'. The need for such a metaphysical grounding for values seems to vary quite widely in intensity from culture to culture and from individual to individual, but the tendency to desire some sort of factual basis for one's commitments seems practically universal; mere conventionalism satisfies few people in any culture... religion, by fusing ethos and world view, gives to a set of social values what they perhaps need to be coercive: an appearance of objectivity.[54]

Paul was engaged in building a new social order which had the gospel as its foundation, and he seemed to think that the norms and values

---

54. Geertz, *The Interpretation of Cultures*, p. 131.

which would constitute a distinctively Christian ethos were intrinsic to that gospel.[55] Although his moral discourse does contain some specific directives, on a conceptual or theological level it served to remind the Corinthians of their shared Christian identity and convictions so that they could decide for themselves how they should behave in the context of a Christian community. Paul wanted to provide the theological motivation for proper Christian conduct. The question which is the focus of attention here is how did he use the symbols of the tradition, specifically the symbol of the cross, to promote an ethos that would be congruous with the world view mediated by the gospel of 'Christ crucified'?

The Word of the Cross as the Foundation of the Ethical Discourse in 1 Corinthians 5–14

For Paul, morality within the Christian community seems to have as much to do with attitudes as it does conduct. In one instance he is just as concerned about the Corinthians' attitude toward a certain behaviour as he is the behaviour itself (cf. 5.1-2), and in other places he identifies the connection between a particular attitude and the conduct in question (cf. 6.12; 8.1; 10.23). Paul is not, of course, interested in psychologizing the ethical crises in 1 Corinthians 5–14, but he does seem to presuppose that how one thinks is the basis for what one does. Although he does not provide extensive analysis of the dispositions of the people who were at the centre of conflict in the community, his perception of the attitudes underlying the controversies is either explicitly or implicitly disclosed in his exhortations. Sometimes it is conveyed by his reiteration of a Corinthian slogan or opinion and other times it must be inferred from how he characterizes a situation, but he usually gives some impression of how the Corinthians' conduct has been prompted by something other than the gospel he first presented to them. Likewise, Paul's ethical injunctions usually contain a recapitulation of the gospel, but because he has related it to a particular situation it is usually not articulated in the kerygmatic language he uses in 1 Cor. 1.18-25 and ch. 15, and elsewhere in his other letters.

In 1 Corinthians 5–14 Paul has interpreted the Corinthian situation in the light of the gospel. On the other hand, he has also allowed the

---

55. Cf. Meeks, *The First Urban Christians*, p. 104; Wuellner, 'Paul as Pastor', p. 73.

situation to shape his formulation of the gospel. Paul's assessment of the problems dealt with in these chapters has been considered from both sociological and theological perspectives, and it has been suggested that a common denominator linking many of these seemingly disparate problems was an individualistic orientation to freedom. From Paul's standpoint it was the Corinthians' unqualified exercise of their freedom in Christ which for him constituted a moral dilemma. Since the theological frame of reference of the moral discourse in 1 Corinthians is his vision of community, it follows that he would try to persuade them to express their freedom in accordance with this vision.

The preceding discussion of the logic of Paul's ethical exhortations has emphasized the way he attempted to ground the Corinthians' identity in a world view defined by the 'word of the cross'. Building on this claim, it seems likely that Paul's gospel is also the basis of his vision of community, and that the gospel and his idea of community are so inextricably bound together that his convictions about how believers should coexist are betrayed in the theological statements of 1 Corinthians 5–14. Conversely, the content of the gospel is at least implicit in the more directive comments which give concrete expression to his vision of community.

Of course for Paul the gospel includes both the death and resurrection of Christ, and although this study is concerned to show the connection between the exposition of the cross in 1 Corinthians 1–4 and the ethical discourse of 1 Corinthians 5–14, he also provides an extensive elaboration of his theology of the resurrection in ch. 15. The death and resurrection of Christ are together the founding events of the new age, and Paul conceives of the church as a community in which the eschaton is proleptically actualized. One way to think about the implications of the explications of the cross and the resurrection in 1 Corinthians for the ethical section sandwiched between them is to understand what Paul has to say about the cross as prospective and what he has to say about the resurrection as retrospective. These two symbols serve as the basis of Paul's moral vision. There is a dialectic between the cross and the resurrection inasmuch as they have significance only in relation to each other, but sometimes he emphasizes the significance of one without reference to the other. Therefore, even though the symbol of Christ's resurrection does inform Paul's moral discourse (e.g. 6.14), the scope of our exegesis of 1 Corinthians 5–14 will be restricted to a consideration of the function of the symbol of the cross. In order to delineate this it is necessary to ascertain how Paul's references to the death of Jesus in 1 Corinthians 1–4 are played out in the paraenesis, and in what sense his conception of this event influenced his idea of community in this letter.

1 Corinthians 5.1-12

As the focus shifts to a more detailed exegetical consideration of 1 Corinthians 5–14, it is important to note the nature of the transition from Paul's treatment of mimetic rivalry in chs. 1–4 to the moral discourse of ch. 5. Although the change in subject matter suggests a rather abrupt transition, Paul's references to the 'arrogance' of certain people in the community are indicative of the continuity between chs. 1–4 and 5–14. Paul does introduce a new agenda in 5.1, but the Corinthians' 'arrogance' regarding the immorality appears to disturb him as much as the incident itself. He is speaking to the community here and so it is their culpability that is in focus.[56] Hence the connecting link between chs. 4 and 5 is the 'arrogance' of 'some' in 4.18-19 and the 'arrogance' of the church in 5.2 and 6.[57]

It is difficult to know whether the Corinthians were arrogant because of or in spite of this man's sexual immorality, but the fact that they were 'boasting' (v. 6) suggests that they may have affirmed it on theological grounds. If so, then the sin would have been regarded as an expression of the believer's freedom in Christ (cf. 6.12; 10.23).[58] In any case, whether their approval of this particular action was explicit or not, it contradicted Paul's conception of the nature of the community.[59] The operative image of the church in this portion of the letter is that of God's holy temple (3.16-17), which suggests that what was ultimately at issue was the purity of the community. The man who was living with his father's wife must be expelled in order to maintain this purity.[60] This concern is further expressed by the imagery of the

56. P. Minear, 'Christ and the Congregation: 1 Corinthians 5–6', *RevExp* 80 (1983), p. 343.

57. Cf. Hurd, *The Origin of I Corinthians*, p. 89 n. 1, followed by G. Fee, *The First Epistle to the Corinthians* (Grand Rapids: Eerdmans, 1987), p. 194. They also point out the tie between the lack of 'power' among the arrogant in 4.19-20 vis-à-vis the 'power of our Lord Jesus' in 5.4.

58. Barrett, *The First Epistle to the Corinthians*, pp. 121-22.

59. J. Ruef, *Paul's First Letter to Corinth* (Philadelphia: Westminster Press, 1971), p. 41.

60. Cf. C. Roetzel, *Judgement in the Community* (Leiden: Brill, 1972), p. 116.

leaven which has to be cleansed out (5.6-7).⁶¹ Leaven was a symbol of impurity and recalled the Feast of Unleavened Bread (Exod. 12.14-20). Moreover, this allusion to the ritual in which the Israelites protected themselves from the dangers of infection by purging their homes of all leaven prompted an allusion to the other more important ritual of Passover, namely the sacrifice of the Paschal Lamb (Exod. 12.6).

In designating Christ as 'our paschal lamb' Paul moves from the idea of purity to the idea of deliverance, though as with Passover the two themes are not unrelated. Barrett is probably right when he says that 'Christ as the Lamb of God summed up God's action for the deliverance of his people; and the context suggests that he delivered them by bearing for them the burden of their guilt and thus removing their sin'.⁶² Thus in v. 7 Paul uses the image of the paschal lamb to remind the Corinthians of the effect of Christ's sacrificial death. The eschatological significance of Christ's death is in view in this context in the sense that it is the new reality wrought by that event that is invoked. Paul urges the Corinthians to become what they already are in Christ, a 'new batch of dough'.⁶³

In the injunction of v. 7 the image of Christ as the paschal lamb who has been sacrificed has corporate connotations. It conveys the image of a community that is holy and pure. But it also calls forth the theme of freedom, which is striking in view of the likelihood that the Corinthians' arrogance is predicated on the conviction that they are free in Christ in an absolute sense. While it may seem surprising that Paul would reply to believers for whom all things had become lawful because they had been liberated in Christ by emphasizing the theological basis of that freedom, it is precisely by establishing the ground of Christian freedom that he can define and qualify the nature of that freedom. The paschal lamb symbolism denotes Christ's sacrificial death through which comes the forgiveness of sins, and in this context the connotation would seem to be that Christ has set the believer free *from* sin not *for* sin. Here again Paul is referring to the eschatological

---

Roetzel points out that in addition to the cleansing of the community judgment also serves the purpose of the redemption of the individual.

61. Newton, *The Concept of Purity*, p. 91, notes that the use of the verb καθαίρω indicates the presence of something unclean which needs to be removed so that the community as the 'new lump' and 'unleavened' can function as intended.

62. Barrett, *The First Epistle to the Corinthians*, p. 128.

63. Cf. Fee, *The First Epistle to the Corinthians*, p. 215.

reality which is the consequence of Christ's death: the believer's transfer from the old aeon to the new aeon, the freedom for new life in Christ.[64]

The new age has, for Paul, been inaugurated by the death and resurrection of Christ, and the new life which is the result of the believer's participation in it continues to be determined by the events on which it is founded.[65] Although Paul does not use the language of participation, the eschatological force of his reference to the death of Jesus in v. 7 suggests that he presupposes an awareness on the part of the Corinthians that their lives have been and are to continue to be shaped by the sacrificial death of Christ. Conzelmann is probably right when he warns that the paschal lamb metaphor is not to be pressed beyond the ideas of sacrifice and covenant,[66] but at the very least, then, it would mean that the character of the New Covenant community in Corinth is to be defined by the sacrifical death of its Lord.

The idea of sacrifice does not itself seem to be central to Paul's understanding of the death of Jesus, especially in the Corinthian correspondence. Fundamentally it refers to the Jewish notion of sacrifice for the forgiveness of sins, and of all Paul's references to the death of Jesus in these two extant letters this is the only one which is connected with sin at all.[67] He emphasizes liberation from sin in this instance, specifically sexual immorality, because he wants to reestablish the theological basis for a new life characterized by 'sincerity and truth' (5.8). But the character of that new life is defined even more precisely by the event on which it is predicated.

This means that the idea of sacrifice denoted by the paschal lamb metaphor here also has an ethical nuance in the sense that it qualifies how the freedom obtained by Christ's death should be lived out. If Paul highlights the ground of Christian freedom in response to a situation in which an abuse of that freedom has been affirmed by the community, it must be because he wants to say something about the proper use of that freedom. This he can do without elaboration because the point he wants to make is implicit in the metaphor of Christ's sacrificial death.

---

64. Fee, *The First Epistle to the Corinthians*, p. 218.
65. This is one of the main arguments of Tannehill's *Dying and Rising with Christ* (see pp. 39-43 and pp. 123-29).
66. Conzelmann, *1 Corinthians*, p. 99.
67. The absence of the idea of forgiveness in Paul's discussion of the significance of the Lord's Supper is conspicuous.

Since Christian freedom was procured through Christ's death on behalf of others, it would be inappropriate to exercise that freedom in self-indulgent disregard for others, as did the man who was living with his father's wife. One might expect that Paul would have spelled out more clearly the implications of Christ's sacrificial death for Christian conduct; but whatever his reasons for leaving them to be inferred, it is evident from 2 Cor. 5.14-15 that Christ's death 'for all' is supposed to provide the motivation to live for others rather than oneself. Therefore, even though he does not explicitly say here that the freedom effected by the death of Christ should be expressed in accordance with what that death signifies, that theme is developed more fully elsewhere in chs. 6–14. And if it is more conspicuously played out in other passages in 1 Corinthians, then it may well be that this is what he had in mind in reminding the Corinthians that they are free because 'Christ, our paschal lamb, has been sacrificed'.

1 Corinthians 6.1-11
In 6.12-20 Paul attends to another type of πορνεία which is also the direct result of an abuse of the believer's freedom in Christ inasmuch as it is legitimated by the slogan 'all things are lawful for me' (6.12). But sandwiched between his discussion of the two episodes of πορνεία is a critique of a situation in which two men were involved in litigation in a civil court. Although 6.1-11 does seem to interrupt two passages that are connected by the common theme of immorality, Paul's remarks about the church's relationship to the world in 5.9-13 provide a smooth transition to his treatment of the lawsuit. More importantly, these verses and his comments in 6.9-11 indicate that what is fundamentally at issue in these two incidents of immorality is holiness, that is, the distinctiveness of the community.

What Paul makes clear in 5.9-11 is that the holiness of God's people in Corinth is endangered not so much by 'the immoral of this world, or the greedy and robbers, or idolaters' as by the immorality and greed of those within the community. The specifics of the incident in 6.1-11 are not disclosed, but it is possible, if not probable, that the term πλεονέκτης in 5.10 betrays Paul's perspective on what is at issue here. The word ἀποστερέω in 6.7-8 suggests that the lawsuit probably concerned material possessions, and if so, then πλεονέκτης would describe the behaviour which he reproves in those same verses.[68] This

---

68. Cf. P. Richardson, 'Judgement in Sexual Matters in 1 Cor. 6.1-11', *NovT*

word group was important in ethical discussions relating to moral conduct in Greco-Roman society and frequently had the connotation of 'to take advantage of someone'.[69]

It is noteworthy that this word occurs again in the list characterizing the unrighteous in 6.10 because the force of what Paul has to say to the Corinthians in these verses hinges on the distinction between the τῶν ἀδίκων and and the τῶν ἁγίων (6.1). Paul provides a rather graphic description of what kind of people the unrighteous are in 6.9-10 in order to emphasize the transformation wrought by Christ in the lives of the Corinthians: 'And such were some of you. But you were washed, you were sanctified, you were justified in the name of the Lord Jesus Christ and in the Spirit of our God' (6.11). However, the contrast is not intended merely as an affirmation of the Corinthians' identity in Christ, rather it serves as the basis for shaming them.[70] In what is probably a play on words, Paul uses the word ἀδικέω in v. 8 (the verb form of the noun translated 'unrighteous' in v. 1) to characterize the behaviour of those who have initiated the lawsuit. The successive questioning in this passage serves to make the Corinthians aware of the absurdity of having the 'unrighteous' make decisions about how the 'saints' should behave. The manner in which he contrasts the two groups, especially in vv. 9-11, together with his use of ἀδικέω to describe the Corinthians' behaviour suggests that he also wanted to stress the incongruity between their identity in Christ and how they were acting in this instance.

More constructively, Paul does suggest what kind of behaviour is appropriate to 'saints' who will judge the world (6.2) by asking two rhetorical questions in v. 7: 'why not rather suffer wrong? why not rather be defrauded?' These questions recall the apostle's own example of self-disregarding behaviour in the hardship catalogue in 4.11-13. As was indicated in the discussion of 1 Cor. 4.9-13, Paul presents

25.1 (1983), pp. 37-58. Richardson thinks that 6.1-11 is connected with the sexual sin of 6.12-20, and this view has gained further support recently from W. Countryman. Countryman argues convincingly that Paul's primary concern in the discussion of sexual ethics in 1 Cor. 5–7 is not purity but property. He observes that when the case of incest is understood as a violation of property rights, that is, taking for one's own a woman who *belongs* to someone else, the subsequent discussion of the lawsuit makes perfect sense (cf. W. Countryman, *Dirt, Greed and Sex* [Philadelphia: Fortress Press, 1988], pp. 200-202).

69. See Delling, 'πλεονέκτης', *TDNT*, VI, pp. 266-68.
70. Cf. Fee, *The First Epistle to the Corinthians*, p. 241.

himself as someone who in his own weakness embodies the weakness of the cross, the significance of which he elaborated on in 1.18-25. In that context his purpose in highlighting the weakness which characterized apostolic existence was twofold. In the first place, it was a way of subverting the cultural values according to which the dominant minority in the community criticized him and boasted of their own superiority. Thus the hardship catalogue served the critical purpose of reproving or shaming those who were 'arrogant', as he calls them. But in these verses Paul also offered his own apostolic existence as an example to be imitated (cf. 4.16), precisely because it conformed to the gospel of Christ crucified.

Paul describes in these verses the apostolic behaviour which he considers to be paradigmatic for all Christians, and 4.12-13 in particular seems to be relevant to his discussion of the litigation in 6.1-11. There is a conspicuous correlation between his own example of blessing when he has been insulted and abused (λοιδορέω), enduring when persecuted, and exhorting when he has been slandered (δυσφημέω), and his counsel in 6.7b: 'Why not rather suffer wrong? Why not rather be defrauded?' In view of the likelihood that Paul's urging the Corinthians to imitate him pertains not only to the concerns expressed in chs. 1–4 but also the subsequent ethical issues, it seems reasonable to assume that his personal example in 4.12-13 also serves to illustrate the self-disregarding behaviour he recommends in 6.7. His apostolate has been shaped by the 'word of the cross', and so likewise he expects the Corinthians to act in a manner that is consistent with the gospel which is the very ground of their identity in Christ, an identity which distinguishes them from the unrighteous of the world (6.9-11). Therefore, the theology of the cross which Paul personifies (4.9-13) is also the basis for, tacitly at least, his admonitions in 6.1-11. Here, as in Paul's own apostolic ministry, the cross signifies the setting aside of one's own self-interests for the sake of others. This kind of other-regarding behaviour is what distinguishes the church from the world, and consequently it is absurd that 'the world' should judge its affairs (6.1-6).

1 Corinthians 8–10
Paul takes up the subject of eating idol meat in chs. 8–10, another issue which had divided the community. Although 1 Corinthians 8 is structured around questions and phrases deriving from the Corinthians themselves, Paul reinterprets the problem so that it reflects his own

3. *The Cross and Moral Discourse*   115

concern for the community as a whole rather than the individual 'rights' (ἐξουσία) of those for whom it was permissible to eat food that was sacrificed to idols.[71] This group's insistence on their 'right' to eat idol meat was based on their 'knowledge' that 'an idol has no real existence' and that 'there is no God but one' (8.4).[72] Despite his concession to the Corinthian slogan that 'all of us possess knowledge' in 8.1, however, Paul points out in v. 7 that, in fact, not all do possess this knowledge. This is followed in v. 9 with a warning which sets his own understanding of the situation in contrast to the Corinthians' view of their behaviour: 'take care lest this liberty of yours become a stumbling block to the weak'. The word ἐξουσία denotes the position of those who perceived their eating to be an expression of their freedom in Christ, while πρόσκομμα registers Paul's concern about the effect their behaviour is having on those whose conscience is weak.[73]

For the Corinthians who were eating idol meat the crux of the matter was knowledge. This knowledge, the content of which is disclosed in v. 4, was evidently the source of their freedom and power.[74] Paul does not dispute its validity, indeed, in principle he agrees with their position. Rather he emphasizes the priority of love over knowledge

---

71. Willis and Fee have made more sense of the whole of Paul's argument in 1 Cor. 8–10 than other interpretations which understand the problem of idol meat as referring to marketplace food by showing that what is at issue is eating sacrificial food at cultic meals in the pagan temples. Not only does this view take seriously 8.10 as the key to understanding the situation implied in 8.1-13, but it is also able to connect Paul's argument in 8.1-13 with his argument in 10.1-22 (W. Willis, *Idol Meat in Corinth: The Pauline Argument in 1 Corinthians 8 and 10* [SBLDS, 68; Chico, CA: Scholars Press, 1985], pp. 7-64; Fee, *The First Epistle to the Corinthians*, pp. 358-63).

72. Theissen and Meeks suggest that the 'strong' in this context belong to the wealthier and better placed minority of the Corinthian community (Theissen, *The Social Setting of Pauline Christianity*, pp. 121-43; Meeks, *The Moral World of the First Christians*, p. 133). However, Willis, while acknowledging that the frequency of eating at pagan sacrificial meals would have varied according to one's social situation and circle of friends, avers that there would have been ample opportunity for most of the Corinthians to have some occasion to participate in such meals (Willis, *Idol Meat in Corinth*, p. 15). Since Paul emphasizes only the matter of 'conscience' in this particular dispute (cf. 8.7-12), it seems unwise to speculate about possible socio-economic distinctions between the 'strong' and the 'weak'.

73. Cf. Fee, *The First Epistle to the Corinthians*, p. 378.

74. Willis, *Idol Meat in Corinth*, p. 111, rightly observes that the word ἐξουσία means both 'power' and 'right' or 'freedom'.

and thereby qualifies their categorical claims to freedom: 'knowledge puffs up, but love builds up' (v. 1). As Willis observes: 'these two slogans in 8.1 capture succinctly the basic conflict between Paul and the Corinthians, not only about idol meat but other issues as well'.[75] In the first slogan φυσιοῖ connotes the arrogance characteristic of someone whose conduct is guided only by the knowledge that they are right, but it also recalls Paul's use of this word in 4.6 where it is used to describe the actual situation of being 'puffed up in favour of one against the other'. Hence the slogan refers to the disposition of the 'strong', a disposition which resulted in their alienating the 'weak' in the community. In the second slogan Paul proposes that love should take precedence over knowledge in any consideration of how one should act in the community because it has the converse effect of knowledge, it 'builds up'. Consistent with the ethical principle which guides him throughout 1 Corinthians, the contrast between φυσιόω, which describes what happens when individuals set themselves up as the norm within the community, and οἰκοδομέω signifies another attempt on his part to get the Corinthians to consider how their behaviour affects the other members of the community.

The activity of those in the community who possessed the knowledge which allowed them to eat idol meat is another example of the individualism which is the target of Paul's moral exhortations. As has been noted, it is likely that their disposition had its antecedents in Hellenistic culture where individual freedom was regarded as the highest good. The Corinthians have simply spiritualized this cultural value. Without undermining their freedom, then, Paul challenges their individualism by setting forth the norm of considering the community. He employs the metaphor of 'building up' in order that their emphasis on the knowledge, power, and freedom of the individual might be superseded by his emphasis on the mutual responsibility believers have to one another.

The ideal of mutual responsibility which is conveyed by this metaphor is given more precise definition and is theologically legitimated in vv. 11-12. There Paul designates the one whose conscience is 'weak' as 'the brother for whom Christ died' (v. 11). He invokes the symbol of Christ's death in order to re-establish the common basis of their life together. The death of Christ, along with his resurrection, is the foundational symbol of the community, and so defines the basis of the

---

75. Willis, *Idol Meat in Corinth*, p. 71.

3. *The Cross and Moral Discourse* 117

community members' relationships to one another. In contrast to the 'knowledge' and 'freedom' which served to distinguish the strong from the weak, the cross here symbolizes the ontological reality which is the ground of their unity in Christ. The Corinthians are to understand themselves as related to one another and to Christ by virtue of the fact that Christ died for them (cf. v. 12).[76] More than that, the symbol of Christ's death functions to relate this ontology to the supreme value or norm which should determine how the members of this Christian community should behave toward one another.[77] If Christ's death is the ground of the believer's mutual responsibility to one another, then what is symbolized by that death also defines the nature of one's obligation to the other members of the community.

Paul explains the ethical norm of regard for others which he recommends with reference to his own ministry in ch. 9. Most interpreters agree that whatever the argument in this chapter discloses about any suspicion in the community concerning Paul's apostolic authority and practices, it is secondary to its primary purpose of providing a personal example of the renunciation of rights which he urges.[78] Although Paul uses the word ἀπολογία to introduce his argument, he is not seeking to prove his right to support so much as arguing from that right.[79] As Willis has pointed out, the reason he establishes his rights so strongly in vv. 4-14 is so that he can make something of his renunciation of them.[80] Paul simply wants to show the Corinthians that he exemplifies

---

76. Paul uses the term ἀδελφός in vv. 11-13 to express relationships within the community that are defined by the death of Christ. Each is to perceive the other as someone for whom Christ died, and therefore to sin against one's brother is to sin against Christ. The switch from the singular in vv. 11 and 13 to the plural in v. 12 ('your brothers') reflects Paul's understanding of the solidarity of Christ with his body. Thus to sin against Christ is also to destroy his body the church. See J. Murphy-O'Connor, 'Freedom or the Ghetto (1 Cor. VIII, 1-13; X, 23-XI, 1)', *RB* (1978), pp. 563-64; Willis, *Idol Meat in Corinth*, p. 107.

77. Cf. Geertz, 'Ethos, World View, and the Analysis of Sacred Symbols', pp. 127-41. According to Geertz, one of the primary functions of sacred symbols, such as the cross, is to relate an ontology to a morality.

78. For a study of the function of 1 Cor. 9 which argues this view see W. Willis, 'Apostolic Apologia? The Form and Function of 1 Corinthians 9', *JSNT* 24 (1985), pp. 33-48.

79. J. Weiss, *Der erste Korintherbrief* (Göttingen: Vandenhoeck & Ruprecht, 1897), p. 233.

80. Willis, 'Apostolic Apologia?', p.35.

the behaviour which he has commended in ch. 8, that is, using one's freedom for the benefit of others.

The correspondence between the arguments of chs. 8 and 9 is conspicuous. In 8.9 Paul exhorts them to be careful that their 'liberty' does not become a 'stumbling block to the weak', and in chapter 9 he use the same word ἐξουσία to designate what he has given up by refusing support. The connection between his personal example and his admonition to the Corinthians in ch. 8 is made even more explicit by his comment in v. 12b: 'we have not made use of this right, but we endure anything rather than put an obstacle in the way of the gospel of Christ'. Doubtless his own non-use of ἐξουσία in order to avoid being an 'obstacle' is intended as a contrast to others in the community who in exercising their ἐξουσία had become a 'stumbling block'. Paul does not spell out here what motivates him to renounce his apostolic rights, he only presents himself as a paradigm for the community. But as Meeks observes, an unstated warrant for the non-use of power has been set out in the early chapters of the letter: it is the model furnished by the crucified messiah.[81] That Paul does indeed have the crucified Christ in mind is shown in the closing remarks of his argument. After characterizing his own apostolic behaviour as 'not seeking my own advantage', he urges the Corinthians to 'be imitators of me, as I am of Christ' (10.33–11.1). Paul imitates the Christ who did not please himself (cf. Rom. 15.2, 3), whose death on a cross epitomized his ethical ideal of setting aside one's own self- interests for the sake of others.

1 Corinthians 11.17-34
In chs. 11–14, the last segment of the paraenetic section of the letter, Paul addresses certain interpersonal problems that have arisen in the context of worship. After speaking briefly to concerns related to women's head covering when praying and prophesying (11.2-16), Paul turns his attention in 11.17-34 to abuses at the Lord's table which belie 'participation in the body of Christ' (10.16). The behaviour of certain Corinthians so contradicted what was signified by the meal that Paul actually warns them that 'it is not the Lord's Supper that you eat' (v. 20). Dennis Smith has shown that there was a standardized form for ritual meals in the Greco-Roman world, and that communal meals did not differ in their forms so much as they differed in the

---

81. Meeks, *The Moral World of the First Christians*, p. 135.

3. *The Cross and Moral Discourse*   119

interpretations given them.⁸² When the Corinthians gathered together the schisms among them indicated that the meal they ate was not in reality communal, and so Paul interprets what the meal means in terms of the sacred tradition in order to promote the unity which should characterize the many who become 'one body' because they 'partake of the one bread' (cf. 10.17).

Paul describes the nature of the divisions in v. 21: 'for in eating, each one goes ahead with his own meal, and one is hungry and another is drunk'. Theissen has argued persuasively that it was the wealthier Christians in Corinth who ate separately the food which they themselves provided for the whole church, and it appears that they began eating before the regular Lord's Supper. Moreover, he suggests that the phrase τὸ ἴδιον δεῖπνον means not only that the wealthy ate their own meals privately, but also that they may have had a greater quantity, or perhaps even a higher quality meal which included meat.⁸³ The plausibility of Theissen's reconstruction of the situation is supported to some degree by Paul's remark in v. 22 in which he distinguishes between those who were wealthy enough to 'have houses to eat and drink in' and 'those who have nothing'. This verse also discloses what he perceived to be the crux of the problem: those who have the means to eat and drink 'despise the church of God and humiliate' those who do not. Paul's use of the word καταισχύνω here implies that he is aware of the social dimensions of the conflict, but his judgment that the wealthy 'despise the church of God' interprets their behaviour with regard to what it says about their attitude toward the church. Thus Paul seems to be most concerned with the theological and ecclesiastical ramifications of their social practice at the Lord's Supper.

While Theissen is right in pointing out that the social causes of the conflict emerge more clearly than do any of the theological ones which previous scholarship has suggested, it is important to differentiate between what the text discloses about the social complexion of the conflict and what it discloses about Paul's perspective on the matter. In addition to his remark in v. 22 that the wealthy 'despise the church of God', there are two words in v. 21 which indicate Paul's orientation

82. D. Smith, 'Social Obligation in the Context of Communal Meals: A Study of the Christian Meal in 1 Corinthians in Comparison with Greco-Roman Communal Meals' (unpublished PhD thesis, Harvard University, 1980). See the statement of his thesis on p. 2.
83. Theissen, *The Social Setting of Pauline Christianity*, pp. 153-58.

in dealing with the situation. The words ἕκαστος and ἴδιον could, as Theissen concedes, denote an exaggerated individualism, and since Paul construes every one of the quandaries in chs. 5–10 and the one in chs. 12 and 14 in terms of self-indulgent behaviours which are fragmenting the community, it seems likely that that is indeed how he conceived of the problem. It is not simply a matter of the community being divided along socio-economic lines into the 'haves' and the 'have nots', but rather an individualistic self-indulgence which is predicated on distinctions of status and wealth.[84] Although the differences in social rank and status may ultimately have been the cause of conflict, from Paul's viewpoint the real problem is that the wealthy are acting as individuals and not as members of the 'body of Christ'. The purpose of Paul's argument in 11.17-34 is to provide that the Lord's Supper truly be a communal meal.[85] Through the 'body of Christ' metaphor Paul is able to relate the theological basis of his ecclesiology to a concrete vision of how the Corinthians should live in relation to each other (cf. 1 Cor. 12–14).

The imagery of the 'body of Christ' is employed here to denote the theological premise upon which Paul's conception of Christian community is founded. In 10.17 Paul related the metaphor to the Lord's Supper in order to establish the ground of Christian unity: 'Because there is one bread, we who are many are one body, for we all partake of one bread'. This statement anticipates the discussion in 11.17-34 where the sacramental 'body of Christ' (vv. 23-26) is interpreted with reference to the social 'body of Christ' (vv. 27-29). In this context the theological and social implications of eating the bread and drinking the cup which symbolize 'the body and blood of the Lord' respectively (v. 27), are set over against the social reality of a disunified community. It is this incongruity between the ideal of community conveyed by the body metaphor and the way the Corinthians are actually behaving which causes Paul to remind them of what it really means to celebrate the Lord's Supper. The traditional interpretation of Jesus' last meal with the disciples cited by Paul in vv. 23-25 defines the 'body' of the Lord

---

84. Cf. Fee, *The First Epistle to the Corinthians*, p. 534. With regard to socioeconomic distinctions Fee observes that 'In a class-conscious society such as Roman Corinth would have been, it would be sociologically natural for the host to invite those of his/her own class to eat in the triclinium, while the others would eat in the atrium'.

85. Cf. Smith, 'Social Obligation in the Context of Communal Meals', p. 195.

in terms of his death, but Paul pushes this tradition to a new conceptualization so that it can also refer to the 'body' which is his church (v. 29). The dual meaning of the metaphor in this context suggests a connection between the understanding of the death of Jesus and the idea of community which it expresses.

The fact that the 'body of Christ' refers in the first place to his body given in death ὑπὲρ ὑμῶν (v. 24) indicates that it is primarily a theological metaphor which has its origins in the words of institution. But the social connotations of the metaphor, which are developed more fully in chs. 12 and 14, are inextricably connected with the theological nuances it has in 11.23-26, even though they are not inherent in the tradition itself. This connection suggests that the vision of community expressed by Paul's use of the 'body of Christ' imagery is somehow predicated on what the sacred tradition cited in 11.23-26 says about the significance of Christ's death. Just as the symbol of Christ's death has both theological and social import throughout 1 Corinthians, so also the 'body of Christ' metaphor is at once both theological and social. As Robert Banks has pointed out, the 'body' and 'covenant' of Christ, symbolized by the bread and the cup, are not simply two ways of referring to the same thing, namely Jesus' death for others sake. While the term 'body' obviously describes the death of Jesus, the term 'covenant' goes on to identify the new relationship with God and one another which results from that death.[86] Therefore, just as the meal is both a social and an eschatological event, so also the bread and the wine represent, respectively, the social and eschatological significance of Christ's death.

In this passage, as both Theissen and Meeks have affirmed, Paul sets the social tensions in the community into a larger symbolic world by making them part of an eschatological drama.[87] The ideal of community derived from the Christian symbol system is here set over against the social realities which characterize the Corinthians' eating of the Lord's Supper. Theissen is right, then, when he says that 'the conflict has its roots in the collision between a consistent theory of community on the one hand and, on the other, behaviour produced by social

---

86. R. Banks, *Paul's Idea of Community* (Grand Rapids: Eerdmans, 1980), pp. 85-86.

87. Meeks, *The First Urban Christians*, p. 159; Theissen, *The Social Setting of Pauline Christianity*, p. 165.

differences'.[88] The tradition of the Lord's Supper functions as a corrective to this dissonance by relating the eschatological reality upon which Paul's theory of community is predicated to an alternative praxis which is congruous with it. The logic of Paul's use of the tradition in this context accords with Geertz's analysis of the function of sacred symbols inasmuch as the symbols of Christ's death, that is, the bread and the cup, serve to promote an ethos or morality which is consistent with the eschatological reality they represent.[89]

For the Christian community reality has been redefined by the death and resurrection of Christ, but the sacrament of the bread and the cup recall specifically the significance of his death. The repeated injunction 'do this as my memorial' indicates that the celebration of the Lord's Supper is understood as a cultic commemoration of the story of the Lord's death.[90] In remembering Jesus' death the Corinthians remember the founding event of the new age in which they participate even now as a community of the new covenant. One of the most important ways in which the reality of the new age is to be actualized in the Christian community is the relativization of all distinctions based on ethnic heritage, status and even sex (1 Cor. 12.13; Gal. 3.28). In Paul's understanding the death of Christ has subverted these human categories of distinction and for that reason is the ground of unity in the body of Christ (cf. 1 Cor. 1.18-31; Rom. 3.21-29). But it is precisely because certain distinctions of status continue to prevail in the Corinthian community that there are divisions when they meet together for the Lord's Supper.

In reminding the Corinthians that in eating the bread and drinking the cup they 'proclaim the Lord's death until he comes' (v. 26), Paul is proposing that what this death represents should influence the manner in which they eat together. If their eating of the Lord's Supper is a 'remembrance' and a proclamation of Christ's death, then it is imperative that their behaviour at the meal reflect what it is they are remembering and proclaiming. Paul makes this point more explicitly in v. 27 where he explains that 'whoever eats the bread or drinks the cup unworthily is guilty of violating the body and blood of the Lord'. Moreover, he makes it clear in v. 29 that eating and drinking 'unworthily' is a matter of 'not discerning the body', which refers to

88. Theissen, *The Social Setting of Pauline Christianity*, p. 162.
89. Geertz, *The Interpretation of Cultures*, pp. 126-27.
90. Cf. Meeks, *The First Urban Christians*, p. 158.

3. *The Cross and Moral Discourse* 123

consideration of the corporate 'body of Christ'. Paul's use of 'body' in this verse recalls his interpretation of the bread in 10.17 where partaking of the one loaf which represents Christ's body given in death is the basis of the unity of the corporate 'body of Christ'.[91]

These two distinct and yet correlative connotations of 'body' in this passage are a *crux interpretum* for ascertaining how Paul employs the symbol of Christ's death as it finds expression in the words of institution to speak to the divisions at the Lord's Supper. He has fused the theological and social nuances of the metaphor so as to insist that what actually happens when the community 'comes together' as 'the body of Christ' is to be governed by what is signified by the one bread of which they all eat, namely the body of Christ given in death. Thus what Paul intends by eating the bread and drinking the cup in a worthy manner (v. 27), and the criterion in terms of which he expects them to 'discern the body' (v. 29), are defined by what the death of Christ means. That he can cite the words, 'This is my body which is for you. Do this in remembrance of me', and can assert that in eating the bread and drinking the wine they 'proclaim the Lord's death' without any elaboration presupposes that the Corinthians share with Paul a fundamental understanding of the implications of Christ's death. And so, when set against the backdrop of the conflict being addressed, the import of what is remembered and proclaimed in the Lord's Supper would be immediately evident. More specifically, when heard by a privileged group within the community which indulged in a private meal of higher quality, Paul's reference to the body of Christ given in death would take on special significance.

The self-giving love of the Lord who gave himself in death for others stands in stark contrast to the self-centredness of those who go ahead with their own meal (v. 21). It is noteworthy, if not ironic, that Paul's interpretation of the problem in v. 22 corresponds in a striking way to the interpretation of Christ's death which is expressed by the the words of institution. As a cultic meal the Lord's Supper was understood as a commemoration of Jesus as a sacrificial victim, and hence what is exemplified by his death is the converse of those who might be classified as victimizers because they 'humiliate those who have nothing' (v. 22). In remembering Jesus death on a cross the community is

---

91. Cf. Fee, *The First Epistle to the Corinthians*, pp. 563-64, for a discussion of the various interpretations of v. 29 and a detailed argument as to why 'body' here refers to the church as the 'body of Christ'.

remembering one who is a victim of shame, and this is a poignant commentary on the behaviour of those wealthier members who by their individualistic self-indulgence shame those of lesser means (cf. 11.22). More positively, though, the community is remembering the Lord who out of love gives himself in death for others. If the community which is his 'body' would allow itself to be governed by what his death signifies, namely the norm of setting aside one's own self-interests for the sake of others, then the unity which was symbolized in their partaking of the one bread (10.17) would become a reality.[92]

In chs. 12–14 where Paul takes up the issue of spiritual gifts, or more specifically the abuse of the gift of tongues, there is no mention of Christ's death. However, he does elaborate further on the social connotations of the 'body of Christ' metaphor which is derived from the tradition cited in 11.23-26. Again, the problem is one of disunity, and, as in 11.17-34, it has been caused by distinctions of status. What distinguishes this controversy from the dissensions at the Lord's Supper is that in the situation implied in 11.17-34 status is spoken of in economic terms, while in ch. 12 it is defined in spiritual terms.[93] Although a detailed exegesis of chs. 12–14 is beyond the scope of this study of the function of Paul's references to the death of Jesus, it is noteworthy that the force of the body metaphor in this context is consistent with how the symbol of Christ's death functions elsewhere in the letter. This is most evident in 12.23 where Paul says that 'those parts of the body which we think less honourable we invest with the greater honour'. This reversal has its foundations in the cross of Christ (1.18-31).

Throughout the letter Paul has appealed to the cross of Christ in order to critique certain cliques which have sought to distinguish themselves in some way from the other members of the community. But he has the more constructive aim of restructuring the emergent social hierarchies so that the members of Christ's body recognize their interdependence.[94] The purpose clause in 12.25 indicates that 'God has

---

92. The importance of imitation in this letter has already been emphasized (cf. 4.16; 11.1). In his interpretation of 'do this in remembrance of me' (v. 24) Barrett follows H. Kosmala ('"Das tut zu Gedächtnis"', *NovT* 4 [1960], pp. 81-94) in seeing a special emphasis on discipleship and imitation of Jesus (*The First Epistle to the Corinthians*, p. 264).

93. Smith, 'Social Obligation in the Context of Communal Meals', p. 193.

94. Cf. Petersen, *Rediscovering Paul*, p. 120.

so composed the body, giving the greater honour to the inferior part (v. 24, cf. 1.26-29), that the members may have the same care for one another'. The vision of community to which Paul exhorts the Corinthians to aspire to is one in which everyone is guided by the love of Christ. This ideal of love is articulated in poetic fashion in ch. 13, which is strategically located between chs. 12 and 14. Although Paul makes no mention of the origin of his characterization of love in ch. 13, it is clear that for him love is defined by the Christ who demonstrates his love by giving his life in death ὑπὲρ ὑμῶν (cf. 2 Cor. 5.14-15). It is evident, therefore, that in 1 Corinthians 1–14, even when Paul does not explicitly invoke the symbol of Christ's death, the paraenesis is predicated on his understanding of the cross as an eschatological event which should shape the corporate life of the church of the new covenant to the extent that it corresponds to what the cross represents: the elimination of all distinctions of status and an other-regarding behaviour which 'builds up' the community.[95]

95. See Tannehill, *Dying and Rising with Christ*, p. 80. Tannehill's thesis is that 'existence in the new dominion takes on a structure which corresponds to the founding events of death and resurrection'.

Chapter 4

FUNCTIONS OF PAUL'S REFERENCES TO THE DEATH OF JESUS
IN 2 CORINTHIANS 4.7–5.19

Introduction

The existential significance of the death of Jesus is nowhere set forth more explicitly than in Paul's reference in 2 Cor. 4.10 to 'carrying in the body the death of Jesus'. As Paul develops his line of thought in this passage he also spells out the behavioural and cosmic implications of this death (cf. 5.14-17). The fundamental theme in 2 Corinthians 1–9 as a whole, considered by most scholars to be a separate and earlier letter than 2 Corinthians 10–13, is apostolic ministry.[1] Paul takes up and develops this theme in response to criticisms initiated by certain rivals in Corinth.[2] These opponents had their own criteria for what constituted apostolic status, and Paul's ministry did not conform to the paradigm they espoused (cf. 2.14–3.6; 4.1-15; 5.11-12; 6.4-10). In addition to undermining his ministry, these opponents also infiltrated

---

1. Cf. V.P. Furnish, *II Corinthians* (New York: Doubleday, 1984), p. 37; R. Bultmann, *The Second Letter to the Corinthians* (trans. R. Harrisville; Minneapolis: Augsburg, 1985), p. 18. Bultmann and Furnish emphasize the apostolic theme in both chs. 1–9 and chs. 10–13 and therefore affirm a thematic coherence in 2 Corinthians in its present canonical form. If their observation is taken a step further it can be said that given this thematic coherence, the abrupt shift in tone and style, as well as subject matter, can be accounted for other than by positing two distinct letters. I would tentatively suggest that Paul's tone is more subdued in the earlier portion of the letter because he is explaining why his ministry is characterized by weakness and suffering, and that the tone becomes sharper in the latter chapters because he uses irony, parody and even sarcasm when he turns his attention to problems in the community (cf. 2 Cor. 12.19-21; 13.5-10). The basis for this commitment to the integrity of 2 Corinthians will be further elaborated in the treatment of 2 Cor. 10–13.

2. There is also a correlation between the criticisms of Paul implied in 2 Cor. 1–9 and those in chs. 10–13, which would indicate that he is dealing with the same opposition throughout the letter in its extant form.

the Corinthian community with what Paul termed εὐαγγέλιον ἕτερον (cf. 2 Cor. 11.4). The style of ministry they advocated was inseparable from this 'other gospel', and together these two elements formed the basis of their attack on Paul.

The Corinthians had apparently been influenced by the opponents' opinion of Paul, and therefore the legitimacy of his ministry was called into question in the community. It is important to keep in mind, however, that Paul's conversation is with the Corinthians, not the interlopers. He is once removed from these outsiders' critique of his ministry, so we cannot know all that it entailed. But what can be inferred from Paul's reply is that the criticisms stemming from the community have to do with certain characteristics of his ministry, namely weakness and suffering (4.7-18; 6.3-10; 10.10; 11.10; 13.3-4), the lack of manifestations of the power of the Spirit (5.12-13; 12.12) and how he supports himself (11.7ff.; 12.13).[3]

Gerd Theissen is right, then, in his observation that the real conflict was between different types of ministries, at least that is how the Corinthians construed it.[4] They had been confronted with two ministries that were distinct in theology and approach, and it seems that it was the opponent's appearance (πρόσωπον) and style of ministry that proved to be decisive in their comparison.[5] Paul's perspective is that style of ministry is determined by one's understanding of the gospel, and so in his response to these criticisms he explains the relationship between the character of his ministry and the gospel he preaches. This is the same gospel which the Corinthians first believed, and it served as the foundation from which he could defend his apostleship. In contrast to the situation underlying 1 Corinthians (cf. 2.1-5), nothing in 2 Corinthians suggests that the Corinthians themselves had deviated

---

3.   Cf. C.J.A. Hickling, 'Is II Corinthians a Source for Early Church History?' *ZNW* 66 (1975), p. 287. Hickling rightly observes that the personal dimensions of the conflict emerge more strongly than doctrinal ones. *Contra* Bultmann who remarks 'Paul's person is at issue only insofar as he is bearer of the apostolic office' (*The Second Letter to the Corinthians*, p. 16).

4.   G. Theissen, *The Social Setting of Pauline Christianity*, p. 40.

5.   The term πρόσωπον is used twelve times in 2 Corinthians and has a variety of nuances. It appears to be a catchword in the comparison between Paul and the opponents. According to BAGD, p. 721, it means 'external things' or 'appearance' in 5.12 and is the opposite of καρδία. Bultmann notes the similarity between ἐν προσώπῳ in 5.12 and boasting κατὰ σάρκα in 11.18 (*The Second Letter to the Corinthians*, p. 150).

from the gospel Paul preached. Rather, they were caught between competing attempts to obtain, or in Paul's case retain, their allegiance. The first seven chapters of 2 Corinthians represent Paul's effort to secure their fidelity to him and the gospel he embodies. Since he discusses the topic of apostleship with a view to convincing the Corinthians that his apostolate was indeed authentic, the significance of his references to the death of Jesus will be examined in terms of how they serve to define and explain his apostolate.

Paul's discourse in 2 Corinthians is multifaceted in that it includes discussion of values, attitudes and behaviour, as well as theology, Christology, soteriology and eschatology, and therefore this examination of the meaning and function of references to the death of Jesus will also include these aspects. Paul's theological assertions are a means by which he attempts to re-establish the vision of reality he imparted to the Corinthian community. In this letter he emphasizes that this vision of reality is associated with a particular way of life, which is underwritten by a corresponding system of values.

When the death of Christ is viewed as a symbol within Paul's symbolic universe, an understanding of symbolic processes can illuminate an examination of the function of Paul's references to the death of Jesus. Symbols can function in a variety of ways, but the primary concern will be with the relationship of the meanings signified by the symbol to individual and community experience of the reality of everyday life. On the most rudimentary level, a symbol functions within the context of the symbolic universe. This function is analogous to the function of the symbolic universe itself, which is to provide a meaningful order for subjective experience. To discern a symbol's meaning within the framework of the symbolic universe entails deciphering how that symbol contributes to the meaningful order supplied by the symbolic universe. In other words, it would be necessary to identify what role that symbol plays in the legitimation of everyday roles, priorities and operating procedures.[6] With regard to the preeminent theme in 2 Corinthians, this would require a consideration of how Paul used the symbol of Christ's death to legitimate his apostolic ministry.

A more dynamic function of symbols concerns the process by which a symbol is applied to specific problems and situations in order to maintain aspects of the world mediated by the symbolic universe.[7] It is

6. Berger and Luckmann, *The Social Construction of Reality*, p. 116.
7. Berger and Luckmann, *The Social Construction of Reality*, pp. 127-29.

distinct from the former function only in that it involves a further elaboration of the objectivated meaning of the symbol. In accordance with this function, the death of Jesus is conceived of as a symbol with a surplus of meaning. Paul emphasized different nuances of the symbol's meaning when reinforcing either the reality represented by the symbol itself or another dimension of reality mediated by the symbolic universe. The meaning conveyed by a symbol functioning in this manner is dependent upon the circumstances which necessitated its use. Paul's contingent application of the symbol of Christ's death resulted in new shades of meaning which the symbol did not possess apart from the given context. The interpretation of the death of Jesus which he inherited from the early church was constantly being expanded as he elaborated on its significance for the community.[8] This study will concentrate on both the contextual meaning of the symbol of Christ's death and on how it serves to reinforce or maintain the vision of reality Paul is arguing for in the letter.

2 Corinthians 4.7-12:
The Death of Jesus and Paul's Apostolic Identity

Paul first mentions the death of Jesus in 2 Corinthians when he shifts the focus of the discussion from the revelation of 'the glory of God in the face of Christ' (4.6), his subject since 3.4, to a qualification of how that glory is presently manifest. He initiates the transition by using the

---

Berger and Luckmann regard theology as one of the major types of conceptual machinery used in universe maintenance.

8. The perspective being proposed here is similar to that of Beker in *Paul the Apostle*. He speaks of Paul's gospel as a 'symbolic structure' which is 'a Christian apocalyptic structure of thought'. Paul's hermeneutic consists in the constant interaction between this symbolic structure (the 'coherent centre') and its contingent interpretation (cf. pp. 11-16). The sociology of knowledge model suggests a dynamic similar to the notion of interaction between coherent centre and contingent interpretation. However, the symbolic universe is inclusive of all experience and interpretation of reality and implies, therefore, that it is inadequate to separate Paul's gospel as a symbolic structure from other symbols or symbol systems through which he construes reality. In other words, it is erroneous to drive a wedge between Paul's theology and his general experience of the reality of everyday life. Also, less emphasis should be put on Paul's 'primordial experience' and more emphasis on the tradition which is constantly being modified as he applies it to contingent situations. See the discussion of Beker in the sections on recent scholarship and method.

image of earthen vessels, which served to establish and explain the distinction between the 'treasure' he had in view and the apostles who dispense it. The antecedent of τὸν θησαυρόν is 'the knowledge of the glory of God in the face of Christ' (v. 6), and ὀστρακίνοις σκεύεσιν refers to those who, as ministers of the gospel, proclaim that knowledge (cf. 4.1-16).[9] The ἵνα clause in 4.7b indicates that the point of the contrast is 'to show that the transcendent power belongs to God and not to us' (cf. 4.7). This differentiation between treasure and vessel was required because the Corinthians had been persuaded that the gospel of glory and power was incongruous with an apostolic ministry which exhibited the frailties of mortal existence.[10] In 4.8-12 Paul defines and illustrates the point conveyed by the image with reference to his own ministry.[11]

Immediately following the introductory remark of 4.7 Paul provides a list of hardships which he has experienced as an apostle (4.8-9; cf. also 1.8-10; 6.4-10). This list is formulated into a series of antitheses to show that weakness actually discloses the power of God.[12] The phrase 'treasure in earthen vessels' and the idea of being given up to death so that the life of Jesus may be manifested express a paradox that is further heightened in the interpretative statements of vv. 10-11.[13] In these verses the paradox is defined explicitly in terms of the

9. So A. Plummer, *A Critical and Exegetical Commentary on the Second Epistle of St Paul to the Corinthians* (Edinburgh: T. & T. Clark, 1915), pp. 125-26; P.E. Hughes, *Paul's Second Epistle to the Corinthians* (Grand Rapids: Eerdmans, 1962), p. 135; C.K. Barrett, *The Second Epistle to the Corinthians* (New York: Harper & Row, 1973), p. 138. Barrett remarks that the contrast is between 'the infinitely precious treasure of the Gospel, and the human bearers of it'.

10. Lietzmann, *An Die Korinther I/II*, p. 115; Furnish, *II Corinthians*, p. 279; R. Martin, *2 Corinthians* (Waco, TX: Word Books, 1987), p. 86.

11. Paul uses the first person plural pronoun in this passage (ἡμεῖς) and it stands in relation to ὑμῖν, which refers to the Corinthians. The we/you language in 2 Corinthians is varied in its use and, as Carrez asserts, the context must be the guide to the sense given it. Carrez delineates two nuances in 4.7-12: (1) Paul distinguishes between the apostles with their mission and other believers, and (2) more specifically, this passage is also a commentary on 1.8-9 and thus required a plural pronoun in order to include his companion Titus (cf. 2 Cor. 2.12-13; 7.5-7) (M. Carrez, 'Le 'nous' en 2 Corinthiens', *NTS* 26 [1980], p. 477).

12. Furnish, *II Corinthians*, p. 280; Bultmann, *The Second Letter to the Corinthians*, p. 113.

13. The πάντοτε of v. 10 takes up the idea of ἐν παντι in v. 8 thus connecting the catalogue of hardships with the interpretive statements of vv. 10-11. Cf.

manifestation of the death and life of Jesus.[14] Most commentators view v. 11 and v. 10 as parallel, with v. 11 elucidating v. 10.[15] Both verses contain purpose clauses which indicate that the manifestation of Jesus' life is the purpose and consequence of being given up to death for his sake. Paul articulates the paradox of life in death in yet another way in v. 12 in order to emphasize that his ministry is for the benefit of those to whom he is an apostle.[16]

The ideas about power and suffering and life and death which are imparted in this passage are not only interdependent, but are set forth in oblique language. The main points are expressed in the form of metaphorical statements, which are by nature 'untranslatable' because they 'disclose a relationship of meaning hitherto unnoticed between terms which were prevented from communicating by former classifications'.[17] Here Paul speaks of his suffering as 'a carrying in the body the death of Jesus' and of his experience of God's power as a manifestation of the 'life of Jesus'. In both instances he is 'cognitively and affectively relating two separate domains by using language appro-

---

J. Lambrecht, 'The Nekrosis of Jesus: Ministry and Suffering in 2 Cor. 4, 7-15', in Vanhoye (ed.), *L'Apôtre Paul*, p. 136, and Plummer, *Second Epistle of St Paul to the Corinthians*, p. 129.

14. A number of commentators have used the idea of paradox to explain Paul's conception of the experience of God's power in weakness. It is G. Güttgemanns who speaks of this paradox in a absolute sense in which Paul's suffering is an epiphany of Christ's power. This is in fact the main thesis of his *Der leidende Apostel und sein Herr: Studien zur paulinischen Christologie* (Göttingen: Vandenhoeck & Ruprecht, 1966): 'die ἀσθένεια ist die irdische Manifestation des Christus selbst' (p. 118); the 'Paradox dass Gottes δύναμις irdische als ἀσθένεια erscheint' (p. 122); 'Gerade der Tod und die Schwachheit sind paradoxe Manifestation des Herrn' (p. 198). Against Güttgemanns, Lambrecht has emphasized that the paradoxical language intends to be provocative and does not offer a complete presentation of the case (Lambrecht, 'The Nekrosis of Jesus', pp. 131-32). The inherent tension of this paradox should not be resolved in such a way that death itself becomes life and weakness power.

15. Furnish, *II Corinthians*, p. 24. He remarks that 'the point of v. 10 is repeated and intensified in v. 11'. Cf. also Bultmann, *The Second Letter to the Corinthians*, p. 119; Barrett, *The Second Epistle to the Corinthians*, p. 140; Bruce, *I and II Corinthians*, p. 197; Plummer, *Second Epistle of St Paul to the Corinthians*, p. 131.

16. Furnish, *II Corinthians*, p. 284; Martin, *2 Corinthians*, p. 89; J. Héring, *The Second Epistle of St Paul to the Corinthians* (trans. A.W. Heathcote and P.J. Allcock; London: Epworth, 1967), p. 32.

17. P. Ricoeur, 'The Metaphorical Process', *Semeia* 4 (1975), pp. 79-80.

priate to the one as a lens for seeing the other'.[18] The metaphors represent Paul's attempt to articulate his experience of the world in terms of the death and resurrection of Christ. Given the presence of these metaphors and the above definition of how they function, it is instructive to ask how these metaphors contribute to Paul's articulation of his experience, and how they function within the context of the letter as a whole.[19]

Paul's consecutive juxtaposition of these two metaphors (vv. 10, 11, 12) indicates that death and life are inextricably connected in apostolic existence. In the same way that the death and resurrection of Christ are perceived as two sides of the one salvation event, so death and life are different features of the same apostolic experience.[20] This perspective is set over against that of those Corinthians who could not reconcile the display of both of these qualities in Paul's ministry. In the face of the challenge instigated by the opponents, he not only acknowledged the reality of suffering in his ministry, but depicted it as intrinsic to his vocation.[21] However, he also made numerous allusions to the evidence of resurrection power (e.g. down payment of the Spirit, 1.22; 5.5; transformation, 3.18; renewal, 4.16; new creation, 5.17; the presence of the day of salvation, 6.2). In contradistinction to the prevailing Corinthian viewpoint, he thus urged that power and weakness, or in his terms life and death, are not mutually exclusive alternatives for an apostle. Rather, the manifestation of Christ's death is the presupposition of the manifestation of his life.[22] This seems to be the thrust of his argument in 4.7-12.

While it is obvious that Paul meant to affirm and explain the manifestation of both the death and life of Jesus in and through his ministry, our concern is with his reference to 'carrying in the body the death of Jesus'. This focus is commensurate with Paul's own aim in writing. There is no indication in this passage that the Corinthians were protesting the lack of manifestations of the life of Jesus in his ministry,

---

18. M. Black, *Models and Metaphors: Studies in Language and Philosophy* (Ithaca, NY: Cornell University Press, 1962), p. 237.

19. According to Ricoeur, 'the ultimate problem raised by metaphor is to know in what respects the transposition of meaning which defines it contributes to the articulation of experience, to the forming of the world' ('The Metaphorical Process', p. 82).

20. Barrett, *The Second Epistle to the Corinthians*, p. 139.

21. Lambrecht, 'The Nekrosis of Jesus', p. 139.

22. Cf. J. Dunn, *Jesus and the Spirit* (Philadelphia: Westminster Press, 1975), p. 329.

4. Paul's References to the Death of Jesus

though it is apparent from 5.12-13 that they had been influenced by the opponents' ideas about how this life was to be exhibited. They had witnessed the 'signs of a true apostle' in previous encounters with Paul, and among these signs were mighty works and other demonstrations of the Spirit and of power (12.12; cf. also 1 Cor. 2.4). What they questioned was the compatibility of the requisite power of the gospel with suffering and weakness. Paul invokes the symbol of the death of Jesus here because it supplies the rationale for his life of hardships. His references to the life of Jesus, though important to his argument, function primarily to show the interrelation of these two aspects of apostolic life. Since it is Paul's suffering and weakness that are at issue in this part of the letter, the main question is how does the metaphor of 'carrying in the body the death of Jesus' serve to explain the character of Paul's life and ministry?

When this metaphor is related to the larger context which begins at 2.14, the correlation between its meaning and the predominant theme of apostleship is evident. Although it was Paul's apostolate that was being challenged in Corinth, his articulation of what is at issue in 2.16b applies to anyone who would claim to be an apostle: 'who is sufficient for these things?'[23] Paul did not pose this question in order to affirm his own sufficiency, but because there were 'many' who in his estimation presumed to be sufficient in themselves.[24] The question is followed by a contrast between those who 'peddle' God's word and Paul's ministry, which is distinguished by its sincerity (2.17). Paul replies to his own question in 3.5 with the confession that 'our sufficiency is from God'. This assertion is both a response to the Corinthians' query

---

23. ταῦτα refers to the responsibilities described in vv. 14-15. Cf. Barrett, *The Second Epistle to the Corinthians*, p. 102; Furnish, *II Corinthians*, p. 190; Héring, *The Second Epistle of St Paul to the Corinthians*, p. 19; Plummer, *Second Epistle of St Paul to the Corinthians*, p. 72. On sufficiency as the fundamental issue in this section see M. Rissi, *Studien zum zweiten Korintherbrief: Der alte Bund—Der Predigt—Der Tod* (Zurich: Zwingli Verlag, 1969), p. 43.

24. Rissi, *Studien zum zweiten Korintherbrief*, p. 22; Furnish, *II Corinthians*, p. 190; D. Georgi, *Die Gegner des Paulus im 2 Korintherbrief. Studien zur religiösen Propaganda in der Spätantike* (Neukirchen: Neukircherner Verlag, 1964), pp. 220-25; J.F. Collange, *Enigmes de la deuxième épître de Paul aux Corinthiens* (SNTSMS, 18; Cambridge: Cambridge University Press, 1972), pp. 36-37. *Contra* Lietzmann (*An die Korinther I/II*, p. 109), Plummer (*Second Epistle of St Paul to the Corinthians*, pp. 72-73), and Héring (*The Second Epistle of St Paul to the Corinthians*, p. 19) who think that Paul asked the question in order to answer it in the affirmative.

about his competence and a subtle denunciation of the opponents' attitude of self-confidence. More importantly, the confession of 3.5b denotes the governing conviction of Paul's apostolate and expresses the reason for his confidence (cf. 1.9). He declares this confidence in 3.4, again in 3.12 and 4.1, and further elaborates on the basis of it in 4.14–5.10.[25] The last and most extensive discussion of confidence (4.14–5.10) is preceded by a discussion of his weakness and suffering, and it was precisely because these were characteristics of Paul's apostolate that sufficiency and confidence are such important themes in 2.14–7.4.[26]

The crux around which the topics of sufficiency, confidence and suffering all revolve is the critical issue of Paul's identity as an apostle. One of the main objectives in writing the letter was to explain to the Corinthians why his apostleship took the form it did.[27] That the tone of 2.14–6.13 is more irenic than polemical means not that Paul did not have apologetic interests, but that the apology is directed to the Corinthians rather than the opponents. His main concern is that the Corinthians understand and thus appreciate his ministry (cf. 6.3-13). The numerous expressions of confidence in the letter reflect above all a desire to be known as he asserts himself to be (cf. 1.12, 15; 2.3; 3.4, 12; 4.1, 13; 5.6, 8, 11; 7.4; 10.8; 11.5; 13.6).[28] Stanley Olson concludes from his examination of these expressions of self-confidence in the light of similar expressions in other Hellenistic literature that Paul's purpose in writing is to make the addressees properly aware of his character.[29] His weakness and suffering, in particular, were features of his ministry that required explanation. The metaphor of 'carrying in the body the death of Jesus' allows him to elucidate their importance in terms of this pivotal symbol.

There is no reason to doubt that Paul was genuinely confident when

25. Furnish, *II Corinthians*, p. 277.
26. Paul may have formulated the question of sufficiency in the letter, but it was probably first raised in the community with regard to his ministry, especially as it was compared to the ministry of the opponents.
27. According to Furnish, this is one of the three main reasons that Paul wrote. The other reasons are: (1) to assure the Corinthian congregation that he is genuinely concerned for them, and (2) to appeal to the Corinthian Christians to strengthen and confirm their commitment to the gospel and to his apostolate (*II Corinthians*, p. 42). Cf. also Tannehill, *Dying and Rising with Christ*, p. 88.
28. S. Olson, 'Epistolary Uses of Expressions of Self-Confidence', *JBL* 103/4 (1984), p. 590.
29. Olson, 'Epistolary Uses', p. 595.

he wrote 2 Corinthians 1–9.³⁰ But the fact that such expressions of confidence usually stand over against an absence of confidence in him on the part of those being addressed suggests that Paul's task was to convince the Corinthians that his confidence was warranted.³¹ The question of his sufficiency was raised as the result of a direct challenge to his apostolate, and hence Paul was compelled to justify the character of his apostolic existence to the Corinthians. He needed to persuade the community that his afflictions were not liabilities which discounted his apostolic status, but rather potential assets because they provided the occasion for the manifestation of the life of Jesus (4.10-11). The hermeneutical key to Paul's positive evaluation of weakness and suffering is the death of Jesus. The meaning he ascribed to this event was the source of the meaning he assigned to his own 'death' experiences. In sociology of knowledge terms, Paul appealed to the symbol of the death of Jesus in order to legitimate his apostolate.³²

The death of Christ, as a constituent symbol of Paul's symbolic universe, served to legitimate the experience of ministry described in 4.8-9. Legitimation is the process of explaining and justifying why things are the way they are.³³ Problematic realities such as suffering are legitimated by being integrated into the symbolic universe, which itself constitutes the highest level of legitimation.³⁴ Reflective

30. Furnish points out that Paul was heartened by Titus's report and is now generally confident of the congregation's loyalty (cf. 7.6-13) (*II Corinthians*, p. 42).
31. Olson, 'Epistolary Uses', p. 587.
32. Theissen and Käsemann both use the term legitimation to describe Paul's defence of his apostleship in this letter. But since their analyses of Paul's legitimation of his apostolate are so dependent on their respective characterizations of the opponents, discussion of their theses will be reserved for the section on the opponents (Theissen, *The Social Setting of Pauline Christianity*, pp. 27-67; E. Käsemann, 'Die Legitimät des Apostels: Eine Untersuchung zu II Korinther 10–13', *ZNW* 41 [1942], pp. 33-71).
33. Berger and Luckmann, *The Social Construction of Reality*, pp. 110-46. This includes both the objectivations of the institutional order and the marginal realities which lie outside the perimeters of everyday life.
34. Berger and Luckmann, *Social Construction*, pp. 111, 123.

> Only after a symbolic universe is objectivated as a 'first' product of theoretical thought does the possibility of systematic reflection about the nature of that universe arise. Whereas the symbolic universe legitimates the institutional order on the highest level of generality, theorizing about the symbolic universe may be described as, so to speak, legitimation to the second degree. All legitimations... may, in turn, be described as machineries of universe- maintenance' (pp. 122-23).

integration of different spheres of reality into the symbolic universe creates a symmetry between subjective reality and objective reality as they are mediated by the symbolic universe. This phenomenon is reflected in the metaphor of 4.10 where objective and subjective reality converge for Paul. He views the death and resurrection of Christ as eschatological events which define objective reality. They are, as Tannehill puts it, the founding events of the new dominion; the 'world' in which Paul dwells.[35] The metaphor 'carrying in the body the death of Jesus' expresses the congruity of Paul's experiences of suffering with the vision of reality mediated by the symbol of Christ's death.

Paul's treatment of suffering in 4.7-12 has in mind not the abstract question of how one understands suffering, but a question which has led to specific criticisms of him: do his experiences as an apostle (i.e. suffering and hardships) correspond to reality as it was defined by the gospel? How the Corinthians would have answered this question would have depended, of course, on their own conception of the relationship between the Christain symbol system and a correlative manner of living. Although Paul may have been the first to preach the gospel to them, they had since learned that there were alternative ways for believers to construe the world and life therein. This had been demonstrated by the different perspective of the opponents. Since Paul could do nothing to change the fact that suffering is intrinsic to his own apostleship, he emphasized the perspective from which apostolic ministry should be appraised. His attitude toward suffering in this context is expressed in the form of a a metaphorical interpretation of the death of Jesus. In addition to describing the relationship between his own experience and the death of Christ, the metaphor also gives rise to a re-interpretation of reality itself.[36]

Paul's legitimation of his apostleship in Corinth was contingent upon a re-interpretation of reality in terms of his gospel. In the interaction between objective and subjective reality it is one's apprehension of the objective world that conditions subjective experience. The symbolic universe, which is comprised of objectivated meanings, provides interpretive schemes which structure human experience and understanding

---

35. Tannehill, *Dying and Rising with Christ*, p. 124.
36. Ricoeur, 'The Metaphorical Process', p. 84. Ricoeur emphasizes the 'new vision of reality' that results from metaphorical interpretation. 'Metaphor is that strategy of discourse by which language divests itself of its ordinary descriptive function in order to serve its extraordinary function of redescription' (p. 88).

4. *Paul's References to the Death of Jesus*

of self and world.³⁷ Religion is a 'sub-universe' within the symbolic universe and functions as the principal interpretive scheme that shapes the entirety of life and thought.³⁸ Although the death of Christ represents only one symbol in Paul's religious symbol system, in 4.7-12 it is the medium through which objective reality is formulated. Paul's subjective experiences of suffering coincide with reality as it is connoted by this particular symbol. For the Corinthians to acknowledge the authenticity of Paul's apostolic status they must apprehend the reality which makes possible his attitude toward suffering. The metaphor has fused Paul's own experience with the reality which it describes so that the truth of one means the truth of the other. Since the significance of Christ's death is not in question, the reality which it symbolizes is re-described in a way that facilitates appreciation of Paul's suffering. The metaphor confronted the Corinthians first with the question of whether their understanding of reality was informed by the meaning of Christ's death, and secondly with the implications of such an understanding for their perception of Paul.

Paul's commentary on this metaphor in v. 11 clarifies his attempt to specify the relationship between the experiences of vv. 8-9 and the death of Jesus. In this verse the death of Jesus is associated more explicitly with the concrete existence of the apostle. Whereas the metaphor only suggests the correlation in a somewhat ambivalent manner, v. 11 makes it clear that Paul is talking about actually 'being given up to death for Jesus' sake'.³⁹ Both verses characterize Paul's experience of the reality

---

37. There is a sense in which objective meanings and objective reality are social products that are the result of the sedimentation of human subjectivity. However, the meanings and reality mediated by the symbolic universe have been objectivated and so are determinative for human subjectivity. I will refer to the subjective dimension of this dialectic later. Cf. Berger and Luckmann, *The Social Construction of Reality*, pp. 65-109. See also G. Lindbeck's study of the theological implications of this phenomenon in *The Nature of Doctrine* (London: SPCK, 1984). Lindbeck devises what he calls a cultural-linguistic model of religion. He compares religion to a culture or language and thus describes it as 'a communal phenomenon that shapes the subjectivities of individuals rather than being primarily a manifestation of these subjectivities' (p. 33).

38. On 'sub-universes' see Berger and Luckmann, *The Social Construction of Reality*, pp. 102-106.

39. Verse 11 explains v. 10 in such a way that it cannot be understood as a reference to a mystical dying with Christ. It defines νέκρωσιν τοῦ Ἰησοῦ in terms of literal sufferings. Cf. Barrett, *The Second Epistle to the Corinthians*, p. 140.

of everyday life and affirm a symmetry between that experience and the death of Christ. Geertz explains the relationship between the reality of everyday life and reality as it is mediated by religious symbol systems as a 'counterpoint' between style of life and the fundamental reality which the sacred symbols formulate.[40] The guiding principle in the encounter between the two is that 'all sacred symbols assert that it is good for man to live realistically'.[41] In this passage realistic would be defined by Paul's refusal to gloss over the fact of his suffering, even though it has proved to be a stumbling block to the Corinthians. The realism reflected by this passage can be contrasted with the idealism of the Corinthians, at least with regard to their expectations of an apostle. The opponents had supplied them with an idealistic stereotype for authentic apostleship, but it was removed from Paul's experience of the reality of everyday life. His conflation of apostolic existence with the determinative reality of Christ's death in vv. 10-11 functions to legitimate his notion of apostleship over against an ideal model of apostleship that is discontinuous with both the objective reality symbolized by Christ's death and the subjective reality which it structures.

The reality symbolized by Christ's death has attained the status of objectivity for Paul and in that sense the meaning of the symbol is fixed. However, Paul has invoked the symbol in the light of his experience and there is also a sense in which the meaning of the symbol in this context is to some extent based on that experience.[42] This can be explained by the fact that symbols have an intrinsic double aspect: 'they give meaning, that is, objective conceptual form, to social and psychological reality both by shaping themselves to it and by shaping it to themselves'.[43] They serve both as models of reality and models for reality.[44] It has already been suggested that the symbol of Christ's death gives meaning and order to Paul's experiences of suffering, but it is also true that those experiences contribute to the meaning of the

---

40. Geertz, *The Interpretation of Cultures*, p. 130.
41. Geertz, *The Interpretation of Cultures*, p. 130. Geertz observes that where they differ is in the vision of reality they construct.
42. Cf. Douglas, *Natural Symbols*, p. 11. Douglas asserts that symbols are a construction upon experience.
43. Geertz, *The Interpretation of Cultures*, p. 93.
44. Geertz, *The Interpretation of Cultures*, p. 93. Both of these statements are made with reference to cultural patterns, but since cultural patterns are none other than sets of symbols for Geertz, they also pertain to the function of specific symbols.

symbol. The latter aspect of this reciprocity is also evident in 4.7-12 where Paul's identity and self-understanding are disclosed primarily with reference to the concrete events of his life. Therefore, the nuance of the symbol of Christ's death in this particular passage depends largely on the character of the experiences to which it corresponds.

In view of the fact that the catalogue of hardships provides the frame of reference for the meaning symbolized by the death of Jesus in this context, the meaning of the symbol can be inferred from the meaning Paul attached to his experiences of sufferings. The focus on apostolic identity and the juxtaposition of the catalogue of sufferings with the question of Paul's sufficiency has led some scholars to conclude that the main purpose for the apostle's references to his afflictions was to exclude the basis for self-trust. Tannehill, for example, thinks that the theme of 2 Cor. 4.7-14 is that suffering forces Paul to rely on God alone. This theme is rooted in the conviction that 'God's redemption of man through the scandal of the cross on the basis of grace alone means the exclusion of man's "boast"'.[45] Similarly, Schrage asserts that the catalogues of sufferings have the same purpose as the doctrine of justification and 'the word of the cross'.[46] Although Paul does express the idea that his sufferings cause him to trust in God and not in himself, there is no reason to think that he has in mind the general problem of human boasting, at least not in the broad theological sense suggested by Tannehill and Schrage. The above interpretation does preserve an aspect of the meaning of the passage, but the force of it is obscured because it is abstracted from its immediate context.[47] The problem of boasting and self-sufficiency reflected in this pericope is a contingent problem which is connected here not with human sinfulness in general, but with a particular group that exemplifies these characteristics.

The occasion for Paul's development of the theme of his sufficiency as an apostle in the light of his weakness and suffering is not a theoretical meditation on boasting as the source of sin, rather it is the doubts the Corinthians have about his apostleship. Furthermore, the general

45. Tannehill, *Dying and Rising with Christ*, p. 89.
46. W. Schrage, 'Leid, Kreuz und Eschaton: Die Peristasenkataloge als Merkmale paulinischer theologia Crucis und Eschatologie', *EvT* 34 (1974), p. 152.
47. Tannehill, for example, imposes on this passage his view that the cross is God's act of grace which frees human beings from sin. In his conclusion he indicates that the problem of boasting is fundamentally connected with the theme of dying with Christ (*Dying and Rising with Christ*, p. 125).

tone of confidence, as well as specific expressions of it, also militates against the view that Paul is concerned with the question of self-sufficiency as an abstract problem in this context. Paul's thesis that 'the transcendent power belongs to God and not to us' (4.7) is set forth in contrast to the opponents' view of the manner in which God's power is manifested. Discussion of the opponents' position will be deferred for the moment, but enough can be inferred from the immediate context to support Rissi's contention that it was their 'consciousness of power' that initiated the underlying dispute.[48] Against their emphasis on power, Paul maintained the distinction between the glory/power of the gospel and the agents of that gospel by using the metaphor of treasure in earthen vessels. In the metaphor of 4.10, then, he related this point to his own ministry, which bears witness to the fact that suffering and weakness provide the context for the demonstration of God's power.

This reference to the death of Jesus in 4.10 is the basis of Paul's legitimation of his apostolate. It serves to show the congruence of his own identity as an apostle with that of the crucified Christ. His positive evaluation of his own weakness and suffering is the consequence of his conviction that his is a lifestyle epitomized in the death of his Lord. The death of Jesus is for Paul a symbol of the same kind of weakness that he experiences. As a symbol belonging to his symbolic universe, it lends authority to and thus legitimates both the experience and his interpretation of it. Rissi's comment on 4.10 conveys the meaning and function of the symbol in this context: 'It is this powerless death of Christ, which has been represented through the life of the preacher, which supports and justifies his own powerlessness'.[49] The authority of the symbol is based on the fact that the one who was crucified in weakness was raised and exalted as Lord (cf. 13.4). This pattern of crucifixion–resurrection is applied by Paul to his own life and then to all believers.[50] Subsequent to his correlation of weakness and suffering with the death of Jesus he asserts that the source of his confidence and hope is his knowledge that 'he who raised the Lord Jesus will raise us also with Jesus and bring us with you into his presence' (4.14).

Although the metaphor 'carrying in the body the death of Jesus'

---

48. Rissi, *Studien zum zweiten Korintherbrief*, p. 43.
49. Rissi, *Studien zum zweiten Korintherbrief*, pp. 51-52.
50. Cf. Meeks, *The First Urban Christians*, pp. 124, 181. Meeks observes that Paul appeals to this pattern when countering those who deny his authority.

serves to validate Paul's apostolate by associating his weakness with the weakness of Jesus in death (cf. 13.4), weakness and suffering are not perceived as meaningful in and of themselves. What is symbolized in the death of Jesus must be understood in conjunction with the power and glory symbolized, and to be realized, in the resurrection of Jesus. Paul's cruciform life is the appropriate mode of existence only until the apocalyptic resurrection of the dead (cf. 5.1-4).[51] During the interim period the powerlessness of Christ on the cross exemplifies the kind of situation in which one encounters God's power and glory.[52] Since ministry presently takes place during this interim, it necessarily follows the paradigm instituted by Christ's death and resurrection. In the same way that Jesus' death was the circumstance for the manifestation of God's resurrecting power, Paul's 'death' experiences provided the occasion for the manifestation of that same resurrection life. The goal of Paul's ministry was the manifestation of this life for the benefit of the community, and it is likely that his opponents had the same objective. The difference was the way in which they thought the life of Jesus should be manifested. Like the rival apostles, Paul affirms the presence of God's power in his life and ministry, but for him the way that power is manifested is qualified by the manifestation of the powerlessness of Jesus' death.[53]

In 4.10-11 Paul indicates by the use of καί that both life and death are manifested in the lives of ministers of the gospel, but in 4.12 he associates death exclusively with apostles and life with his readers.[54] The ὥστε of v. 12 introduces the consequence of what Paul has just said in the preceding verses.[55] As a result of Paul's 'carrying in the body the death of Jesus', the life of Jesus is manifested in the Corinthian community. That Paul changes the recipients of the manifestation of

51. Cf. Beker, *Paul the Apostle*, p. 300.
52. Cf. Rissi, *Studien zum zweiten Korintherbrief*, p. 50. Rissi remarks that 'In seiner Ohnmacht hat uns der Christus den Ort vor Gott angewiesen, an dem uns Gott begegnen will mit seiner Dynamis und Doxa'.
53. Rissi, *Studien zum zweiten Korintherbrief*, p. 52: 'Schwachheit und Wehrlosigkeit ist vielmehr die Voraussetzung und nicht die Offenbarung der Wirksamkeit der Lebenskraft selbst'.
54. According to Lambrecht, Paul uses 'we' and 'you' in this context to separate the apostles with their mission from those who believe but are not apostles ('The Nekrosis of Jesus', pp. 125-26).
55. Cf. C.F.D. Moule, *An Idiom Book of New Testament Greek* (Cambridge: Cambridge University Press, 1953), p. 144.

that life from ἡμεῖς in vv.10-11 to ἡμῖν in v. 12 reflects both the orientation of his apostolate and another nuance of his reference to the death of Jesus. The fact that his apostolic ministry is characterized by weakness is related to the fact that it is a ministry for others. The character of his ministry is inseparable from its purpose. In addition to legitimating his life of weakness and suffering then, the death of Jesus is also the basis for understanding his identity in terms of ἀσθένεια. The death of Jesus here symbolizes not just weakness, but weakness for the sake of others (cf. 4.15). This meaning is only tacitly present in 4.12 because Paul is preoccupied with the character of his own apostolic ministry. But in 5.14-15 Paul again takes up the theme of the death of Jesus in order to assert that it provides the motive and purpose of apostolic service.

2 Corinthians 5.14-15: The Death of Jesus and Existence for Others

In 5.14 Paul asserts that it is the love of Christ that compels him in his ministry to the Corinthians, and his conception of that love is symbolized in the death of Jesus.[56] In addition to its association with his own ministry, this symbolization of love is also the basis for the behavioural goal of the 'all' for whom Christ died: 'that those who live might live no longer for themselves but for him who for their sake died and was raised' (5.15). Paul first defines the meaning of the symbol of Christ's death as love, and then prescribes the appropriate response to it. And yet Paul is not concerned with proper Christian behaviour *per se* in this passage, but with giving the Corinthians cause to be proud of his ministry (5.12). This is evident especially in v. 14 where he interprets the symbol with reference to his own apostolate. In v. 15 Paul moves to a more general reflection on its significance for all believers, but the context suggests that he still has his own ministry in view and so v. 15 must also be connected in some way

---

56. There is general agreement among commentators that ἀγάπη τοῦ Χριστου is a subjective genitive. For the arguments in support of this view see Furnish, *II Corinthians*, p. 309. The verb συνέχω has a wide range of meanings, as is evidenced by a variety of different interpretations. Bultmann translates συνέχειν here as 'to rule' (*The Second Letter to the Corinthians*, p. 51), and Furnish prefers 'to lay claim to' because it covers a large spectrum of meanings (pp. 309-10). However, Furnish does refer to 'the rule of love' which is established through Christ's death (p. 321).

with his attempt to solicit the Corinthians' respect. He states that this is his objective in v. 12 and follows it in v. 13 with the declaration that his ministry has been conducted sober-mindedly (σωφρονέω) for them (v. 13).[57] The γάρ of v. 14, which is linked with v. 15 by καί, indicates that these two verses together elucidate and provide the support for this claim.[58] Although the οὖν of v. 11 joins this pericope with what immediately precedes it, the phrase 'commending ourselves' (v. 12) was introduced in 3.1, and Paul's assertion that his ministry is for the sake of the Corinthians (v. 13) is a reiteration of 4.15. These verses continue the theme of apostleship, but from a different point of view. In 4.7-12 Paul wanted to help the Corinthians to understand why his ministry took the form it did. Now that he has explained that, he hopes not only to retain his apostolic status in their eyes, but also to obtain their personal approval. What is different about Paul's approach to the subject of apostleship in this passage is that he has changed the focus from an interpretation of his experiences of suffering in terms of the death of Jesus to a more conceptual treatment of the implications of that death. Put succinctly, in 4.7-12 precedence is given to Paul's experience, and the meaning symbolized in the death of Jesus in that context is primarily an idiom for interpreting that experience. In 5.14-15 the symbolic meaning of the death of Jesus is construed in such a way that it is presented as the model for reality upon which Paul's model of apostleship is predicated.[59]

The situation to which Paul is responding is most evident from vv. 12-13. Paul has rejected self-commendation in v. 12a (cf. also 3.1), but his desire nonetheless is that the integrity and sincerity of his ministry will be apparent to the Corinthians (cf. 5.11b). In v. 12a he uses the term καύχημα in his appeal to the Corinthians, here as well as in 1.14 and 9.3 it has a positive meaning. But the frequency of the καύχημα word-group in the letter suggests that the matter of legitimate

---

57. The verb σωφρονέω, which means 'to be of sound mind', is set in contrast to ἐξίστημι and expresses Paul's concern for the community (U. Luck, 'σωφρονέω', *TDNT*, VII, p. 1102).

58. Furnish, *II Corinthians*, p. 325, points out that v. 14 follows closely on v. 13 and explains that being in one's right mind means being responsive to the claim of love.

59. The idea of a model *of* reality and a model *for* reality are not mutually exclusive, rather they are reciprocal and reflect either the priority of experience or the priority of theoretical development. As Berger points out, it involves a dialectical process.

versus illegitimate boasting was an important part of the dispute between Paul and his Corinthian rivals at this time.⁶⁰ More specifically, Paul contrasts those who boast ἐν προσώπῳ with those who boast ἐν καρδία (5.12b).⁶¹ His distinction between the two grounds for boasting reflects the opponents' criticism that he failed to produce as evidence of his apostleship the kind of ecstatic experience they valued.⁶² Paul deliberately obscured the specificity of the debate in order to discuss the criterion by which apostleship should be judged. If ἐξέστημεν refers to ecstatic experiences, which Paul asserts are between God and the believer, then σωφρονοῦμεν must refer to what he has maintained is most important throughout the discussion, that is, his ministry to the Corinthian community.⁶³ By characterizing his apostolic ministry as a service to the Corinthians out of response to the love of Christ, Paul differentiates his motive from that of the opponents. While they esteem external qualities (ἐν προσώπῳ), Paul gives priority to genuine love and concern for the community (ἐν καρδία).

The love which guides Paul in his relationship with the Corinthians finds paradigmatic expression in the death of Christ (5.14-15). What makes Christ's death a personification of love is the fact that it is a representative death ὑπὲρ πάντων.⁶⁴ For Paul this death denotes the

---

60. Furnish, *II Corinthians*, p. 307.
61. Bultmann, *The Second Letter to the Corinthians*, p. 150.
62. Furnish, *II Corinthians*, p. 324. Most scholars agree that ἐξέστημεν refers to ecstatic experience. The contrast between boasting ἐν προσώπῳ and ἐν καρδία corresponds to the distinction between ἔξω and ἔσω person in 4.16 and even τὰ βλεπόμενα and μὴ βλεπόμενα. These antitheses reflect competing value systems which will be discussed later.
63. As Käsemann points out, 'Hier wird ja offensichtlich der Bezirk des privaten religiösen Lebens, der in Ekstasen kulminiert, von dem Bereich des apostolischen Dienstes an der Gemeinde, der als σωφρόειν beschrieben ist, abgegrenzt' (Käsemann, 'Die Legitimät des Apostels', p. 67).
64. The idea of representation is a distinctive Pauline emphasis which builds on the tradition of the early church but moves beyond it. K. Kertelge explains Paul's development of the tradition in this way: 'ergibt sich eine bemerkenswerte Verschiebung des Gedankens der stellvertretenden Sühne Jesu zugunsten des Stellvertretungsmotivs... Paulus entfaltet hier nicht so sehr die Sühne als Tilgung der Sünden, sondern die schicksalhafte Verbundenheit aller mit Christus' ('Das Verständnis des Todes Jesu bei Paulus', pp. 121-22). Others who emphasize the centrality of representation in this reference to the death of Jesus are Dunn, 'Paul's Understanding of the Death of Jesus', pp. 130-41; H. Windisch, *Der zweite Korintherbrief* (Göttingen: Vandenhoeck & Ruprecht, 1924), pp. 182-83; Plummer,

self-surrender of God's Son on behalf of humanity and therefore defines love as existence for others (v. 15). As a symbol, it re-presents an historical manifestation of love that has been reified and thus now has an objective and ontological character.[65] The meaning of love which it symbolizes has been objectivated and determines not only Paul's understanding of love, but, more importantly, his activity as an apostle. The objectivity of this conception of love is reinforced by his emphasis on the eschatological significance and universal scope of Christ's death. These aspects are brought out by Paul's use of the schema of representation of the all through the one.[66] He will not elaborate on the eschatological consequences of the death of Christ until 5.16-17, but the idea is introduced here in order to show that his apostleship is a response to the eschatological rule of love instituted by Christ's death.[67] It is love as an eschatological phenomenon, and not merely as an abstract ideal or a subjective experience, that motivates Paul in his ministry to the Corinthians.

The eschatological criterion of love which Paul establishes in these verses stands in contrast to the criterion of ecstatic experiences (v. 13a) which certain Corinthians had imposed upon him. The subjective and arbitrary basis of their criterion caused him to supply a standard of apostleship which was grounded in the new reality instituted through the death and resurrection of Christ. Here he defines that reality exclusively with reference to the death of Christ. The phrase ἀπέθανεν ὑπὲρ (5.14) constitutes the core of the most important confessional formula about Christ's death in the Pauline epistles, and it is frequently connected with the idea of love (cf. Rom. 5.8; 8.34-35; Gal. 2.20).[68]

Second Epistle of St Paul to the Corinthians, p. 174.

65. Berger and Luckmann define reification as 'the apprehension of the products of human activity as if they were something other than human products—such as facts of nature, results of cosmic laws, or manifestations of divine will' (*The Social Construction of Reality*, p. 106).

66. Kertelge, 'Das Verständnis des Todes Jesu bei Paulus', p. 122.

67. Love is eschatological because it is defined by the eschatological Christ-event and because it is a characteristic of the eschatological new creation. With reference to God's demand for love, Bultmann asserts that 'it is just in this that eschatological existence becomes reality' (*Theology of the New Testament*, p. 344). See also V. Furnish, *The Love Command in the New Testament* (Nashville: Abingdon Press, 1972), p. 93.

68. According to Hengel, 'the constitutive elements of both the longer and the shorter formulae are the subject χριστός; the aorist ἀπέθανεν, which refers to a

This confessional formula has its origin in the primitive Christian tradition and finds its most complete expression in Paul in the creedal statement of 1 Cor. 15.5.[69] Paul has modified the tradition in this context to serve his purpose. The distinctive characteristic of the formula here is Paul's use of πάντων instead of the more usual ἡμῶν.[70] The plural pronoun is a means of stressing the eschatological-universal significance of Christ's death rather than its personal or existential significance. If the love symbolized in Christ's death is to be the yardstick for evaluating Paul's apostleship, then it must be based on reality as revealed in the Christ-event and not just on another type of experience (cf. v. 13a). The eschatological rule of love which Paul is speaking about is something that has affected the world and thus cannot be reduced to subjectivity. Likewise, apostleship is decided not by ecstatic or spiritual manifestations, but by whether it corresponds to objective and eschatological reality as determined by the death and resurrection of Christ.

Although Paul modified the traditional interpretation of Christ's death by stressing the idea of representation and using πάντων, it was nevertheless a fundamental element of the sub-universe of faith which he shared with the Corinthians and he appealed to it as such. We know from 1 Cor. 15.3 that the confession 'Christ died for our sins' was an essential part of the tradition which Paul delivered to the community. Together with the other items from the tradition listed in that passage (vv. 3-7) it formed the foundation of this sub-universe of faith which, as a symbol system comprised of these primary symbols from the tradition, served as a medium of reality for the believer. The tradition itself is evidence of the fact that the world created by the symbol system has been objectified. However, that does not guarantee that what has

---

unique, unrepeatable event of the past (cf. Rom.6.9f.); and the preposition ὑπέρ with the genitive, which contains the soteriological interpretation' (*The Atonement*, p. 36).

69. Hengel, *The Atonement*, pp. 36-39.

70. Sanders thinks that the idea of 'for all' doubtless comes from the tradition but provides no evidence (*Paul and Palestinian Judaism*, p. 465). It seems more likely that Paul has broadened the horizons of the tradition, maybe as the result of his missionary activity, by making the effect of Christ's death inclusive of all humanity. Thus I agree with Dunn that it is a mistake to confine the 'all' of 5.14 to believers ('Paul's Understanding of the Death of Jesus', p. 131). Furnish, *II Corinthians*, p. 327 and F. Hahn, '"Siehe jetzt ist der Tag des Heil": Neuschöpfung und Versöhnung nach 2. Korinther 5,14–6,2', *EvT* 33 (1993), p. 248, also understand 'all' as inclusive in an unqualified sense.

been presented as objective reality has been subjectively incorporated into the life of the believer. There are always alternative definitions of reality which challenge the one which prevails, and this is precisely what occurred in the church at Corinth. The competing definitions of apostleship which emerge in the letter are inextricably bound to respective definitions of reality. Therefore, Paul sees the legitimation of his apostolate as being contingent upon maintenance of the reality mediated by the sub-universe of faith, the reality upon which the community was founded. The most effective vehicle for reality-maintenance, and the one which Paul adopts in the form of epistles, is conversation.[71] As he talks through the problematic situation which has arisen, the sub-universe of faith is itself modified.[72]

Paul employed the conversational apparatus and other conceptual machineries of universe-maintenance to draw out new theoretical implications within the tradition so that the reality which it represented could be made subjectively plausible and relevant to the community, and thus reinforced. The tradition, and in this instance specifically the traditional interpretation of Christ's death, provided the frame of reference for reality-maintenance. Paul may not have been able to assume that the meaning of Christ's death had been integrated by the Corinthian believers or that their understanding of that death was the same as his, but he can assume that this symbol had a certain authority for them because it was a constituent element of the Christian symbol system. It is possible to go a step further and say that he could at least presuppose that the Corinthians comprehended the confession 'Christ died for our sins'. In the context of 5.11-15 this tradition is the given from which Paul maintains the reality which it represents. This accords with Berger and Luckmann's assertion that 'the greater part of reality-maintenance in conversation is implicit, not explicit', that is, 'it takes place against the background of a world that is silently taken for granted'.[73] In 5.14-15 Paul applies the taken for granted tradition to the problem of apostleship which is at issue. He uses the tradition to

---

71. Berger and Luckmann, *The Social Construction of Reality*, p. 173
72. Cf. A. Schutz and T. Luckmann, *The Structures of the Life World* (Evanston, IL: Northwestern University Press, 1973), p. 14; 'previous explications stored in my stock of experience do not suffice for the solution of that which is problematic in the current situation. I am now motivated to proceed with the explication until the solution appears to be sufficient as well for the actual problem under consideration.'
73. Berger and Luckmann, *The Social Construction of Reality*, p. 172.

define the love which motivates him and establishes this love as the standard by which his apostleship should be evaluated. In the process the tradition itself is pushed beyond its original form to a new conceptualization.[74]

It has already been noted that conceptualizing love in terms of the death of Christ is not unique to this passage. What is most distinct about this particular reference is the performative force which it has in this context. Of the four passages in which Paul connects the idea of love with the death of Jesus, only here does he mention the appropriate behavioural response to that love (5.15). First he deduces from the tradition which states that Christ has died for all that 'all have died' (v. 14). The assertion that 'all have died' is best understood in the light of Paul's statement in v. 17 that 'the old has passed away, behold the new has come', but it also attests to the comprehensive effect of Christ's love.[75] It marks a transition from Paul's focus on Christ's love as the specific motive of his ministry to the universal implications of that demonstration of love. Having established the inclusive scope of Christ's death, Paul then discloses the behavioural consequence of this death for all believers in v. 15: 'that those who live might live no longer for themselves but for him who for their sake died and was raised'. This statement does not serve to indict the Corinthians or the opponents for they would have agreed with it and claimed themselves to live for Christ. Rather Paul's point is that faithfulness to a Lord who gives himself in death for others requires a corresponding mode of conduct which is not dictated by one's self-interests. Stated positively, the self-giving love epitomized in Christ's death impels the believer to live for others. In these verses the self-giving love of Christ in his death for others is presented as a model for authentic Christian behaviour. But in this instance Paul is not concerned with the

74. Berger and Luckmann, *The Social Construction of Reality*, p. 125.
75. This phrase will be dealt with in more detail in the next section. It is difficult to ascertain in what sense Paul can say that 'all have died'. Since elsewhere he asserts that participation in Christ's death is realized only through faith, Bultmann (*The Second Letter to the Corinthians*, p. 152) and Barrett (*The Second Epistle to the Corinthians*, p. 168) must be right in saying that his representative death on behalf of all humanity provides the possibility for anyone to make Christ's death their own, especially in the sense described in v. 15. But in making this inclusive statement Paul seems most concerned to emphasize the cosmic and eschatological consequences of Christ's death and the fact that all without exception are the objects of God's love (cf. Furnish, *II Corinthians*, p. 327).

Corinthians' behaviour as he is with their impressions of his. Therefore, although the love symbolized in Christ's death encompasses all humanity, he appeals to it here because it represents the reality upon which his own apostleship is modeled and the criterion by which he wishes it to be judged.

The progression of thought in vv. 14-15 is indicative of the legitimating function of this reference to the death of Jesus. The context (vv. 11-13) reveals that Paul is preoccupied with the Corinthians' attitude toward his apostleship. He expresses his desire for them to be proud of him (v. 12) and points out that his ministry has been conducted sober-mindedly for their benefit (v. 13). The premise for appreciation of his ministry given in v. 13 is then supported and explained by the affirmation that 'the love of Christ controls us' (v. 14a).[76] Since the entire discussion leading up to Paul's remarks about the eschatological-universal significance of Christ's death (vv. 14b-15) relates to his apostolate, these verses must also be understood in the light of that theme. There is a logical sequence of ideas in these verses from specific to general, and by way of circular reasoning the climatic generalization of v. 15 confirms the specific claim of vv. 13-14b. Paul has asserted in v. 14a that his behaviour as an apostle is a response to the love expressed and symbolized in Christ's death and in v. 15 he indicates that the *purpose* (ἵνα) of the death of this one for all is that those who live might live no longer for themselves, that is, that their lives might exemplify the kind of love symbolized by Christ's death.[77] Consequently, Paul's behaviour is seen as a fulfillment of the behavioural goal of all those for whom Christ died. There is no way of knowing whether the Corinthians inferred this from Paul's statements, but if they had adopted this symbolization of Christ's death as their criterion they would indeed have been 'proud' (v. 12) of him.

In 4.7-12 Paul used the symbol of Christ's death to clarify the relationship between his apostolic identity and his experiences of

---

76. Furnish, *II Corinthians*, p. 325; Bultmann, *The Second Letter to the Corinthians*, p. 152. *Contra* Martin, *2 Corinthians*, p. 128, who says that 'in 5.14, Paul is not looking back to 5.11-13'.

77. This in contrast to the majority of commentators who think that Paul is saying that what is true of his apostleship is true of every believer. I am proposing that Paul has deduced from the shared conviction that Christ died for all that the all, or 'the living', should live no longer for themselves, and therefore that he aims to show that his apostolate is consistent with what should be true of everyone.

hardship. Here he invokes another meaning inherent in the symbol in order to commend his conduct as an apostle to the Corinthians. In his competition with the opponents to win the Corinthians' allegiance, the legitimation of his apostolate is based on his existence for the community. Gerd Theissen terms this functional legitimation and remarks that 'wherever Paul is attacked, he refers to his "workmanship". This is what proves he is a legitimate apostle...' (cf. 1 Cor. 9.1-2; 2 Cor. 3.2; 10.12-18).[78] Theissen contrasts Paul's ministry with opponents he describes as itinerant missionaries who appeal to a charismatic legitimation supplemented by a traditional one.[79] The differences between Paul and his rivals will be examined in more detail in the next chapter. Suffice it to say at this point that they can be distinguished by the reasons which undergird their arguments for the legitimation of their respective ministries.

The opponents attempt to persuade the Corinthians by drawing attention to certain charismatic experiences (5.13) and by appealing to their Israelite lineage (11.22) and letters of recommendation (3.1). In Paul's estimation, 'they measure themselves by one another, and compare themselves with one another' (10.12). The authenticity of Paul's apostleship, on the other hand, depends ultimately on the Corinthians themselves; they are his letter of recommendation (3.2; cf. also 1.24; 4.2). Furnish is right when he says that 'his apostolate is validated by nothing else but the congregation's own experience of having been established and nurtured by its preaching and its pastoral care'.[80] Since Paul knows that the Corinthians are the ones who must decide the truth of his apostleship, he can do nothing but assist them in the decision making process by reminding them of what he has done for them and by showing them that his ministry is inspired by and patterned after the love exemplified in Christ's death for all. This symbolic meaning of the death of the one who is Lord of the community is the source and criterion of authentic Christian existence and thus of true apostleship.

2 Corinthians 5.16-19: The Death of Jesus and the New Creation

The motive of Christ's love which provides the impetus for Paul's conduct as an apostle is, as Barrett remarks, not a private but a

78. Theissen, *The Social Setting of Pauline Christianity*, p. 51.
79. Theissen, *The Social Setting of Pauline Christianity*, p. 53.
80. Furnish, *II Corinthians*, p. 325.

universal motive.⁸¹ It has as its referent the death of Jesus, which has affected the entire cosmic order. The universality of the motive coheres with the universal-eschatological significance of Christ's death. One reason Paul emphasized this aspect of the meaning of Christ's death in the context of 5.11-15 has already been suggested, but he develops the implications of it more fully in 5.16-21. Hence what Paul has to say about epistemology, new creation and reconciliation in the subsequent section (vv. 16-19) is inferred from the comments he made about the death of Christ in vv. 14-15, as is evidenced by the presence of ὥστε in v. 16.⁸² These verses advance both the topic and the line of argument of 5.11-15. The assertion that 'one has died for all; therefore all have died' is foundational, then, in two respects. In the first place, as has been noted, it symbolizes the objective eschatological reality of love to which his apostolate corresponds, and therefore substantiates the model of Christian existence after which he patterns his apostleship. Secondly, in 5.16-17 it is foundational in the sense that it serves as the basis for the appropriate eschatological perspective for apprehending his understanding and display of authentic apostleship. These two functions of this reference to the death of Jesus are interrelated in that an apprehension of Paul's theological explanation of his apostleship in 5.14-15 hinges on the eschatological perspective set out in 5.17.

Although the eschatological significance of Christ's death was only tacitly important in vv. 14-15, in vv. 16-17 it becomes an integral factor in Paul's continued effort to legitimate his apostleship. The fact of the objective eschatological reality represented by the symbol of Christ's death was affirmed in the former context, but the nature of that reality and its implications are elucidated in the latter. Paul's undivided attention is here directed to the maintenance of this reality, and the theological ideas present in this passage, especially the eschatological ones, constitute theconceptual machinery employed in this endeavour.⁸³

81. Barrett, *The First Epistle to the Corinthians*, p. 167.
82. According to Moule, ὥστε is in this context an inferential particle (*An Idiom-Book of New Testament Greek*, p. 144).
83. There is a question as to whether eschatology belongs to the mythological or theological type of conceptual machinery. Berger and Luckmann define mythology as 'a conception of reality that posits the ongoing penetration of the world of everyday experience by sacred forces'. They distinguish theology from mythology only by the degree of theoretical systematization. 'The cosmos may still be conceived of in terms of the sacred forces or beings of the old mythology, but these entities have been removed to a greater distance.' In view of this distinction Paul's escha-

Reality-maintenance in this instance concerns the eschatological-cosmological world view mediated by the sub-universe of faith, and thus is a vehicle for the ultimate type of legitimation in which behaviour and attitudes are located within a cosmological frame of reference.[84] According to Geertz, it is the function of sacred symbols to relate an ontology and a cosmology to an aesthetics and a morality.[85] Understood in terms of this dynamic, the death of Christ serves as a sacred symbol which synthesizes the ethos promoted in 5.14-15 and the eschatological world view of 5.17. Geertz explains this phenomenon from an anthropological perspective:

> the ethos is made intellectually reasonable by being shown to represent a way of life implied by the actual state of affairs which the world view describes, and the world view is made emotionally acceptable by being presented as an image of an actual state of affairs of which such a way of life is an authentic expression. This demonstration of a meaningful relation between the values a people hold and the general order of existence within which it finds itself is an essential element in all religions.[86]

Paul, having designated love as the most important value for Christian and apostolic existence, creates a symmetry between that value and the eschatological world view which is also derived from the symbol of Christ's death.

Paul succinctly describes this eschatological world view as a 'new creation' in which 'the old has passed away, behold, the new has come' (v. 17). Through this eschatological language he articulates the world which provides a metaphysical grounding for the value of love that has been previously affirmed.[87] Amos Wilder has asserted that eschatological rhetoric is by nature mythopoetic, 'meaning that it makes an implicit claim to provide valid representation of the world and dramatization of existence'.[88] Reversing this order, Paul has in 5.14-

---

tology should probably be classified as theological conceptual machinery (Berger and Luckmann, *The Social Construction of Reality*, pp. 128-29).

84. Berger and Luckmann, *The Social Construction of Reality*, pp. 114-15.
85. Geertz, *The Interpretation of Cultures*, p. 127.
86. Geertz, *The Interpretation of Cultures*, p. 127.
87. Geertz, *The Interpretation of Cultures*, p. 126: 'Never really metaphysics, religion is never merely ethics either. The source of its moral vitality is conceived to lie in the fidelity with which it expresses the fundamental nature of reality.'
88. A. Wilder, *Jesus' Parables and the War of Myths* (Philadelphia: Fortress Press, 1982), p. 7.

4. Paul's References to the Death of Jesus 153

15 dramatized Christian existence as love, and in 5.17 provided a representation of the world as a new creation where the love of Christ is the operative power and principle. Another comment from Geertz sheds more light on the relationship between ethos and world view as reflected in this passage: 'between the approved style of life and the assumed structure of reality there is conceived to be a simple and fundamental congruence such that they complete one another and lend one another meaning'.[89] This is the case in this context where both ethos and world view are fused in the symbol of Christ's death. But it is the world view, constructed on the basis of the eschatological significance of Christ's death (v. 17), that is the given point of reference from which Paul can legitimate the model of authentic existence which in 5.14-15 is also constructed on the basis of the eschatological significance of Christ's death. This eschatological world view lends meaning and authority to the pattern of existence affirmed in 5.14-15. In the legitimation process 'knowledge' precedes 'values'.[90] Here the knowledge of the eschatological world view contributes to the legitimation of the way of life which Paul advocates by giving it an appearance of objectivity.[91]

The objective state of affairs depicted in 5.17 is that believers have been drawn into a new sphere of existence as the result of their participation in Christ's death (cf. 5.14), and, in fact, the new creation is itself the consequence of this death. Paul is interested in the more temporal aspects of this new order, but he can discuss these only after he has established in v. 14 that those for whom Christ died have in some objective sense decisively broken with the past. Participation in Christ's death, then, is the condition which provides for a movement from the old way of life to the new.[92] This is the factual basis from which Paul can expound upon the values that are characteristic of the new creation. Having summarized the ethos associated with the new order as existence for others (5.15a), in v. 16 he assigns perception κατὰ σάρκα to the old age and therefore shifts the focus to a means of valuation that is to be abandoned by participants in the new way of life. He begins this verse with a transitional clause (ἀπὸ τοῦ νῦν) that reinforces the presence of the new, as well as discontinuity with the

---

89. Geertz, *The Interpretation of Cultures*, p. 129.
90. Berger and Luckmann, *The Social Construction of Reality*, p. 111.
91. Geertz, *The Interpretation of Cultures*, p. 131.
92. Cf. Tannehill, *Dying and Rising with Christ*, p. 66.

past. This point is reiterated again in v. 17: 'the old has passed away, behold, the new has come'. Paul has in v. 15 designated the ethos that is congruent with the new, but in v. 16 his concern is with what belongs to the old.

The emphasis on discontinuity with the past, symbolized by the death of all human beings in Christ's death, is set in contrast to the opponents' emphasis on continuity with the past.[93] This contrast is first evident in 3.7-11 where Paul compares the διακονία of death and condemnation with the διακονία of righteousness. The mention of Moses and the old covenant in this passage supports Käsemann's contention that tradition was important to the opponents.[94] But an even more crucial issue which separated the opponents from Paul was their comprehension of πνεῦμα.[95] They featured outward manifestations of the Spirit as evidence of the presence of the future, and probably also regarded them as a mark of apostleship (cf. 12.12). That their particular brand of spirituality was at issue in the Corinthians' negative appraisal of Paul's apostleship is indicated by his subtle use of ἐξέστημεν in 5.13 and his allusion to their τοὺς ἐν προσώπῳ καυχωμένους in 5.12. John Schütz explains how these two elements are combined in the perspective of the opponents in this way: '"tradition" turns "gospel" into their spiritualistic, realized eschatology'.[96] But not only has Paul stressed discontinuity with the past in response to their esteem of tradition, he has also in 5.1-10 asserted the provisional character of the eschatological future with the phrase τὸν ἀρραβῶνα τοῦ πνεύματος and thus replied to their enthusiasm. However, even though he has discounted the two main components underlying the opponents' conception of apostleship and the Corinthians' criticism of his, he nevertheless makes it clear that there is a real sense in which the new creation and the day of salvation (6.2) are present. The eschatological future does influence Christian existence and so also Paul's understanding of apostleship, but with reference to behaviour and perspective, not spiritual performance.

The role of the more suppressed realized eschatology of 5.14-15 where Paul has accented the believer's death with Christ to the past in order to discuss the behaviour which is characteristic of the present

93. Schütz, *The Anatomy of Apostolic Authority*, p. 176.
94. Käsemann, 'Die Legitimät des Apostels', pp. 56-58.
95. Schütz, *The Anatomy of Apostolic Authority*, p. 173.
96. Schütz, *The Anatomy of Apostolic Authority*, p. 175.

new life has already been noted. There he alludes to and assumes awareness of the new creation of 5.17, but does not explicitly refer to it. But in 5.16 this eschatological perspective comes much more to the fore of the discussion. Bultmann rightly observes that ἀπὸ τοῦ νῦν is the terminology of eschatology and remarks that 'ever since the event of verse 14 the world is new (v. 17; 6.2)'.[97] Paul's orientation to death to the old, which frees one to live for Christ and humanity, has given way to talk about the presence of the new. Both aspects are inherent in the idea that 'one has died for all; therefore all have died' (v. 14), so the shift in focus is just a matter of emphasis. What becomes important in 5.16 is that a knowing κατὰ σάρκα is not consistent with reality as it has been portrayed in 5.14-15, nor, as v. 17 indicates, with the new creation. Although the point of v. 16 is inferred from what Paul has said about the death of Christ in vv. 14-15, it is v. 17 that extends the thought of v. 16. This epistemological insight is grounded in the eschatological reality of the new creation. The emphasis of eschatology may be different in this context, but its function is essentially the same as in 5.14-15. It is noteworthy that what might be called the negative side of the eschatological coin (death) is used to reinforce the positive value of love, while the more positive side (new creation) is employed to negate a knowing according to the flesh. Nevertheless, both aspects of Paul's eschatology are seen to be the result of Christ's death, or better, both consequences of his death (discontinuity with the past as well as participation in the new) inform his eschatology. This is what distinguishes his realized eschatology from that of his opponents, who are concerned only with manifestations of the power associated with the advent of the new age.

Paul's discussion of epistemology in v. 16 is also similar to his discussion of the love of Christ and authentic Christian behaviour in vv. 14-15 with respect to its relationship to the recurrent theme of apostleship. In 5.16ff. his immediate concern is still the Corinthians' perception of his apostolate, and here he addresses the issue of perception or epistemology forthrightly within a cosmological-eschatological horizon. The subject of v. 16 is not, as Bultmann suggests, how a person should be understood and judged.[98] The epistemological point is inseparable from the eschatological one and therefore epistemology

---

97. Bultmann, *The Second Letter to the Corinthians*, p. 154.
98. Bultmann, *The Second Letter to the Corinthians*, p. 154.

cannot be reduced to a matter of individual subjectivity.[99] Paul precludes a subjective epistemology and argues instead for one that is based on the eschatological reality which is determined by the death and resurrection of Christ, and which determines the everyday reality of the believer. He uses the apocalyptic concept of 'new creation' to depict this reality, and it is important to emphasize with Stuhlmacher the ontological status it has for him.[100] What he asserts through this eschatological terminology is that the turn of the ages has occurred in the Christ-event.[101] The fundamental eschatological reality is that Christians stand at the juncture of the ages, and this is the decisive fact upon which the epistemological statement of v. 16 is founded. Paul declares that such an understanding of reality determines one's perception of Christ. He cites this as an example because it is the most extreme case of a transformed perception of others.[102] But it is Paul's apostolate that was being scrutinized by the Corinthians, so, arguing from the greater to the lesser, he suggests by inference that their perception of him should likewise be dictated by this eschatological reality.[103]

Since vv. 16 and 17 are interdependent, with v. 17 extending the thought of v. 16, the eschatology of v. 17 must be understood in the light of the epistemology of v. 16. That is to say, the scope of v. 17 cannot be taken literally and therefore is determined by the context. Paul cannot mean unconditionally that there is a new creation in that the old has passed away and the new has come. His main point is that for the believer the possibility of an epistemology which belongs to the old aeon is excluded, as are the values of the old aeon. They have

---

99. Cf. J.L. Martyn, 'Epistemology at the Turn of the Ages: 2 Corinthians 5.16', in W. Farmer, C.F.D. Moule, and R.R. Niebuhr (eds.), *Christian History and Interpretation* (Cambridge: Cambridge University Press, 1967), p. 274.

100. P. Stuhlmacher, 'Erwägungen zum ontologischen Charakter der *kainé ktisis* bei Paulus', *EvT* 27 (1967), p. 27. This is the main thesis of Stuhlmacher's article and he points out that even in the apocalyptic tradition καινὴ κτίσις has an ontic depth-dimension. Stuhlmacher observes that

> Für Paulus ist ja, wie unser Textzusammenhang eindrücklich zeigt, die Christustat die Speerspitze des in die alte Weltzeit hereinbrechenden neuen Äons. Die Offenbarung gilt dem Apostel folglich als ein äonenhaftes, räumliches, im Wort anwesendes Phänomen, in das eingegliedert zu werden, nur individuelle Applikation der durch Christus heraufgeführten Zeitwende bedeutet' (p. 5).

101. Martyn, 'Epistemology at the Turn of the Ages', p. 271.
102. Furnish, *II Corinthians*, p. 332.
103. Furnish, *II Corinthians*, p. 331.

been replaced by a new value system which is apprehended by means of a new epistemology; both are determined by the new eschatological reality. The eschatological vision of the new creation in this context provides the cosmological frame of reference within which the new value system and epistemology are legitimated. They are congruous with this vision of reality and their authenticity and authority are contingent upon acceptance of it as an objective picture of the world. Thus Stuhlmacher is right when he says that the Pauline contrast between old aeon and new creation is not immediately existential or an exclusively anthropological phenomenon.[104] And yet Paul does establish the objective transformation of reality effected by Christ's death with a view to discussing the more subjective aspect of it. The subjective dimension of this transformation concerns 'the total re-orienting of one's values and priorities away from the world (self) and toward the cross (Christ, others) vv. 15bc, 16'.[105]

The value system which is consistent with the eschatological world view presented in these verses operates on the basis of a way of knowing which does not depend solely upon sense perception.[106] It is a way of knowing granted not to the natural person, but to those who are able to discern the eschatological significance of Christ's death and who view reality in terms of its consequences. From this perspective salvation is realized under the sign of the cross. But the fact that it is indeed realized means that the believer's life is characterized as a 'life in departure' as opposed to a 'life in delay'.[107] Nevertheless, the realized eschatology of these verses is a matter of perception, and the presence of the 'new' (v. 17) must be understood in the light of the epistemological point of v. 16. It is noteworthy that where we might expect knowing κατὰ πνεῦμα to be the antithesis of knowing κατὰ σάρκα Paul provides no explicit alternative to his negation of the way

104. Stuhlmacher, 'Erwägungen zum ontologischen Charakter der *kainé ktisis* bei Paulus', p. 8.
105. Furnish, *II Corinthians*, p. 332.
106. Martyn says that for a philosophically inclined citizen of Corinth Paul's expression γινώσκειν κατὰ σάρκα would have meant to know on the basis of sense perception. It was the way of knowing characteristic of the natural man ('Epistemology at the Turn of the Ages', pp. 276, 278). Schütz is correct in saying that in this context knowing κατὰ σάρκα is the equivalent of ἐν προσώπῳ καυχωμένους (*The Anatomy of Apostolic Authority*, p. 176).
107. Hahn, '"Siehe jetzt ist der Tag des Heils"', p. 245. Hahn contrasts Paul's understanding of 'life in departure' with the Jewish view of 'life in delay'.

of knowing which is characteristic of the natural person.¹⁰⁸ Yet, as Martyn points out, it is clear from the context that the implied opposite of knowing κατὰ σάρκα is knowing κατὰ σταυρόν.¹⁰⁹ Martyn asserts that the essential flaw in the epistemology of the Corinthians 'lies in their failure to view the cross as the absolute epistemological watershed'.¹¹⁰ The cross marks the present as the eschatological time of the turn of the ages and suggests a corresponding way of knowing which understands the Christian life as a 'life in departure' lived in the midst of death.¹¹¹

At the centre of Paul's argument in this passage lies the conviction that epistemology, eschatology and the nature of Christian existence are inextricably related and reflect different aspects of the significance of Christ's death, which is itself the absolute watershed. It is his repeated appeal to and conceptualization of the death of Christ that gives the argument its coherence. The epistemological comment of v. 16 is retrospective of Paul's explanation of the character of apostolic existence in 4.7-12, and is contingent upon the eschatological insights of vv. 14 and 17. What is elucidated in 4.7-12 can only be comprehended and appreciated from the eschatological perspective of vv. 14 and 17. The cross symbolizes the turn of the ages and this means that the old-age way of knowing is relegated to the past. Conversely, the presence of the new creation means that there are new standards for identifying an apostle. The value which Paul most wants to infer from the fact that the believer stands at the juncture of the ages is that a true

---

108. Martyn thinks that the super-apostles must have agreed with the pneumatics depicted in 1 Corinthians that the true way of knowing is κατὰ πνεῦμα. By that expression they meant γινώσκειν κατὰ πρόσωπον or γινώσκειν κατὰ δυνάμεις ('Epistemology at the Turn of the Ages', p. 283).

109. Martyn, 'Epistemology at the Turn of the Ages', p. 285. It could be argued that the antithesis of knowing κατὰ σάρκα should be knowing κατὰ καινὴ κτίσις, but since Paul understands the new creation to be effectuated by Christ's death and since it is the cross which determines the character of the new creation, the cross seems to be the more definitive of the two symbols.

110. Martyn, 'Epistemology at the Turn of the Ages', p. 285: 'He who recognizes his life to be God's gift at the *juncture* of the ages recognizes also that until he is completely and exclusively in the new age, his knowing κατὰ πνεῦμα can occur only in the form of knowing κατὰ σταυρόν.'

111. Martyn, 'Epistemology at the Turn of the Ages', p. 272: 'For that is what the turn of the ages means—that life is manifested in death.'

apostle is not powerful, but weak.[112] Thus the conclusion he draws constitutes a reversal of values. Given this perspective on reality, the Corinthians should be able to distinguish between true and false apostles and therefore recognize that Paul's apostolate is authentic.

---

112. Martyn, 'Epistemology at the Turn of the Ages', p. 273.

Chapter 5

THE SOCIAL SIGNIFICANCE OF THE DEATH OF JESUS:
2 CORINTHIANS 10–13

The Purpose of Chapters 10–13

In the previous chapter I argued that Paul's references to the death of Jesus in 4.7–5.19 function to explain why his apostolate was characterized by weakness. His weakness is also the main theme of chs. 10–13, but in this section explanation has been supplanted by polemic. The radical change in tone is not the only thing that distinguishes the two sections, Paul also appears to have a different objective in chs. 10–13. His purpose in chs. 1–9 was to effect a mutuality of pride between him and the Corinthians, and this entailed responding to criticisms that his weakness was incompatible with being a minister of the gospel.[1] The bulk of chs. 10–13 also consists of replies to similar charges against Paul, yet he expressly states in 12.19 that he has written not to defend himself, but rather with a view to 'building up' the community. The idea of 'building up' (οἰκοδομή) also occurs in 10.8 and 13.10 where it stands in sharp contrast to 'tearing down' (καθαίρεσις). Paul emphasizes the negative side of this antithesis in 10.4-6 where he makes use of warfare imagery. Although his desire is to use the authority the Lord has given him to 'build up' the community, the existence of certain 'strongholds' (ὀχύρωμα) and 'reasonings' (λογισμός) which are apparently inhibiting the obedience of the Corinthians requires that he confront these obstacles with weapons that are 'powerful for God' (10.4).[2]

The warfare imagery is introduced in 10.2 with an allusion to the charge that Paul is 'acting in a worldly way' (κατὰ σάρκα περιπα-

---

1. Cf. Fitzgerald, *Cracks in an Earthen Vessel*, p. 149. Fitzgerald rightly affirms that 1.12-14 states the theme and purpose of the whole of chs. 1–7.
2. For an explanation of this translation of δυνατὰ τῷ θεῳ see BDF, p. 192.

τοῦντας), and it is with reference to this charge that he asserts that 'though we live in the world we are not carrying on a worldly war' (10.3). The reference to the war which is not fought κατὰ σάρκα immediately broadens the horizons of the discussion and relates the suspicion about Paul's behaviour to his concern for the Corinthians' obedience to Christ (10.5-6; cf. also 11.3-4). That the battle to which Paul is referring is fought primarily in the interest of securing their obedience is indicated by the fact that 'building up' is correlated with 'tearing down'.[3] Thus the warfare in which Paul is about to engage has a constructive purpose which extends beyond apology. That constructive purpose is supported by his claim in 13.10 that he has written so that when he arrives he will not have to be severe in his use of the authority the Lord has given him 'for building up and not tearing down'. The threat the opposition poses to Paul's apostleship has not receded in this section, but it is viewed in terms of its bearing on the community itself. There is a sense in which criticisms against him, his reply to these criticisms and his anxiety about the Corinthians' conduct are all interrelated. Paul's dialogue with his critics is not so much a defence of himself as it is an attempt to tear down the 'strongholds' erected by his opponents.

The term 'strongholds' (ὀχύρωμα) in 10.4 refers to reasoning faculties (λογισμοί) that are exalted against the knowledge of God (10.5). Paul has in mind here the logic behind the accusation that his behaviour is inconsistent, that is, that he is humble when present and confident when he is away (10.1-2; cf. 10.10). His comments in 10.4-5 are reminiscent of the Cynic–Stoic debates in which the Cynic who appears in humiliating circumstances and garb is actually at war.[4] As with the contest between Cynics and Stoics, the confrontation between Paul and his adversaries has to do with self-understanding, or better apostolic understanding, but Paul is more interested in the reasoning behind the definition of apostleship which is in conflict with his. Paul's

---

3. Cf. J. Hainz, *Ekklesia: Strukturen paulinischer Gemeinde-Theologie und Gemeinde-Ordnung* (Regensburg: Verlag Friedrich Pustet, 1972), p. 163. Hainz notes that Paul's claim that the authority the Lord gave him is for building up rather than tearing down (10.8) stands in a certain opposition to 10.3-6 where Paul speaks of the necessity of tearing down strongholds. See also Windisch, *Der zweite Korintherbrief*, p. 303; Lietzmann, *An die Korinther I, II*, p. 162.

4. Cf. A. Malherbe, 'Antisthenes and Odysseus, and Paul at War', *HTR* 76 (1983), p. 170.

war is not merely a personal one; it is directed against everything which obstructs the knowledge of God (10.5), and in this case the arguments of the rival apostolate are perceived to be such an obstruction.[5] Much more is at stake then in these chapters than just an understanding and appreciation of Paul's apostleship. The 'reasoning' of the opposition (10.4) is the object of Paul's counterattack not only because it is the source of their attack on him, but, more importantly, because it has impeded and even distorted the 'knowledge of God' (10.5) in the community. Therefore, he takes up the weapons appropriate to this kind of battle (δυνατὰ τῷ θεῳ) and proceeds to dismantle those arguments which, although they are leveled against him personally, imperil the very truth of the gospel (cf. 11.4).

On the surface, Paul's preoccupation with criticisms of his apostleship suggests that he is primarily concerned with vindicating himself, but the fear he expresses in 11.3 indicates that his battle is, in part at least, on behalf of the Corinthians. It is their 'thoughts' which are in danger of being 'led astray from a sincere and pure devotion to Christ' (11.3), and consequently it is their 'thoughts' which he wants to take 'captive to the obedience of Christ' (10.5). Although the warfare imagery is introduced in 10.3 with a reference to questions about Paul's conduct, by 10.6 the focus of attention has become the Corinthians' conduct, that is, the completion of their obedience. Paul's allusion to the suspicions about his behaviour and the concern he expresses about the Corinthians' obedience suggests that even though the discussion is oriented to 'reasoning' (10.4), 'thoughts' (10.5; 11.3) and rhetorical arguments (11.1–12.10), what is really at issue is conduct.[6] As to the matter of whose conduct is in dispute, it would depend on to whom the question was addressed. From the numerous criticisms stemming from the opposition in Corinth it would seem that Paul is the one on trial, but from Paul's point of view it is the Corinthians who need to

---

5. Malherbe thinks the confrontation is a personal one and that Paul is defending himself against the criticisms recounted in 10.1 and 10.10 ('Antisthenes and Odysseus, and Paul at War', p. 172). However, as Malherbe himself has shown, what was at issue between Cynics and Stoics was the more fundamental matter of lifestyle. Likewise, it would seem that from Paul's viewpoint his conflict with the opposition was about lifestyle and hence involved more than just a personality contest.

6. Malherbe, 'Antisthenes and Odysseus, and Paul at War', p. 172. Malherbe, however, presumes Paul is concerned only with defending his own conduct.

5. *The Social Significance of the Death of Jesus* 163

'examine' and 'test' themselves to see whether they are holding to the faith (13.5). Paul's arguments in chs. 10–13 promote this self-examination, and, more importantly, the account of his conduct which emerges from the reply to his critics constitutes the model of authentic Christian existence which is to serve as the yardstick.

In 12.19 Paul asserts that, despite all appearances, the preceding arguments have not been in self-defence, rather his intention all along has been the 'upbuilding' of the community. The concrete reasons for this aim are given in 12.20-21 where he supplies an extensive list of behavioural problems which he anticipates when he arrives. Earlier Paul expressed a general concern about the Corinthians' obedience and disclosed his fear that their 'thoughts' would be led astray from Christ. In 12.20-21 his fear of misguided thoughts has become fear of the behavioural consequences of those thoughts, and from the exhortation to self-examination in 13.5 it can be inferred that the catalogue of negative behaviours in these verses heads Paul's agenda in chs. 10–13. Nevertheless, the connection between erroneous thoughts and misconduct is inextricable, and so Paul must 'tear down' the thinking which is the cause of such behaviour before he can 'build up' the community. Barrett rightly contends that the negative behaviours listed in 12.20 relate to the sort of situation that would be brought about by the incursion of rival apostles.[7] Building on this observation, it would seem that the brunt of Paul's argument in this section is devoted to undermining the opponents' claims and their rationale because of the 'quarreling, jealousy, anger, selfishness, slander, gossip, conceit and disorder' they had aroused in the community (12.20; cf. Rom. 16). If this was his strategy, then the pressing question is how he did expect these destructive arguments to accomplish the constructive end of building up the community? The burden of this chapter will be to show that the cutting edge of both the destructive and constructive aspects of his argument is his theology of the cross.

The Criticisms of Paul's Apostleship Reflected in 2 Corinthians 10–13

Criticisms of Paul dominate 2 Corinthians 10–13 and are thus the point of departure for his argument and for any attempt to understand what he is trying to accomplish in this letter. These criticisms stem

---

7. Barrett, 'Paul's opponents in 2 Corinthians', p. 75.

from an opposition in Corinth which appears to have gained control in the community and persuaded the majority against Paul.[8] It has been suggested that the negative effect this opposition had in the community was of primary importance to Paul, but this is not to deny that his apostolic status was also in jeopardy as the result of their influence. These are two concomitant problems which have as their common denominator critical questions regarding the character of Christian existence. On the one hand, the Corinthians are suspicious of Paul's conduct and question the authenticity of his apostleship. Paul, on the other hand, is confident that he is faithful to Christ and his apostolic calling, and his concern is with the Corinthians' conduct.[9] These are two independent interests that converge on the general theme of Christian conduct, and Paul addresses this theme from the perspective of both interests—his and the Corinthians'—with reference to his apostleship. But his own agenda is so intertwined with the Corinthian agenda to which he is replying that their criticisms of him are also the vehicle for his critique of what he deems to be a deficient understanding of the nature of Christian existence. In more than one sense, then, the criticisms of Paul recounted in chs. 10–13 are the crux of his dialogue with the Corinthians.

Paul opens this section in 10.1 with an exhortation relating his own 'humble' presence to the 'meekness and gentleness of Christ'. This exhortation must be understood in terms of specific criticisms leveled against him, a synopsis of which is given in 10.10: 'his letters are weighty and strong, but his bodily presence is weak, and his speech of no account'. Paul is here quoting his opponents, and even though he mentions other criticisms in subsequent verses, this quotation is inclusive of all the other criticisms. The sum and substance of this comprehensive charge is that his entire 'physical presence' (παρουσία τοῦ σώματος) has been perceived as 'weak' (ἀσθενής), and this is associated first and foremost with a manner of speaking which excites contempt (ὁ λόγος ἐξουθενημένος).[10] In one form or another, all of the

---

8. Most commentators agree that the opponents have gained control in the community. Cf. also Marshall, *Enmity in Corinth*, p. 263, and Theissen, *The Social Setting of Pauline Christianity*, p. 57.

9. There is no reason to suppose that the confidence expressed in chs. 1–7 has been supplanted by insecurity. Paul's conviction is that his competence is from God, and therefore it is not subject to changing whims (cf. 2.14–3.6).

10. Furnish, *II Corinthians*, p. 479; Barrett, *The Second Epistle to the*

criticisms cited reflect a particular expression of this weakness. Thus the attack on Paul can be subsumed under the general heading of weakness, which in conjunction with power emerges as the central theme in the letter (cf. 10.1, 10; 11.21, 29, 30; 12.5, 9, 10; 13.3-4, 9).[11]

Betz has shown that the content of the accusation in 10.10 pertains to the σχῆμα of the apostle; a concept which has its background in debates about the σχῆμα of the true philosopher dating from the time of Socrates.[12] Paul's σχῆμα is disparaged because 'his bodily presence is weak', but it is evident from other criticisms in chs. 10–13 that weakness denotes more than just physical appearance, though it obviously includes that.[13] The form of his λόγος was also considered to be an aspect of his appearance,[14] and the fact that he refers to the accusation that he is 'unskilled in speaking' (ἰδιώτης τῷ λόγῳ, 11.6) more than any of the other criticisms suggests that it was the characteristic of weakness most despised by the Corinthians (cf. 10.10; 11.6; 13.3).[15] Such a conception of weakness, that is, one that is defined by a lack of rhetorical skill, is indicative of the social connotations of the opposition's criticisms of him.[16] Paul was judged weak because his style

Corinthians, p. 261; Lietzmann, *An die Korinther I, II*, p. 142.

11. Schütz, *Paul and the Anatomy of Apostolic Authority*, p. 214.

12. Betz, *Der Apostel Paulus und die sokratische Tradition*, pp. 42-47. The decisive criterion in debates among the philosophical schools was appearance, their whole garb. The true philosopher was the one who had the *appearance* of a philosopher.

13. Some scholars think of Paul's weakness just as physical weakness. See J. Jervell, 'Der schwache Charismatiker', in *Rechtfertigung*, p. 191; B. Holmberg, *Paul and Power: The Structure of Authority in the Primitive Church as Reflected in the Pauline Epistles* (Philadelphia: Fortress Press, 1978), p. 78; Fitzgerald, *Cracks in An Earthen Vessel*, pp. 138-39.

14. Betz asserts that λόγος is the outer form of γνῶσις and that this outer form is the exclusive concern of chs. 10–13 (*Der Apostel Paulus und die sokratische Tradition*, pp. 58-59).

15. Marshall suggests that the disparagement of Paul's personal bearing, ἡ παρουσία τοῦ σώματος ἀσθενής, is a concomitant of the dispraise of his rhetorical style (*Enmity in Corinth*, pp. 325-26).

16. See the discussion of the social connotations of the terms δύναμις and ἀσθένεια in Chapter 3. According to Forbes, '"weakness" is the state of those without power or status, and "strength", is the state of those who do have status. "Weakness" connotes humiliation in the eyes of others, rather than inadequacy in one's own' ('Comparison, Self-Praise and Irony', p. 19). Marshall (*Enmity in Corinth*), Betz (*Der Apostel Paulus und die sokratische Tradition*) and Theissen

of speaking fell short of Greco-Roman rhetorical conventions, and weakness understood in the light of those conventions signified inferior social status. From the opposition's viewpoint, then, his weakness is essentially a matter of low social status with respect to the cultural values of Greco-Roman society.[17]

The connection in 11.7 between Paul's 'humility' and his financial policy of self-support is further evidence that he was demeaned by the Corinthians largely because they perceived him to be socially inferior. Although there is no explicit reference to Paul's work as a craftsman in this verse, it is likely that he continued his trade of tentmaking during his ministry at Corinth (cf. Acts 18.1-3), and that this was a bone of contention between him and the Corinthians (cf. 1 Cor. 9.3-18). Among itinerant philosophers of that time, working at a trade was considered the least appropriate means of earning a living. On the basis of this understanding of the popular attitude toward work, Ronald Hock asserts that Paul carried on as a tentmaker at the expense of considerable loss of social esteem.[18] He relates the phrase ἐμαυτὸν ταπεινῶν (11.7) to Paul's practice of supporting himself at a trade, and concludes that his tentmaking was largely responsible for his humiliation.[19] The social stigma attached to the apostle's work is also demonstrated in the hardship catalogue in 1 Cor. 4.9-13. In this passage Paul assumes the position of someone who is socially and economically disadvantaged, and he credits this partly to the fact that he works with his hands (4.12).[20] The description of Paul as 'weak' and 'humble' was not solely the result of his working at a trade, but the stigma attached to physical labour does attest to the social dimension of his negative persona in the community.

In addition to the dishonour associated with working for a living, there is another aspect of Paul's decision to support himself which contributed to the deterioration of his relationship with the Corinthians.

('The Strong and the Weak in Corinth: A Sociological Analysis of a Theological Quarrel' in *The Social Setting of Pauline Christianity*, pp. 121-43) also emphasize the social connotations of these terms.

17. Judge points out that one of the fundamental principles upon which the Greek status-system rested was the belief that fine form is congruent to truth ('Cultural Conformity and Innovation in Paul', p. 13).

18. Hock, *The Social Context of Paul's Ministry*, p. 59.

19. Hock, *The Social Context of Paul's Ministry*, p. 64. Hock cites the example of Lucian who deemed taking up a trade to be humiliating.

20. See the discussion of this passage in Chapter 3.

5. *The Social Significance of the Death of Jesus* 167

With a touch of sarcasm, he asks in 11.7 if he has committed a 'sin' by preaching the gospel to the Corinthians without cost. This question recalls the discussion in 1 Cor. 9.3-18 where Paul defended both an apostle's right to be financially supported for preaching the gospel (9.4, 14), and his prerogative to refuse that privilege (9.12, 15-18). Dungan has argued with reference to the *Sitz im Leben* of 1 Corinthians that Paul's refusal of aid was the main cause of conflict, and he goes on to suggest that 1 Corinthians 9 represents the first stages of the conflict seen in 2 Corinthians 10–12.[21] By the time 2 Corinthians was written the situation had degenerated considerably, and consequently chs. 10–13 is characterized by hostility and invective. The personal offence of what is treated as a matter of principle in 1 Corinthians 9 is disclosed in 2 Cor. 11.8-11. The Corinthians have inferred from Paul's acceptance of support from other churches (11.8) that they 'were made inferior to the rest of the churches' (12.13). Paul redresses their deduction by reaffirming his love for them (11.11; 12.15), but he makes no apologies for his unwillingness to be a burden to them (11.9; 12.14).

Although Paul was reluctant to be a burden to the Corinthian church, his acceptance of support from the Philippians (Phil. 4.15), who in 2 Cor. 8.2 he describes as being in 'severe poverty', indicates that this was not his only reason for turning down the Corinthian offer. The Corinthian offer of a gift constituted an offer of friendship, and, in accordance with Greco-Roman conventions of friendship, it was intended to place Paul under obligation.[22] Moreover, giving and receiving was an integral part of the status apparatus, and as such was linked with the notions of honour and shame.[23] The purpose of bene-

---

21. D. Dungan, *The Sayings of Jesus in the Churches of Paul* (Philadelphia: Fortress Press, 1971), p. 19. See also Marshall, *Enmity in Corinth*, p. 231.

22. Marshall, *Enmity in Corinth*, pp. 232-33. See also R. MacMullen, *Roman Social Relations* (New Haven: Yale University Press, 1974), pp. 106-107 and S.C. Mott, 'The Power of Giving and Receiving: Reciprocity in Hellenistic Benevolence', in G.F. Hawthorne (ed.), *Current Issues in Biblical and Patristic Interpretation* (Festschrift Tenney; Grand Rapids: Eerdmans, 1975), pp. 60-72.

23. Marshall, *Enmity in Corinth*, p. 242; E.A. Judge, 'The Social Identity of the First Christians: A Question of Method in Religious History', *JRH* 11 (1980), p. 214. Judge observes that this cultural understanding of friendship is the reason Paul refrains from using the familiar language of friendship and instead develops his own ideal of partnership in labour, which was 'surely meant as provocation to a society that considered physical toil demeaning'.

faction was to enhance the giver's status and to win honour and recognition. In rejecting the offer of financial assistance Paul was, in effect, rejecting the protocol of social rank imposed by the practice of benefaction.[24] However, as the result of declining the Corinthian offer of friendship he found himself engaged in the process of ritual enmity.[25] Thus in addition to personal criticisms of Paul, there was also a relational dimension of the Corinthian attack on his apostleship. As with the personal criticisms, the enmity between Paul and the Corinthians concerned the matter of status. Conventions of friendship in the Greco-Roman world comprised a transaction in which the greater conferred a status on the lesser.[26] As Furnish observes, the point at issue was not only Paul's status as an apostle, the status of the congregation was also involved. By labouring as a tentmaker and refusing support from the community, he not only demeaned himself and undermined his own status, his action was perceived by the Corinthians as a renunciation of their status as a patron congregation.[27] Paul's financial self-sufficiency rendered to them the same dishonour they disdained in him.

The remaining criticisms of Paul reiterated in chs. 10–13 are of a religious nature. They are distinguished from the aforementioned criticisms in that they designate specific items of comparison between him and his rivals in Corinth. Although the accusations are not as flagrant in 1 Corinthians, objections to Paul's lack of status and eloquence (1.17; 2.1-4), his working for wages (4.12) and his refusal of financial assistance (9.1-23) are reflected in that letter before the interlopers arrived on the scene. The presence of these so called 'superlative apostles' (11.5) in Corinth highlighted other weaknesses which Paul had, and thus took the Corinthians' disenchantment with Paul a step further. In comparison with this rival apostolate Paul is seen to be deficient with regard to certain religious qualifications required of an apostle, such as visions and revelations (12.1-10), miracles (12.12), and pure Jewish background (11.22). These 'religious' criticisms which

24. Judge asserts that he refused the benefaction they offered 'because he preferred financial and therefore social independence' ('The Social Identity of the First Christians', p. 214).
25. On Greco-Roman conventions of friendship and enmity see the first chapter of Marshall, *Enmity in Corinth*, pp. 1-70.
26. Judge, 'Cultural Conformity and Innovation in Paul', p. 15.
27. Furnish, *II Corinthians*, p. 508. Furnish observes that Paul's rivals seem to have encouraged this perception.

5. *The Social Significance of the Death of Jesus* 169

have the 'superlative apostles' as their point of reference are the ones to which Paul replies in 11.1–12.10, and will be discussed in more detail in a subsequent section. Suffice it to say here that even these religious criticisms are status related. What is fundamentally at issue in Paul's dispute with the Corinthians are certain measures of status they have in common with the larger society, and, as Meeks correctly observes, 'they have superimposed on these some specifically religious qualifications'.[28]

From the above survey of the various criticisms of the apostle there emerges a fairly consistent portrait of one who was socially inferior in terms of the cultural values of Greco-Roman society. According to Marshall, the deprecatory remarks seem to pertain to the encomiastic topics of physical appearance, education and achievements.[29] Taken together, they form the description of him as one who is 'weak' and 'humble', terms which denote the baseness of someone low in status, as it was defined by literary and artistic cultivation.[30] To put it crudely, Paul embarrassed the Corinthians because they thought he should assume the role of a leader in the socially accepted sense.[31] Moreover, in the light of Judge's contention that Paul 'was a person highly placed in every social scale that mattered in the social centres where he worked',[32] it appears that he deliberately adopted the posture of a socially and economically disadvantaged person. The reason for this

28. Meeks, *The First Urban Christians*, p. 72. E. Ellis remarks that in pre-Christian usage the term Hebraioi (11.22) 'appears to denote a dignity or status associated with traditional Jewish values and customs' ('Paul and his Opponents', reprinted in *Prophecy and Hermeneutic in Early Christianity* [Grand Rapids: Eerdmans, 1980], p. 106).
29. Marshall, *Enmity in Corinth*, p. 327.
30. Judge, 'Cultural Conformity and Innovation in Paul', p. 13. 'Cultivation in the literary and artistic sense was thus the means of legitimising the status of those who could afford it. And precisely because it made a conspicuous difference to a person's public appearance it became the means by which the social inferiority of the uncultivated was imposed on them as a felt distinction.'
31. Judge, 'Cultural Conformity and Innovation in Paul', p. 13. See also Judge, 'St Paul as a Radical Critic of Society', p. 197. Judge remarks that 'the formal recital of affronts is itself a deliberate embarrassment to those he is addressing as well as a mark of his own sensitivity to questions of status' ('St Paul as a Radical Critic of Society', p. 192).
32. Judge, 'St Paul as a Radical Critic of Society', p. 191. According to Judge, Paul's style of speech and writing place him in the mainstream of educated public figures, but most decisive was his Roman citizenship.

will be discussed later. Here it is enough simply to point out such a posture had serious consequences in a culture where honour and shame were the pivotal social values.³³ Paul's style of apostleship was a source of shame for those Corinthians who held to the accepted cultural values of Greco-Roman society, and therefore they attempted to humiliate and shame him by ridiculing him as a man who lacked culture.³⁴

The Source of the Criticisms: Paul's Opposition in Corinth

Attempts to identify the opposition behind the derisive critique of Paul in chs. 10–13 have for the most part been preoccupied with locating the rival apostles within the appropriate history of religions category. There is a wide range of opinions about the category to which this group belongs, but the basic presupposition underlying all of these investigations is that the criticisms of Paul mirror the predominant features of the opponents. The problem is that when this presupposition is rigorously held to, the resulting profile is one of Jewish missionaries, perhaps from Palestine, who are skilled in the art of rhetoric and exhibit the qualities of a cultivated person in Hellenistic society, and there is no known group in early Christianity which combines all of these characteristics. The many and diverse solutions that have been proposed to resolve this problem consist of attempts to reconcile these disparate features, but inevitably one or two of the traits are considered to be preeminent and the others are either subordinated or ignored.³⁵ For the purposes of this study, an answer to the history of religions

---

33. Malina, *The New Testament World*, pp. 25-35: 'Honour might be described as socially proper attitudes and behaviour in the area where the three lines of power, sexual status, and religion intersect' (p. 27).

34. Marshall asserts that Paul's use of the terms αἰσχύνω (10.8) and ἀτιμία (11.21) indicate that the criticisms were aimed at humiliating and shaming him (*Enmity in Corinth*, p. 327).

35. Usually the Hellenistic features are set over against the Jewish ones or vice versa. Käsemann ('Die Legitimität des Apostels: Eine Untersuchung zu II Korinther 10–13') and Barrett ('Paul's Opponents in II Corinthians') distinguish between the 'false apostles' and the 'superapostles' in order to explain the disparate Palestinian Jewish and Hellenistic features. Ellis thinks the rival apostles' pneumatic powers have their background in pentecostal manifestations in the Jerusalem church ('Paul and his Opponents', p. 127). While it is possible to reconcile the emphases on Jewish background and pneumatic powers, none of the attempts to do so recognize the importance of rhetorical skills in the conflict.

question is neither necessary nor expedient because it detracts from the more immediate and important exegetical questions raised by the criticisms of Paul.[36] However, since Paul is replying to these criticisms in chs. 10–13, it will be necessary to ascertain their source. I intend to show that this endeavour is not equivalent to the task of designating and assigning a label to a homogenous group of rival apostles.

One reason there is no consensus of opinion as to who these rival apostles were is that the situation which necessitated the writing of 2 Corinthians involved more than a confrontation between them and Paul. Something of a social triangle can be inferred from 2 Corinthians in which the Corinthians interact with both Paul and the rival apostles, but Paul and these intruders have no personal contact with each other. Although the rival apostles appear to have made a significant contribution to the degeneration of Paul's relationship with the Corinthians, his conversation is with the Corinthians, and the opponents are no more than silent partners in the dialogue. Paul is competing with the rival apostles for the allegiance of the Corinthians, but his rejoinder to the charges against him is directed to the Corinthians because it is their loyalty he is interested in,[37] and only they can decide whether or not he is an authentic apostle. The rival apostles, then, are further in the background than has often been thought, and it is therefore erroneous to assume that the Corinthians are caught in the middle of a conflict between Paul and these interlopers when it is clear that it is they who are in the position of power.

The prominence of the Corinthians in the dispute also means that the identity of the rival apostles cannot be directly inferred from the criticisms of Paul, for it is the Corinthians who are exercising control over the comparison of the two apostolates. The rival apostles must have exemplified many, if not most, of the attributes Paul was accused of lacking, but it is necessary to distinguish between what the criticisms

---

36. The best treatment of the *Religionsgeschichte* question is still Georgi's *Die Gegner des Paulus im 2 Korintherbrief: Studien zur religiösen Propaganda in der Spätantike*. In general I follow his description of the rival apostles as itinerant charismatics who stand on a Jewish missionary tradition. However, C. Holladay has shown that the 'divine man' category he is so dependent on is more fluid than Georgi suggests and therefore this aspect of his description must be disregarded (*Theios Aner in Hellenistic Judaism: A Critique of the Use of this Category in New Testament Christology* [SBLDS, 40; Missoula, MT: Scholars Press, 1977]). Georgi also is not aware of the importance of rhetorical skills to this group.

37. Hainz, *Ekklesia*, p. 161.

imply about the Corinthians' expectations of an apostle, and what they imply about the opponents' compliance with these expectations. Given the importance of the Corinthians' position in this social triangle, it would seem that these criticisms of Paul reflect above all what *they* sought in an apostle, and that the critical issue in the dispute was the extent to which Paul and his rivals were willing, or in Paul's case unwilling, to accommodate their demands.

The appearance of the rival apostles in Corinth was undoubtedly a factor in the assault on Paul's apostleship, but the seeds of discontent with Paul are already evident in 1 Corinthians. The correspondence between the criticisms of Paul in 1 and 2 Corinthians were noted in the preceding section. A further examination of the background and character of the objections to his apostleship in 1 Corinthians will clarify the connection between the opposition to Paul in the two letters. As this connection is developed it will be possible to delineate the fundamental causes of the conflict behind chs. 10–13, and the nature of the Corinthians' relationship with the rival apostles.

Nils Dahl has argued that in 1 Corinthians the strife among the Corinthians reported to Paul by Chloe's people is associated with an opposition against him within the community.[38] It is evident from Paul's remark in 4.3: 'But with me it is a very small thing that I should be judged by you or any human court' that some criticism of him had been voiced in Corinth, and from other statements in 1.10–4.21 it is possible to deduce the content of these criticisms. Phrases like 'not with eloquent wisdom' (1.17), 'not in lofty words of wisdom' (2.1), 'not in persuasiveness of wisdom' (2.4) and 'milk, not solid food' (3.2) taken together with the Corinthians' understanding of themselves as pneumatics (cf. 3.1) leads Dahl to conclude that in their eyes Paul lacked rhetorical ability and the gift of pneumatic wisdom.[39] The hardship catalogue in 4.11-13 provides even more insight into the criticisms of Paul. In these verses Paul emphasizes not so much his apostolic sufferings, but rather his lack of honour and status.[40] This is also the point of the preceding v. 10 where Paul contrasts the fact that he is 'foolish' (μωρός), 'weak' (ἀσθενής) and 'dishonoured' (ἄτιμος) with a description of certain Corinthians who are 'wise' (φρόνιμος), 'strong' (ἰσχυρός), and 'honoured' (ἔνδοξος). These antitheses probably reflect

38. Dahl, 'Paul and the Church at Corinth', p. 49.
39. Dahl, 'Paul and the Church at Corinth', p. 48.
40. Fitzgerald, *Cracks in an Earthen Vessel*, p. 140.

5. *The Social Significance of the Death of Jesus* 173

the status of Paul's opposition, as well as their attitudes toward him.[41]

Marshall asserts that the key to understanding the antithetical comparisons and hardship catalogue in 4.9-13 lies in the meaning of vv. 6-8.[42] Paul's description of some Corinthians who are 'puffed up in favour of one against another' in 4.6 is correlative with the ironic description in 4.8 of those who are already 'filled' (κορέννυμι), 'rich' (πλουτέω), and 'ruling' (βασιλεύω). According to Marshall, the nuance of status is present in the terms κορέννυμι and πλουτέω, and they betray the social standing of these Corinthians.[43] The term φυσιόω in v. 6 (cf. also 4.18-19; 5.2; 8.1; 13.4) denotes the arrogance which is typical of people from the upper class, such as are depicted in v. 8.[44] Moreover, the language of v. 7 describes behaviour characteristic of the wealthy and powerful.[45] Thus the contrast in 4.10, as well as in 1.26-28, is a social one in which certain Corinthians belonging to a 'cultivated social elite' are distinguished from Paul and other members of the community of lowly status.[46] As Theissen points out, the Corinthians who enjoyed high social status were a minority, but a dominant minority in the sense that they were probably the most active and influential members in the community.[47] They esteemed the same cultural values as other members of the social elite in Greco-

41. Marshall, *Enmity in Corinth*, p. 210.
42. Marshall, *Enmity in Corinth*, p. 181.
43. Marshall, *Enmity in Corinth*, p. 209.
44. Marshall, *Enmity in Corinth*, pp. 204-206. Marshall classifies the opponents as 'hybrists', a designation he derives from the term ὕβρις. He cites several examples of behaviour of the ὕβρις kind in 1 and 2 Corinthians, but in general the term denotes excessive behaviour. In this context the behaviour implied by Paul's questions in 1 Cor. 4.7 is typical. With regard to this verse Marshall says that 'implicit in such language is the notion of freedom in regard to one's actions of being unrestricted, of an independence which is tantamount to the pursuit of self-interest. This is characteristic of the behaviour of the wealthy and powerful in discussions of ὕβρις and associated ideas in Greek authors' (p. 205).
45. Marshall, *Enmity in Corinth*, p. 205.
46. Marshall, *Enmity in Corinth*, p. 210. See also Theissen, *The Social Setting of Pauline Christianity*, p. 72; S. Bartchy, *First Century Slavery and I Corinthians 7.21* (SBLDS, 11; Missoula, MT: Scholars Press, 1973), p. 141; Meeks, *The First Urban Christians*, pp. 69, 185; and E.A. Judge, 'The Early Christians as a Scholastic Community', *JRH* 1 (1960), pp. 128-30.
47. Theissen, *The Social Setting of Pauline Christianity*, pp. 73, 96. Judge identifies forty people who belong to a cultivated social elite ('The Early Christians as a Scholastic Community', pp. 128-30).

Roman society such as character, education, reputation, wealth and power, and in 1 Cor. 1.10–4.21 these values are the basis of this select group's opposition to Paul.[48]

The objections to Paul's apostleship evident in 1 Cor. 1.10–4.21 bear a striking resemblance to the criticisms in 2 Corinthians 10–13, and this suggests some continuity between his opposition in the two letters. On separate occasions he has been judged weak and dishonoured with respect to the cultural values and conventions of those of high status, and in both instances he is derided for the same reasons: a lack of eloquence in speech (1 Cor. 2.1-4; 2 Cor. 10.10; 11.6; 13.3), an unimpressive physical demeanor (1 Cor. 4.11; 2 Cor. 10.10; 12.10), and working as a craftsman and refusing financial support (1 Cor. 4.12; 9.3-18; 2 Cor. 11.7; 12.13). Also, there is an emphasis on pneumatic performance in both letters. In 1 Corinthians Paul is concerned with the arrogance and excessive behaviour of the pneumatics in Corinth (2.14–3.4; 5.1-2; 8.1ff.; 12–14), while 2 Corinthians reflects their misgivings about his pneumatic deficiencies (12.1-10, 12). That Paul's behaviour, rather than the Corinthians', has become the main focus of attention in 2 Corinthians 10–13 is, in fact, the thing which most distinguishes it from 1 Corinthians, and this must be accounted for by the intrusion of the rival apostles. However, since there was already opposition to Paul from within the community before the rival apostles arrived on the scene, responsibility for the criticisms which comprise the challenge to his apostleship cannot lie solely, or even primarily, with these interlopers. In the light of these factors, it seems likely that the anti-Pauline group in Corinth formed an alliance with the rival apostles and together they engaged in anti-Pauline polemic.[49]

Although the fact of this alliance can be established on the basis of the correspondence between the opposition from within the community in 1 Corinthians and the outside opposition referred to in 2 Corinthians, it is more difficult to ascertain the nature of the relationship between these two groups. This is mainly because the identity of the rival

---

48. Marshall, *Enmity in Corinth*, p. 290. Marshall remarks that these social conventions were the things by which those of high social standing commanded respect (τιμή, δόξα), and through which they exercised influence.

49. Forbes, 'Comparison, Self-Praise and Irony', p. 15; Marshall, *Enmity in Corinth*, pp. 232-33, 263ff.; G. Lüdemann, *Paulus, der Heidenapostel, Band II. Antipaulinismus im frühen Christentum* (Göttingen: Vandenhoeck & Ruprecht, 1983), pp. 128-32.

apostles is still a matter for debate, and hence it is impossible to discern everything they had in common with Paul's enemies in the community. Among those who recognize the collaboration of these two distinct groups, Forbes thinks that the rival apostles are Judaizing Christians engaged in a deliberate anti-Pauline mission on behalf of the Judaizing wing of Palestinian Christianity, while Lüdemann contends that they are attacking Paul because he is pneumatically deficient.[50] But neither of these explanations makes sense of the correlation between the internal opposition of 1 Corinthians and the external opposition of 2 Corinthians. Lüdemann is not justified in subsuming all the criticisms of 2 Corinthians 10–13 under the heading of *Pnuematikertum*, and Forbes's claim that it was an *ad hoc* alliance for diverse social and theological purposes does not sufficiently account for the common perspective shared by the opposition in both 1 and 2 Corinthians. Marshall, on the other hand, sustains the continuity between the opposition in the two letters and asserts that the upper class Christians in Corinth initiated the alliance when they invited apostles of their own to oppose Paul.[51] On the basis of the characteristics implied by the comparisons in chs. 10–12 he places the rival apostles in the mainstream of Greco-Roman cultural convention, and suggests that they more closely represented the social and cultural interests of some of the Corinthians than did Paul.[52] The influential Corinthians sought out the rival apostles because they were better able to fulfill their expectations of an apostle.[53]

While in Corinth these more cultivated rival apostles entered into comparisons among themselves in accordance with common rhetorical

---

50. Forbes, 'Comparison, Self-Praise and Irony', p. 15; Lüdemann, *Paulus, der Heidenapostel, Band II*, pp. 128-32. Forbes suggests that together the two groups constituted a 'united front' with the rival apostles holding a dominant position. Although Lüdemann realizes that the anti-Paulinism in 1 Corinthians is not associated with pneumatic deficiencies on Paul's part, he thinks that his lack of *Pneumatikertum* is the point on which the two anti-Pauline groups converge (p. 132). He sees a connection between the rival apostles and the Jerusalem conference, but argues that they are themselves not from Jerusalem (p. 141).

51. Marshall, *Enmity in Corinth*, p. 265. They did this by letters of recommendation.

52. Marshall, *Enmity in Corinth*, pp. 276-77.

53. Marshall remarks that the rival apostles do not necessarily have better credentials than Paul. Their acceptance must be seen against the background of the Corinthians growing disenchantment with Paul (*Enmity in Corinth*, p. 276).

conventions of σύγκρισις, but, as Forbes suggests, 'the real cutting edge of the comparisons was directed against Paul' (2 Cor. 10.12-13).[54] In 10.12 Paul refers to them as τῶν ἑαυτοὺς συνιστανόντων, which used together with the term συγκρίνω implies that they considered themselves superior.[55] The phrase ἐν ἑαυτοῖς ἑαυτοὺς μετροῦντες means that that they themselves represented the measure, and the standard by which the measuring was done consists of the values which required anapostle to be a cultivated man.[56] Their κανών (10.13b, 15, 16) was one of Greek respectability, comprising the norms of a cultured society,[57] and it is this κανών which is the basis of their criticisms of Paul. Unlike his adversaries, who 'boast beyond measure' with reference to their social κανών, Paul plans to abide by τὸ μέτρον τοῦ κανόνος assigned to him by God (10.13). Nevertheless, even though he has rejected their κανών and their practice of self-comparisons, he goes on to boast as a 'fool', and with biting irony compares himself with his opponents (cf. 11.1–12.10). His use of irony and his conviction that boasting in the manner of his opponents is 'foolish' (11.1, 16) indicates that he has an ulterior motive for entering into comparisons with his rivals. A more detailed examination of 11.1–12.10 will further illuminate the nature of Paul's argument in this passage.

Paul's Reply to the Opposition

Paul depicts the rival apostles as self-recommenders who boast excessively in their mutual comparisons and thus show that they are without understanding (10.12-13). But despite his negative appraisal of their comparisons and boasting, in 12.11 he claims that the Corinthians have forced him to engage in the very practice he has just

---

54. Forbes, 'Comparison, Self-Praise and Irony', p. 15. He agrees with Marshall's claim that Paul was at enmity with the Corinthians, and suggests that studied mutual comparisons would have been the expected thing between enemies. For a detailed discussion of the methods of σύγκρισις, see pp. 2-8.

55. Marshall, *Enmity in Corinth*, p. 199. According to Marshall συγκρίνω, συνίστημι and μέτρον are technical terms from rhetoric which were central to the nature of the conflict between Paul and his enemies.

56. Marshall, *Enmity in Corinth*, pp. 326-27.

57. Marshall, *Enmity in Corinth*, pp. 368-69. Marshall asserts that κανών, like μέτρον, is used by Greek authors with a moral sense to denote the limits of appropriate conduct and can be translated as 'standard' or 'measure'.

5. *The Social Significance of the Death of Jesus* 177

renounced because they have themselves failed to commend him. Throughout chs. 10–12 Paul employs the same rhetorical techniques of σύγκρισις as his opponents, but, in contrast to them he regards the whole enterprise as 'foolishness' (11.1, 16, 17; 12.11). This judgment expresses not only his opinion about the practice of boasting itself; it is also an ironical indictment of the rival apostles and, to a lesser extent, the Corinthians. Betz has shown that in Hellenism 'self-glorification' falls into the category of ἀλαζόεία, and the ἀλαζών is the 'fool'. Understood in this context, the 'fool' is someone who has lost awareness of his own human limitations, and this is precisely what Paul has accused the rival apostles of in 10.12-13.[58] By playing the 'fool' in 11.1-33, he is simply mimicking their excessive conduct, and thus by implication suggesting that it is they who are really the 'fools'.[59] Moreover, he sarcastically insinuates that it is necessary for him to assume the guise of a 'fool' for the sake of the Corinthians because they 'gladly bear with fools', as is evidenced in their willingness to be taken advantage of by the intruders (11.19-20). Having designated his role as the 'fool', Paul then goes on to indulge the opposition in their own game of σύγκρισις, and in so doing he demonstrates his ability to utilize popular rhetorical devices.

It is significant that the rhetorical skills which the alliance prized so highly, and criticized Paul for lacking, are skilfully employed by Paul in this section to refute, or 'tear down', the case they have constructed against him. Judge asserts that it is beyond doubt that Paul was familiar with the rhetorical fashions of the time, and therefore it is reasonable to assume that up to this point he had deliberately refrained from exploiting any competence he had in this area.[60] In these chapters, however, he is completely unrestrained in his use of rhetorical

---

58. Betz, *Der Apostel Paulus und die sokratische Tradition*, pp. 24-25.

59. Marshall (*Enmity in Corinth*), Forbes ('Comparison, Self-Praise and Irony'), Betz (*Der Apostel Paulus und die sokratische Tradition*) and E.A. Judge ('Paul's Boasting in Relation to Contemporary Professional Practice', *Australian Biblical Review* [1968]) all think that 10.12-13 is the key to the boasting passage. According to Marshall, Paul is drawing on the language of moderation to commend his own apostolic behaviour, and of immoderation to discredit his enemies (*Enmity in Corinth*, pp. 201-202).

60. Judge, 'Paul's Boasting', p. 41. In another article Judge characterizes Paul as 'a person highly placed in every social scale that mattered', and this included his style of speech, which placed him in the mainstream of educated public figures' ('St Paul as a Radical Critic of Society, p. 191).

conventions. Paul's main rhetorical weapon here is 'parody', which according to Betz is a polemic device that uses irony to expose opponents.⁶¹ He provides two parodies of aretologies which represent criteria of apostleship that are important to the opposition. First, the appeal to visions and revelations in 12.1-10 may on the surface appear to be a concession to their demand for him to exhibit the 'signs of an apostle' (12.12), but Paul gives this account of his being 'caught up into Paradise' (12.2, 4) an ironic twist when he tells the Corinthians of the 'unspeakable' things which he heard (12.4). The conspicuous absence of the content of the visions and revelations renders them 'useless' (οὐ συμφέρον), as he had warned they would be in 12.1.⁶² The second parody concerns a 'healing miracle' with no results, and thus also 'useless' (12.7-9). Both parodies illustrate in an impressive way that one could claim to display 'the signs of an apostle' without producing the evidence, and this in turn exposes the 'foolishness' of the criteria in terms of which his opponents boast.

Speaking as a 'fool' in 12.1-10 Paul has effectively demonstrated that pneumatic experiences are no real cause for boasting, but (as has been suggested) pneumatic phenomena were neither the most important criterion or criticism in the opponents' attack on Paul. The purpose of the parody, though, was not only to undermine the ground of his rivals' boasting, but also to establish what he considered the only legitimate ground of boasting—his weakness (12.9-10). Betz is right, then, when he says that all of Paul's statements in the 'foolish discourse' have a double meaning. In addition to refuting his adversaries' concept of καυχᾶσθαι δει, he also affirms theslogan in his own way.⁶³ Paul

---

61. Betz, *Der Apostel Paulus und die sokratische Tradition*, pp. 82-84. Betz points out the similarities between Paul's discourse and the literary form of the 'foolish discourse', but he pushes the parallel to extremes when he suggests that Paul is dependent on the literary form. Parody was a common rhetorical device apart from this particular use.

62. Betz, *Der Apostel Paulus und die sokratische Tradition*, pp. 89-92. Betz shows that Paul makes his ironic point by a play on words. The phrase ἄρρητα ῥήματα can mean two things, 'unspeakable' in the sense of 'ineffable', and 'not to be told'. The expected meaning with regard to heavenly revelations is 'ineffable', but Paul refers to the other meaning according to which he is not allowed to reveal esoteric revelations. R. Spittler designates this phrase an oxymoron and asks: how can 'words' be 'unutterable'? ('The Limits of Ecstasy: An Exegesis of 2 Corinthians 12.1-10', in *Current Issues in Biblical and Patristic Interpretation*, p. 263).

63. Betz, *Der Apostel Paul und die sokratische Tradition*, pp. 93-94.

concludes the parody by asserting that he can boast legitimately, that is, not as a 'fool', only of his weakness (12.9). He puts forward the thesis that God's 'power is made perfect in weakness', and thereby redefines boasting and weakness from the perspective of the gospel.[64]

In 11.21b-33 Paul, again 'speaking as a fool', provides another parody of his opponents' self-advertisement, but here his use of irony is more constructive. In addition to undermining the achievements his opponents boasted of, he also presents an antithetical set of values and criteria by boasting, even if ironically, of his weakness. First, he merely acknowledges their claim to be 'Hebrews', 'Israelites' and 'descendants of Abraham' while maintaining that he can boast of the same credentials (11.22);[65] but with reference to their claim to be 'servants of Christ', he asserts that he is a better one because of his 'greater labours', 'more imprisonments' and 'countless beatings' (11.23). Paul's point is not that he is superior to his rivals because he has suffered more than they, but rather that being a 'servant of Christ' is defined by weakness, not the qualities which they boasted about. As Spittler remarks, the hardship catalogue of 11.22-28 is not an attempt to outdo the rivals, but a polemical shift to a different ground for boasting, namely weakness.[66] In the hardship catalogue Paul describes in detail the things which show his weakness. Although the catalogue consists of the same features of his apostolate for which he was criticized, here they are the basis of his boasting (11.30). What begins in 11.16 as a highly ironical comparison with the rival apostles and a parody of their self-praise,[67] becomes, with the introduction of the hardship catalogue, a serious attempt to establish the criteria which make one an authentic 'servant of Christ'. Paul deliberately pictures himself as inferior according to the oppositions' standards, and boasts of the things which mark him as a man of shame according to socially accepted values.[68]

64. A.B. Spencer, 'The Wise Fool (and the Foolish Wise): A Study of Irony in Paul', *NovT* 23 (1981), p. 357.
65. Betz points out that the matter of one's 'good breeding' was a standard topic of Hellenistic rhetoric. In claiming the same credentials Paul is following the conventions of σύγκρισις (*Der Apostel Paulus und die sokratische Tradition*, p. 97).
66. Spittler, 'The Limits of Ecstasy', p. 260.
67. Forbes, 'Comparison, Self-Praise and Irony', p. 2. Paul is being ironic, even sarcastic, in 11.18-21 when he says in v. 21 that he was 'too weak' to take advantage of the Corinthians in the same manner as the rival apostles.
68. Marshall, *Enmity in Corinth*, pp. 351-52.

In 11.21a Paul, with tongue in cheek, concedes that he was in fact 'too weak' to take advantage of the Corinthians as the opponents had done. If being weak means refusing to manipulate those whom the apostle serves, then Paul prefers to be weak. Although this ironic statement is a counter-criticism of the rival apostles and the Corinthians who 'gladly bear with fools', Paul also develops the positive significance of his weakness in the hardship catalogue in 11.23-28. His affirmation of the social humiliation implied by the catalogue is not just an ironic comparison with the excessive and abusive behaviour of the rival apostles, but, more importantly, an attempt to set forth an alternative conception of authentic apostolic existence.[69] One reason Paul can positively appraise his weakness is that it enables him to participate in the weakness of those he serves as an apostle. This is the meaning of the rhetorical question in 11.29: 'Who is weak, and I am not weak? Who is made to fall, and I am not indignant?' This verse is the summary and climax of 11.21-29.[70] It explains that Paul boasts only of the things that show his weakness because it is out of this weakness that he is able to identify with the 'weak' in the community, and it is the ability to comfort those who are 'weak' which by his standards qualifies him as a 'better' servant of Christ (cf. 2 Cor. 1.3-7; 1 Cor. 12.26). This corresponds to other places in chs. 10–13 where Paul boasts of his care and concern for the community (cf. 11.2, 10-11; 12.14-15).

With this interpretation of his weakness, which reverses the negative verdict of his opponents, Paul is indirectly approaching the idea of οἰκοδομή. He insisted at the outset that this was the aim of his boasting (10.8) and later on asserts that it is the purpose of his polemic (12.19; 13.10), but his use of irony and parody bear witness to the subtlety of his argument and the covert means by which he intended to accomplish this goal. Nevertheless, the hardship catalogues and his consistent endorsement of weakness throughout the letter provide the key to his strategy. Paul has been criticized by the opposition for various charac-

---

69. Forbes correctly observes that although Paul boasts ironically in order to satirize the boasting of his opponents, this does not rule out the possibility that his boasting contains serious points. He remarks that 'Paul is presenting a case for a radically different conception of authority through his irony' ('Comparison, Self-Praise and Irony', p. 20).

70. M.L. Barre, 'Paul as Eschatological Person: A New Look at 2 Cor. 11.29', *CBQ* 37 (1975), pp. 517.

5. *The Social Significance of the Death of Jesus*

teristics which mark him as socially inferior according to the social values current in Greco-Roman society. Instead of denying the accusations against him and making an effort to defend himself, Paul accentuates his social inferiority in order to distance himself as much as possible from their conventional values. Not only does he deride himself with reference to these values, he glories in his failure to attain the ideal of the cultivated person which they have imposed on him. The consequences of this response are twofold. On the one hand, his parodies of the rival apostles' self-praise function to refute the values and conventions on which it is based. On the other hand, and in a more positive vein, the characterization of his life of weakness, with all of its social connotations, functions more constructively to define a contrary set of values which is derived from the gospel, and which he embodies in his apostolic ministry. These are the values which facilitate οἰκοδομη. They have a christological foundation in the crucified Christ (13.4), and it is the weakness exemplified in the crucifixion in particular which in this context informs Paul's understanding of apostolic and Christian existence and has caused him to renounce those things which were equated with power and status in Greco-Roman society.

Paul makes express mention of the death of Christ only in 13.4 where he invokes the image of the Christ who 'was crucified in weakness and lives by the power of God'. But it is apparent that his affirmative assessment of his own weakness has its origins in this interpretation of the Christ-event. This is evidenced especially in the fact that he emphasizes the weakness of the crucified Christ in order to demonstrate the christological basis for his own weakness.[71] In other places Paul grounds his identity, as well as Christian identity in general,

---

71. The importance of the christological foundation of Paul's argument in chs. 10–13 is supported by his opening remark in 10.1 where he links the 'humble' presence for which he has been criticized (cf. 10.10) with the 'meekness and gentleness of Christ'. Whether Paul is here referring to the characteristics of the earthly Jesus (so Plummer, *Second Epistle of St Paul to the Corinthians*, p. 273; Kümmel, Supplemental notes to Lietzmann's *An die Korinther I, II*, p. 208) or to the kenotic Christology of Phil. 2.6-11 (so Bultmann, *The Second Letter to the Corinthians*, p. 182; Furnish, *II Corinthians*, p. 460) is, as Barrett remarks, not as important as the fundamental emphasis on the parallel between Jesus' behaviour and his own (Barrett, *The Second Epistle to the Corinthians*, p. 246, and Martin, *2 Corinthians*, p. 302 emphasize the relationship between the earthly life of Jesus and his condescension in becoming incarnate).

in the death of Christ (e.g. Rom. 6.1-11; Gal. 2.20; 6.14) and understands his suffering as participation in that death (e.g. 2 Cor. 4.8-12; Phil. 3.10). But it is notable that in chs. 10–13 he focuses exlusively on weakness—both his and Christ's (10.10; 11.21, 29-30; 12.5, 9-10; 13.4, 9).[72] The perspective underlying these chapters is that his weakness is authorized by the weakness represented in the crucifixion of Christ. Thus Paul's reference to the weakness of the crucified Christ in 13.4 validates the preceding explanation of the theme of weakness as it relates to his apostleship.[73] But since the main connotation of weakness as it pertains to Paul throughout chs. 10–13 is social shame according to the cultural values of Greco-Roman society, the primary significance of the death of Christ must also be social in this context. In his argument Paul rejects the values which are shared by the opponents from within and without the community in Corinth, and substitutes in their place an antithetical set of values based on a christological paradigm that affirms the continued efficacy of the weakness of the crucified Christ (13.4a).

The negative function of Paul's double-edged polemic is to undermine the very foundation upon which the opposition has constructed its attack against him, but this is only a means to an end. His main objective is to 'build up' the community (13.10), and he can accomplish this only if he discredits the opponents. He needs to 'tear down' the 'strongholds' (10.4) erected by these intruders not just because their arguments have called his authority as an apostle into question, although this seems to be the case, but above all because their influence has resulted in the disobedience of certain Corinthian Christians (cf. 10.5-6; 11.1-4; 12.20-21). Although the Corinthians have doubts about his status as an apostle, the issue for him is whether he will have to be severe in his use of the authority the Lord has given him when he returns to Corinth (13.10; cf. 10.8). It seems unlikely that Paul is insecure about the matter of his authority, even if the Corinthians have given him reason to be, for it is something he presupposes. Rather, his concern is with the behaviour of the Corinthians. The reason Paul felt he might have to exercise his apostolic authority for a purpose other than that which was intended is that he suspects the Corinthians' behaviour will not reflect their commitment to Christ, that is, that

---

72. This is also true in 1 Cor. 1–4, which reflects the same problems at issue in chs. 10–13 (cf. 1 Cor. 1.18–2.5; 4.1-13).

73. Cf. Furnish, *II Corinthians*, p. 577.

5. *The Social Significance of the Death of Jesus* 183

'there may be quarreling, jealousy, anger, selfishness, slander, gossip, conceit and disorder' (12.20). Therefore he wrote to secure their obedience to Christ.

The Conflict in Values Underlying Paul's Dispute with the Corinthians

Paul's response to the opposition's criticisms of his behaviour and his apprehensiveness about the Corinthians' behaviour are both fundamentally related to a quandary centred around values. I have argued that the conflict between Paul and his opponents concerned the validity of Greco-Roman social conventions, and that Paul deliberately rejected their ideal of the cultivated person in favour of weakness. If I am right in contending that Paul's agenda is different from the Corinthians in that he is more concerned about their behaviour than he is about their opinion of his, then his commentary on weakness, personal though it may be, must have implications for the interpersonal problems within the community. Therefore the weakness motif will be examined in more detail, keeping in mind that the cultural values and conventions that Paul repudiates are adhered to by an elite group of Corinthian Christians who are of high social standing. This group was a source of the divisions in the community which Paul addressed in 1 Corinthians (cf. 1.10-17; 11.17-22), and together with the rival apostles they are also the cause of the problems he has in view in 2 Corinthians. Since his conversation is with the Corinthians, and not the rival apostles, it seems likely that this group is the target of his polemic.

The question, of course, is what does Paul's christological interpretation of weakness have to do with his concern about the Corinthians' misconduct, and how does he expect it to effect οἰκοδομή in the community? In order to ascertain how these community concerns coalesce with his reply to the criticisms against him, it is necessary to consider his discussion of weakness in conjunction with the converse theme of power. In both the christological formulation in 13.4 and the anthropological application of that Christology in 12.9-10 there is a dialectical relationship between weakness and power which is integral to Paul's argument. The dialectic is grounded theologically in the death and resurrection of Christ (13.4a), but its importance with respect to the situation Paul is confronting in the community is disclosed in 13.3b where he says: 'He is not weak in dealing with you, but is powerful in you'. A touch of irony can be detected in this remark. Moreover, it suggests that the Corinthians thought of Christ as being powerful in them, and it is this consciousness of Christ's power which prompted them to require Paul to supply proof that Christ was working in him, either through eloquent speech (13.3) or pneumatic phenomenon (12.12).[74] Thus the criticisms of his apostleship and the basic charge that he was weak have their origin in a perspective which equated power with the overt display of personal qualities which were characteristic of a cultured person of high status: impressive physical appearance (10.1, 10), eloquent speech (10.10; 11.6; 13.3), achievements (12.1-10) and so on.[75]

This understanding of power was also the cause of the kind of behaviour depicted in 12.20, and thus it is the common denominator connecting the oppositions' attack on Paul with his attempt to 'build up' the community in the light of his concern about the apparent incongruity between their lifestyle and the gospel he preached to them (10.6; 11.2-4; 13.5-7). Paul's objective was to reform this distorted notion of power which had set the Corinthians against him and against one another, but in order to do that he had to subvert the values in which it was embedded. His positive assessment of weakness and his appeal to the weakness of the crucified Christ in 13.4 is not, then, primarily an attempt to legitimate his own weakness in the face of criticisms. Rather, he juxtaposes the theme of weakness with the theme of power in order to argue for an alternative, even if paradoxical, way of construing power.[76] If Paul's intention was merely to defend his own weakness, then he should have emphasized only that Christ 'was crucified in weakness' (13.4a). However, the ἀλλά connecting the two clauses of the christological assertion is an adversative stressing the fact that Christ now 'lives by the power of God'.[77] The importance

74. It was noted in the section on the criticisms of Paul that eloquent speech was most important to his opponents within the community. According to Betz, rhetorical skill could have been regarded as proof of a speaker's possession of the Spirit (*Der Apostel Paulus und die sokratische Tradition*, pp. 58-59).

75. Barrett rightly notes that the Corinthians judged between Paul and the rival apostles 'on essentially Hellenistic grounds' ('Paul's Opponents in II Corinthians', p. 80). Martin similarly describes the Corinthian notion of power as the display of 'an aggressive and a mighty personality', but he does not recognize the Hellenistic cultural origins of this understanding (Martin, *2 Corinthians*, p. 477).

76. Meeks, *The First Urban Christians*, p. 183.

77. BDF, p. 448.

5. *The Social Significance of the Death of Jesus* 185

of Paul's interpretation of weakness, which is grounded in the fact that Christ was 'crucified in weakness', is that it informs the conception of power he is advocating.

Paul sets a christological conception of power which incorporates the weakness of the crucifixion over against the misconception of power which stands behind the criticisms of him and the interpersonal problems in the community. These two contrary conceptions of power can be differentiated in terms of the values to which they correspond. Values can be concisely defined as 'criteria for judgement, preference, and choice', or 'standards in terms of which evaluations are made', and it is such criteria or standards that are fundamentally at issue throughout the letter.[78] With regard to the charges against him, Paul has conceded that most of them are warranted and he admits that by the standards in terms of which he is being evaluated he is indeed weak. So it is not so much the criticisms as the criteria which are the basis of those criticisms that he challenges in his counter-argument.

Values, 'as standards (criteria) for establishing what should be regarded as desirable', also influence behaviour and in that sense the values held by the Corinthians pertain to any social discord that occurred within the community. Although values are not the same as norms for conduct, they provide the ground for accepting or rejecting particular norms.[79] The same values according to which Paul is deprecated as an apostle are also the cause of 'quarreling, jealousy, anger, selfishness, slander, gossip, conceit and disorder' (12.20), and therefore he responds to the personal criticisms leveled against him at a foundational level with a view to reforming them. Before considering how Paul aims to accomplish this, it will be helpful to discern in more detail the conflicting values underlying the dispute. It is possible to identify the socially effective standards that are actually operating in a group or society 'by observing which behaviours are praised and other-

---

78. Cf. R. Williams, 'Values', in the *International Encyclopedia of the Social Sciences*, XVI, p. 283.

79. Williams, 'Values', p. 284. The main difference between norms and values is that values 'are standards of desirability that are more nearly independent of specific situations'. However, 'as one moves along a scale of increasing generality, in which norms become more and more detached from particular circumstances, a point eventually will be reached at which "norm" becomes practically indistinguishable from "value"'.

wise rewarded and which are criticized, condemned, or punished'.[80]

The values which the Corinthians imposed on Paul in their critique of his apostleship have been identified as those which were normative among the social elite in Greco-Roman society. Despite their socio-cultural origins, however, these values have a distinctively theological character for the Corinthian Christians. The decisive element common to both the social and theological formation of these values is an emphasis on the external exhibition of power. This power could be manifested in a variety of ways, both secular and religious; but in Corinth any such outward displays of power would have been interpreted theologically, even if there was nothing inherently theological about them, as for example with rhetorical skills and physical appearance. The Corinthians did have a special affinity to specifically religious manifestations of power such as charismatic phenomena, miracles, visions and revelations, but irrespective of whether or not the external manifestations of power which they prized were essentially religious or secular they were equated with God's power. Moreover, the demonstration of God's power through manifestations of the Spirit and glory of Christ was thought to make the person who mediated it powerful (cf. 2 Cor. 13.3b).

Paul confronted these values and the notion of power associated with them in 3.7-18 where his midrash on Moses and the old covenant opposes the Corinthians' dependence upon external qualities as evidence of the glory of God.[81] His allusion to the activity of the rival apostles in the community in 3.1-6 suggests that his exposition is a protest against the claim that their ecstatically radiant faces verify that they are true messengers of God (cf. 5.12).[82] The Corinthians had apparently been seized by the impressive appearance of these rival apostles, who convinced them that their faces resembled the glory of Moses' face. They accentuated Paul's weakness and stirred up further doubts about the authenticity of his apostleship. Against the rival apostles' appeal to the face of Moses as the paradigm of the visible display of

80. Williams, 'Values', p. 285. Williams asserts that 'content analysis of verbal materials is often a suitable technique in this connection; identification of implicit assumptions in social discourse often reveals values not otherwise readily discovered'.

81. W.H. Smith, Jr, 'The Function of 2 Corinthians 3.7–4.6 in its Epistolary Context' (unpublished PhD dissertation, Southern Baptist Theological Seminary, 1983), p. 156.

82. W.H. Smith, Jr, 'The Function of 2 Corinthians 3.7–4.6', p. 156.

God's glory, followed of course by the Corinthians, Paul points to the face of Christ (4.6) as the definitive revelation of God's glory (3.10-11). He asserts that the observable glory of Moses' face has been superceded by 'the knowledge of the glory of God in the face of Christ' (4.6). The designation of Christ as the 'image of God' (4.4) and his face as the place where God's glory is manifested must have for Paul incorporated the significance of his death on the cross. In fact, Paul's intention in this passage may have been to declare a clear relationship between the glory of God and the crucified Christ.[83] In 1 Cor. 2.8 it is evident that for him it is precisely as the crucified one that Christ is 'the Lord of glory', and it is because this revelation of God's glory in Christ is paradoxical that his gospel is veiled to those who are unable to recognize it (4.3-4).[84]

The conception of glory Paul responds to in Corinth has more in common with the Greco-Roman values than his own gospel, but because glory is intrinsic to the gospel he attempts to modify their understanding of it rather than dismiss it wholesale. He does this not only by emphasizing that 'the gospel of the glory of Christ' is veiled (4.3), but also by showing the provisional and indirect way in which it is apprehended. This is the point in 3.18 where Paul says that 'we all, with unveiled faces, beholding the glory of the Lord, are being changed into his likeness from one degree of glory to another'. He uses the verb κατοπτρίζω in order to make the point that to behold the glory of the Lord is to have only a mirror-type reflection of it in the gospel.[85] This is not a direct vision of the Lord or his glory, and, by the same token, the Christian's being transformed ἀπὸ δόξης εἰς δόξαν does not entail the full realization of this glory. Both the apprehension and manifestation of the glory of God accord with the provisional and paradoxical character of the gospel. Most importantly, Christians are transformed into 'the same image' reflected in 'the gospel of the glory of Christ', which means that the glory they exhibit is analogous to the glory of the crucified Lord. Thus Paul affirms in 4.7-12 that in his apostolate God's glory is manifested in the context of adversity.

Paul advances the theme of glory in 4.7-12 where he elaborates on

---

83. W.H. Smith, Jr, 'The Function of 2 Corinthians 3.7–4.6', p. 163.
84. Furnish, *II Corinthians*, p. 248. Smith says that 'the linkage of the glory of God and the face of Christ further clarifies Paul's assertion of a "veiled gospel" (4.3)' ('The Function of 2 Corinthians 3.7–4.6', p. 163).
85. J. Lambrecht, 'Transformation in 2 Cor 3,18', *Bib* 64 (1983), p. 250.

it with reference to his own apostleship. I have examined the relationship of the glory motif to other themes in this passage in the preceding chapter, and I am interested in it here only as it reflects the values underlying his two-dimensional dispute with the Corinthians. The two conceptions of glory which Paul contrasts in 3.7–4.18 are indicative of the incongruous values which correspond to them, and it is these values that are the crux of the conflict.

The predominant notion of glory among the Corinthians implies values or 'criteria for judgment' which were oriented exclusively to external appearance and demeanour, and other Christians, including apostles, are either praised or criticized accordingly. From Paul's point of view, the problem with these values and the respective understanding of glory is that eschatological reserve is excluded. Hence, in 4.13-18 he attempts to reinstate his eschatological perspective in the community by referring the 'eternal weight of glory' (which the Corinthians think they have witnessed in the rival apostles) to the future (4.17), and by distinguishing between 'the external' (ὁ ἔξω, which is 'wasting away') and 'the inward' (ὁ ἔσω, which is 'being renewed every day') and by emphasizing the priority of 'eternal' (αἰώνια) things that are 'unseen' over the 'transient' (πρόσκαιρα) things that are 'seen' (4.16-18). This eschatological perspective is further developed in 5.1-10, and (as has been seen) culminates with the epistemological insight of 5.16-17. What is significant with regard to values is that both epistemology and glory, concepts that imply criteria by which evaluations are made, are defined in terms of an eschatological conception of reality which has as its focal point the death of Christ.[86] The result is that value judgments can no longer be made κατὰ σάρκα because temporal norms and values that give prominence only to that which is seen have been abrogated by the proleptic arrival of the new creation (5.16-17). The values which replace them are derived from the eschatological Christ-event. In other words, the Christ who 'was crucified in weakness, but lives by the power of God' (13.4) has become the definitive standard of evaluation for those who participate in the new age.

The different ideas of glory delineated in the above excursus betray certain values which were attached to them. The oppositions' values conform to Greco-Roman social values, but they find expression in

---

86. This accords with Berger and Luckmann's claim that *knowledge* precedes *values* (*The Social Construction of Reality*, p. 111).

5. *The Social Significance of the Death of Jesus* 189

theological symbols such as glory, Spirit, the power of God and so on. The one constant uniting the theological symbols ascribed to them is that they all represent divine power in one form or another, and it can be inferred from Paul's remarks that the divine power they symbolize serves to legitimate the social display of power with which they appear to be preoccupied. This kind of power was one of the lines that marked off the principal value of honour, which in the Mediterranean world was understood as 'a claim to worth along with the social acknowledgement of worth'.[87] This pivotal value of honour and its concomitants, especially power, determined the opposition's understanding of the gospel in such a way that it was devoid of an adequate eschatological perspective and an appreciation of the significance of Christ's death. In addition to that, it also determined his critic's negative attitude toward Paul and the problematic social stratification within the community. The centrality of this value for them is supported by the onesidedness of their theology, at least as it is described by Paul.

Once the connection between the theological and social aspects of the dispute is recognized, the ulterior social considerations underlying the entire theological dialogue can be discerned. This is as true for Paul as it is for the opposition, and so he proposes an alternative set of values which is constructed on an eschatological interpretation of the Christ-event. For example, in chs. 1–7 love is the positive value which sums up his 'system of criteria by which conduct is judged and sanctions applied'.[88] He argues that the authenticity of apostolic existence, and for that matter Christian existence in general, is to be decided on the basis of whether or not it corresponds to the love exemplified in Christ's death for all (5.14-15). Paul affirms that love is the absolute value established by the eschatological event of Christ's death which has relativized the temporal values implied by the notions of the glory, power and Spirit of God that he is countering.[89]

87. Cf. Malina, *The New Testament World*, pp. 25-35.
88. Williams, 'Values', p. 288. This is a concise definition of a value system. 'Theoretically, it is the patterned or structural criteria, explicit and implicit, by reference to which evaluative behaviour becomes intelligible. Functionally, it is the set of principles whereby conduct is directed and regulated and a guide for individuals and the social group.'
89. Paul puts forward a similar argument in 1 Cor. 13 where he concedes the immediate value of spiritual gifts for the life of the community but then goes on to recommend the more excellent way of love, which, unlike spiritual gifts, belongs to the age to come.

The same values which are at issue in chs. 1–7 are disclosed in a more explicit manner in the criticisms of Paul's apostleship in chs. 10–13. In the former section where Paul explains the nature of his apostleship, the fundamental discrepancy of values is couched in theological terms because his intention is to provide a theological interpretation of his apostolate. However, in chs. 10–13 the values which are implicit in the previous theological discussion come expressly to the fore as the debate becomes more focused on the personal characteristics of the two competing apostolic ministries. The oppositions' values are revealed in their criticisms of Paul, while Paul makes known the values he is trying to instate—or perhaps reinstate—in his response to these criticisms. In this context Paul and the rival apostles personify the values they represent, and the Corinthians' disenchantment with Paul reflects the Greco-Roman social values they had in common with the intruders. These interlopers were only able to gain a foothold in the community because an elite group of Corinthian Christians already had a predisposition to such things as honour, status and power, the very features they sought to exemplify in their apostleship. Thus the place of theology in the Corinthians' attraction to the rival apostles and their critique of Paul was probably secondary.[90] Both the Corinthian opposition and the rival apostles subordinated theology to performance, which is consistent with Berger and Luckmann's analysis of this type of social conflict. They assert that in a rivalry such as this judgments are based on a kind of pseudopragmatism, and the outcome is decided primarily by extra-theoretical, or in this case extra-theological interests.[91] The rival apostles were preferred to Paul because what they had to offer was seen to be more pragmatically relevant to the collective needs and interests of the community, at least as they were defined by the dominant group of higher status Christians.[92] In a word, they reinforced the Greco-Roman social values espoused by this group.

90. Cf. Hickling, 'Is the Second Letter to the Corinthians a Source for Early Church History?', p. 287; Furnish, *II Corinthians*, p. 53.

91. Berger and Luckmann, *The Social Construction of Reality*, p. 138. They assert that 'a theory is *demonstrated* to be pragmatically superior not by virtue of its intrinsic qualities, but by its applicability to the social interests of the group that has become its *carrier*'.

92. Since authority among members of the community seems to lie primarily in the hands of the higher status Christians, it is their needs and interests that are determinative for the whole community.

5. The Social Significance of the Death of Jesus 191

It was with reference to these values that Paul was criticized for being weak, and it is against this backdrop that he develops the power in weakness theme which pervades chs. 10–13. Against the opposition's view that weakness and power are mutually exclusive, he argues for the coherence of these two seemingly antithetical characteristics. Paul's position is distinguished from theirs, however, not only by the fact that he holds that weakness and power are indissoluble, but because the ground of this conviction is the theological dialectic of the death and resurrection of Christ. In contrast to the opposition, for him weakness and power have an objective point of reference in the theological symbols of the death and resurrection of Christ. Existentially these symbols refer to a Christian lifestyle defined by the objective reality which they mediate. Although there is always a dialectic between symbols and the experience they shape, Paul gives priority to the theological meaning of these symbols in order to influence the social life of the community. He seems to think that the opponents have reversed this process, appealing to certain theological symbols in order to legitimate an interest in social power. Käsemann probably expresses Paul's viewpoint when he says that the opponents have no objective basis for the lifestyle they exemplify (cf. 10.12).[93] Since values and behaviour are the decisive points at issue in his dialogue with the Corinthians, this perceived difference between him and his opponents is the cutting edge of the conflict.

Paul has been judged weak by his opponents solely with respect to the social conventions of Greco-Roman society, but with the christological paradigm of 13.4 he introduces the theological aspect of both weakness and power. The two apostolates personify not only the diametrically opposed values implied by the terms weakness and power, they also embody respective interpretations of Christian life and reality which coincide with these values, and it is in this sense that the dispute involves more than a personal contest. According to Berger and Luckmann reality is socially defined, but the definitions are always embodied, that is, 'concrete individuals and groups of individuals serve as definers of reality'.[94] What I am suggesting is that although it is the personal features of the two apostolates that are highlighted in the comparisons in chs. 10–13, Paul and his opponents embody two radically diverse representations of Christian reality which have

93. Käsemann, 'Die Legitimität des Apostels', p. 59
94. Berger and Luckmann, *The Social Construction of Reality*, p. 134.

important consequences for the social life of the community. His concern about the Corinthians' obedience, along with his stated purpose of building them up (10.6, 8; 12.19; 13.5-6, 10) and the reference to specific behavioural problems in 12.20, all allude to the negative effect the opposition has had in the community. In the light of this and the fact that Paul has in a more irenic tone already provided a theological explanation of his weakness in 4.7-12, I contend that his polemic is addressed primarily to this situation. The difficulty is that the two incongruous interpretations of the Christian life in question are inseparable from the apostles who embody them.[95] Thus Paul sets forth values appropriate to an authentic model of Christian existence by demonstrating how his apostleship reflects the weakness *and* power of the crucified and risen Christ.

The Social Significance of the Weakness and Power of Christ

The terms weakness and power have a dual meaning for both Paul and his opponents in that they are used as rhetoric of status and to refer to existential participation in the death and resurrection of Christ. These two nuances overlap to the extent that in some contexts it is difficult to differentiate between them. The one difference that has been noted with respect to the two apostolates is that of sequence. While the opponents give every indication of working from their compliance with Greco-Roman conventions of status emphasizing honour and power to a legitimation of that compliance through recourse to theological symbols such as glory and pneumatic power, Paul advocates a distinctively Christian order of status and values shaped by the symbols of Christ's death and resurrection. It is not, then, just in giving precedence to these symbols, but rather in preserving the dialectical relationship between death and resurrection, weakness and power, that Paul is distinguished from his opponents. Although weakness is epitomized in the cross of Christ, a symbol of immense authority for Christians, the opponents thought that any material display of it was inconsistent with

---

95. Schütz's observation that the problem of criteria is central to the dispute is similar to my contention that the conflict is fundamentally one of values. However, he does not recognize the implications of this problem for the wider community. He is right, nevertheless, when he says that neither Paul's nor the opponents' criteria, or κανών is detachable from their apostolic ἐγώ. This, he suggests, is what makes the argument so elusive (*The Anatomy of Apostolic Authority*, p. 171).

the pneumatic power and glory characteristic of the Christian life because for them it denoted social inferiority. Paul, on the other hand, affirmed his experiences of weakness precisely because they identified him with the crucified Christ, but this did not for him preclude the coterminous experience of the power of God (cf. 12.9-10; 13.4). The logic which controls his consolidation of weakness and power is the key to ascertaining the social significance of these twin themes in chs. 10–13. The conception of power he sets over against that of his opposition is inseparable from his interpretation of weakness; but since it is on the nature and function of weakness that he elaborates, the meaning of power must be delineated in terms of its correlation to weakness.[96]

The purposefulness with which Paul embraces his weakness, that is, his social humiliation, makes the position which he adopts in chs. 10–13 even more radical than if he had merely defended himself as a victim of circumstance. In view of the educational background reflected by his proficiency in rhetoric and his Roman citizenship, Judge has argued that Paul intentionally abandoned the security of established status in his own life, and he explains the reason for his conscious debasement in this way:

> As a convert to the persecuted Jesus, paradoxically discovered from the very depths of that humiliation to be anointed Israel's Messiah (Acts 2.36), Paul consciously sought the reversal of his own socio-cultural expectations. It was the expression of his identification with Christ in weakness, and he expected his converts to follow him in it.[97]

In contrast to the notions of self-cultivation and self-preservation associated with the ideal person in Greek culture, Paul was led by analogy with Christ crucified to an opposite ideal of the man who gives himself for others (cf. 2 Cor. 5.14-15).[98] Thus he affirms that he is weak in Christ (13.4) not because there is any intrinsic value in being weak *per se*, but because in the weakness of the crucifixion Christ epitomizes existence for others.[99] It is by virtue of his identification with the weakness of Christ that Paul can say he is a better servant of Christ (11.23), for his definition of weakness is derived from his understanding of the death of Christ. Nonetheless, the correspondence

---

96. Cf. G. O'Collins, 'Power Made Perfect in Weakness: 2 Cor 12.9-10', *CBQ* 33 (1971), pp. 528-37.
97. Judge, 'Cultural Conformity and Innovation in Paul', p. 14.
98. Judge, 'St Paul as a Radical Critic of Society', p. 195.
99. See the discussion of 2 Cor. 5.14-15 in Chapter 4.

between his weakness and the weakness of the crucified Christ includes more than just the idea of service or self-sacrifice, as the hardship catalogue following his claim to be a better servant of Christ indicates (11.23-28). He endures the same kind of suffering and social humiliation associated with death on a cross, and it is the social stigma in particular that is accentuated in these chapters (cf. 1 Cor. 1.18-25).[100] Paul's social humiliation is no less separable from his existence for others, that is, being a διάκονος Χριστοῦ (11.23),[101] than it was for Christ on the cross. These two aspects belong together christologically, and in Paul's own apostolic ministry.

Following the paradigm of Christ crucified in weakness, Paul integrates the weakness motif with the διακονία motif and thereby transforms the meaning of both. The two motifs converge in 11.23-33 where, for the sake of 'foolish' comparison, he grants that the rival apostles are servants of Christ (11.23), and then goes on to elaborate on his conception of being 'a better servant of Christ' by referring to a lengthy catalogue of his weaknesses (11.24-29).[102] It matters little whether the designation a διάκονοι Χριστοῦ stems from Paul or the rival apostles. The important thing is that he appealed to it in order to define the character of his apostolic ministry (cf. also 1 Cor. 3.5; 4.1), and by associating it with weakness he has given it a different meaning than it must have had for his opponents. Georgi has observed that apart from 12.10 all of the catalogues of weakness include the notion of διακονία (cf. 4.8-10; 6.4-10; 11.23-33).[103] This would seem to signify an attempt on Paul's part to make plain his conviction that even though his weakness connotes social shame and has resulted in criticisms of his apostleship, it is constitutive of the constructive aim of serving Christ and the community. He gives some indication as to how his weakness fulfills this purpose in 11.29, which Forbes appropriately paraphrases as follows: 'who among Christians find themselves

---

100. On the social stigma attached to the crucifixion see Hengel, *Crucifixion*, pp. 69-83.

101. Schütz refers to the connotation of debasement that is evident in the διακονία word group in classical Greek literature (*The Anatomy of Apostolic Authority*, p. 178). In the light of this, however, it is difficult to see why he thinks the designation διάκονοι Χριστοῦ (11.23) was coined by the rival apostles.

102. Cf. Forbes, 'Comparison, Self-Praise and Irony', p. 18; Schütz, *The Anatomy of Apostolic Authority*, p. 180.

103. Georgi, *Die Gegner des Paulus im 2. Korintherbrief*, p. 244. In the case of 4.8-10 the idea is carried over from 4.1.

in a state of humilation, and I do not share their experience? And their shame? Who is put to shame for Christ's sake, and it does not reflect my own humiliation?'[104] If Paul is going to indulge in boasting, then he will boast only of the things which show his weakness because they are the mark of his solidarity with those who are in need of comfort (11.30; cf. 1.3-7). It is in this sense that weakness contributes to the building up of the community.

There is a certain reciprocity between these two motifs in that while on the one hand weakness denotes διακονία for Paul, on the other hand, the connotation of abasement is inherent in the διακονία word group, as is evidenced in its use in classical Greek literature.[105] This nuance underlines the social connotations of the idea of serving and thus its connection with his weakness. The way these motifs are interrelated in this context is reminiscent of 4.5 where the polemical edge is even more apparent.[106] Paul tacitly incriminates the rival apostles when he remarks that 'what we preach is not ourselves, but Jesus Christ as Lord, with ourselves as your servants for Jesus sake'.[107] The idea of being a servant is in 4.8-11 followed by a hardship catalogue. In these two passages and 6.4-10 Paul concisely articulates a model of apostleship in which weakness is intrinsic to ministry or service, and he does this in contradistinction to the rival apostles' pattern of apostleship. While he describes his apostolic service as 'spending and being spent' for the Corinthians (12.15), his representation of the rival apostles is the exact opposite. With forceful sarcasm he asserts that instead of being servants to the Corinthians, they have made the Corinthians *their* slaves by exploiting them for their own self-serving goals (11.20; cf. also 1.24).[108] In his weakness Paul is a slave to the Corinthians, but they have themselves become slaves to the rival apostles.

In the same way that διακονία is the counterpart to Paul's weakness, the rival apostles' conduct is the counterpart to the cultural values of honour and power which comprise their ideal of apostleship, and it is on this behavioural level that Paul wants to conduct the 'foolish' com-

---

104. Forbes, 'Comparison, Self-Praise and Irony', p. 20.
105. H. Beyer, 'διακονέω', *TDNT*, II, p. 82: 'In Greek eyes serving is not very dignified. Ruling and not serving is proper to a man.'
106. Schütz, *The Anatomy of Apostolic Authority*, p. 181.
107. Furnish, *II Corinthians*, p. 249.
108. Furnish, *II Corinthians*, p. 250.

parison. His argument is that although his weakness reflects social inferiority according to the values in which his opponents are entrenched, it serves the purpose of building up the Corinthians (cf. 10.8; 12.19; 13.10) and reveals the priority of his love and care for them (cf. 11.2, 10-11, 28-29; 12.14-15). In this respect he is superior to the rival apostles (11.23), who, precisely because they exhibit the qualities of the cultivated person in Greco-Roman society and display concomitant signs of pneumatic power, tyrannize the Corinthians and arouse 'quarreling, jealousy, anger, selfishness, slander, gossip, conceit and disorder' among them (12.20). This notwithstanding, the Corinthians have been bewitched by the outward form of the rivals' apostolate and as a result have denigrated Paul for his 'weak bodily presence' (10.10), but this is because they are 'looking only on the surface of things' (10.7, NIV).[109] In order to transform their superficial perspective, Paul discredits the rival apostles and at the same time demonstrates his superiority as an apostle according to his criteria of διακονία, οἰκοδομή, and love for the Corinthians by playing the fool and ironically comparing himself with his enemies.[110] It is evident from 11.1-6 that his 'foolish' boasting is intended to divert them from the rival apostles and their values to the gospel he preached to them not because his apostleship is in question, though in their eyes it is, but rather because he fears that their 'thoughts will be led astray from a sincere and pure devotion to Christ' (11.3b), and it seems likely that this fear is related to the fear he expresses about their conduct in 12.20-21.

The comparisons then, as far as Paul was concerned, involved more than a personal contest between him and the rival apostles. As was suggested in the previous section, the two apostolates embodied

---

109. Barrett (*The Second Epistle to the Corinthians*, p. 256), Furnish (*II Corinthians*, p. 465), Martin (*2 Corinthians*, p. 307) and the majority of commentators translate βλέπετε as an imperative on the ground that it is virtually always used in the imperative sense in the Pauline letters. However, πρόσωπον recalls the κατὰ πρόσωπον of 10.1 and probably the ἐν προσώπῳ καυχωμένους in 5.12, and both of these suggest an exclusive orientation to outward appearance on the Corinthians' part. Thus we follow J.A.T. Robinson who takes it as an indicative mood and ironically (*The Body: A Study in Pauline Theology* [London: SCM Press, 1952], p. 26; also Forbes, 'Comparison, Self-Praise and Irony', p. 28 n. 26). Bultmann may be correct in reading the clause as a question: 'Do you look to what can be seen outwardly?', but this would mean essentially the same thing as when it is rendered as an indicative (*The Second Letter to the Corinthians*, p. 187).

110. Marshall, *Enmity in Corinth*, p. 353.

alternative interpretations of the gospel. In 11.4 he mentions the rival apostles' 'other' gospel, but he nowhere contrasts the content of this gospel with the one he preaches because he thinks of it more in terms of consequences than content.[111] These consequences are precisely what he is referring to in 11.3 and 12.20-21, and it is not difficult to see the connection between the anxiety he conveys about the Corinthians in these passages and the understanding of the gospel which is the source of the charges against him. The oppositions' judgment that Paul is 'weak' in terms of the prevalent social conventions—taken together with their conviction that Christ is powerful in them in the form of rhetorical proficiency, impressive physical appearance, visions and revelations, signs and wonders and so on (13.3)—means that they thought of power as the exhibition of external qualities which in some form or another made the individual superior to others. Just as the accusation that Paul was weak had social implications with respect to his standing with the Corinthians, so their penchant for power, comprehended in this way, affected social interaction within the community, and 12.20 provides a glimpse of what sort of affect it probably had. Without denying his social inferiority, Paul has in 11.23-29 revalued his weakness by asserting that it enables him to be a better servant of Christ, but in order to counteract the social repercussions of the interpretation of the gospel embodied by his opponents he also redefines the meaning of power by showing its dialectical relationship to weakness as it takes concrete form in his own apostolic ministry.

As a 'fool' Paul has boasted of his weakness in the hardship catalogue in 11.23-29 and in the subsequent account of his escape from the governor of Damascus, which is also a story of humiliation, and has argued that it is in the best interest of the Corinthians. He continues his foolish boasting in 12.1-10, but here he moves from the social to the spiritual sphere. In v. 7 he recounts an experience of another kind of humiliation in which he was given a 'thorn in the flesh' to keep him 'from being too elated by the abundance of revelations'. The point of the narrative, however, is his reiteration in v. 9 of the Lord's reply to his prayer for the thorn to be removed: 'My grace is sufficient for you, for my power is made perfect in weakness'. This word from the Lord has led him to boast of his weakness so that (ἵνα) the 'power of Christ' may rest upon him, and to conclude that 'when I am weak, then I am strong' (12.9-10). These paradoxical statements in 12.9-10

111. Schütz, *The Anatomy of Apostolic Authority*, p. 175.

constitute the thesis of Paul's argument in this section, but they raise questions about the character of God's power, the manner in which it is manifested, and the nature of the relationship between that power and human weakness. The question of how Paul understands God's power and expects it to be displayed in the community is more fundamental to the aim of his argument, but it can be answered only in the light of his explanation of the weakness–power dialectic.

The declaration that 'power is made perfect in weakness' stands in stark contrast to the opposition's perspective that God's power is something which makes the individual powerful in some observable way. For them power had the opposite social connotations of weakness, and hence they were necessarily incompatible characteristics. Paul challenges this view that weakness precludes the manifestation of God's power by asserting the *simultaneity* of weakness and power (12.9-10).[112] His affirmation of weakness in the parody of the rival apostles' boasting is immediately followed by the claim that he 'was not at all inferior to these super apostles', even though he is 'nothing', and he goes on to remind the Corinthians that 'the signs of a true apostle were performed among you in all patience, with signs and wonders and mighty works' (12.11-12). The same pneumatic phenomenon exhibited by the rival apostles also occur in his ministry, the only difference is that unlike them 'his bodily presence is weak' (10.10).[113] Therefore, despite the fact that Paul can profess consubstantial credentials in terms of pneumatic performance, his conception of 'power' and related ideas is 'diametrically different' from that of his opponents.[114]

The problem is that in 12.9-10 Paul does not spell out what he

---

112. O'Collins, 'Power Made Perfect in Weakness', pp. 31, 536.

113. Jervell rightly observes that this is indeed the paradox: 'Der Apostel ist und bleibt als Pneumatiker genau was er als Mensch immer gewesen ist, nämlich der Schwäche', that is to say, 'die Gotteskraft durch die Ohnmacht, die Krankheit und die Schwäche arbeitet' (Jervell, 'Der schwache Charismatiker', pp. 196-97). *Contra* Güttgemanns who says that the paradox is that the weakness of the apostle is 'δύναμις des gekreuzigten Kyrios', or the 'Epiphanie der göttlichen Kraft des Gekreuzigten' (*Der leidende Apostel und sein Herr*, pp. 168-69). Jervell correctly states that 'Die ἀσθένεια ist fur Paulus nicht identisch mit Dynamis, sondern Ort der Kraftoffenbarung' (p. 197 n. 63).

114. Jervell, 'Der schwache Charismatiker', p. 190. Thus on the one hand Jervell can say that 'Er redet nicht von denselben Phänomenen wie sie', but on the other hand, 'dass die charismatischen Phänomene, als Phänomene betrachtet, für Paulus und seine Widersacher dieselben sind' (p. 191).

means by power. The closest thing to an explicit definition in this context is the synonymous use of ἡ χάρις μου in his reiteration of the word from the Lord in v. 9.[115] The term χάρις has a wide range of meanings and is frequently used in this letter, but the christological commentary in 8.9 is perhaps the best guide to its basic connotation: 'For you know the grace of our Lord Jesus Christ, that though he was rich, yet for your sake he became poor, so that by his poverty you might become rich'. In addition to its primary soteriological sense, this shorthand kenotic Christology also implies something about the nature and significance of grace, and this is in fact its main function in this passage. Paul explains grace theologically as the saving event of Christ' incarnation and death, but he is interested in it here as a power which actualizes itself in the Church, for example, in the Jerusalem collection (2 Cor. 8).[116] His paraenetic appeal to Christ's act of grace (8.9) is meant to inspire a financial contribution that reflects the consequences and character of that grace in the community. Despite the versatility of the notion of grace even in the Corinthian correspondence, Paul consistently refers to it as a *power* which, as the result of what God has done in Christ, is operative both in his apostolic ministry and the life of the Church (cf. 1 Cor. 1.4-5; 3.10; 15.10; 2 Cor. 1.12; 4.15; 6.1; 8.1; 9.8, 14; 13.13). As Dunn remarks, 'for Paul grace is not merely an act of God in the past; it is also and more characteristically, the act of God in the present'.[117] This nuance is essential to the principle set forth in 12.9-10.

Paul further clarifies this understanding of grace/power as defined by the kenosis of Christ, especially in his death,[118] by emphasizing that

---

115. O'Collins, 'Power Made Perfect in Weakness', p. 532.
116. H. Conzelmann, 'χάρις', *TDNT*, IX, p. 395.
117. Dunn remarks that 'for Paul grace means power, an otherly power at work in and through the believer's life' (*Jesus and the Spirit*, p. 202). Barrett's comment on 12.9 confirms and expands on what we have said about grace: 'Grace has been so frequently and widely used in the epistle that it is unlikely that it here means the special grace that makes Paul an apostle. It may be added, however, that it is grace by which any man becomes the sort of Christian that he is and does the sort of service that he does (6.1; Rom.12.6; 1 Cor.1.4)... Grace however is also, and more fundamentally, the movement in love of God to man that takes effect in Christ (8.9)' (*The Second Epistle to the Corinthians*, p. 316).
118. In Gal. 2.21 Paul refers to 'the grace of God' exclusively in terms of the death of Christ (cf. 2.20). With reference to the christological definition of grace in 2 Cor. 8.9 Furnish draws attention to the connection with 5.14-15 where Paul uses

it is brought to fulfillment in weakness (12.9). This maxim is the antithesis of the oppositions' view that weakness is *ipso facto* an exclusion of power, and he undoubtedly intended it as such. Only this qualified notion of power is appropriate to the eschatological Christ-event in which the weakness of the crucifixion is the context for the manifestation of the power of the resurrection (13.4), to the intrinsic meaning of grace as 'an act of wholly unmerited generosity on God's part', and to Paul's own experience of the gospel working powerfully through his own weakness in Corinth (1 Cor. 2.3-5).[119] All of these things militate against the opponents' conviction that divine power manifests itself by making the believer powerful. The social consequence of their way of thinking was the sort of mimetic rivalry that caused the dissensions reflected in 1 Cor. 1.10-17 and to which he alludes in 12.20. Such an individualistic pursuit of power could only result in the sort of competitive environment which was counter-productive to the realization of community. Contrary to this, weakness signifies inferiority and vulnerability, the opposite of the opponents' boasted superiority, which in turn engenders an interdependence that creates community.[120] Although Paul formulates the paradox of power in weakness (12.9-10) with reference to his own apostolate, his stated aim of 'building up' the community (cf. 10.8; 12.19; 13.10) suggests that his thesis is directly applicable to the Corinthian Christians and the particular situation he is confronting in the community (cf. 12.20-21).[121] Just as the opponents are the exemplars of a conception of power which is destructive, so Paul is the exemplar of a paradoxical understanding of power which he intends to serve the constructive purpose of his letter, namely οἰκοδομή.

Paul substantiates this paradoxical understanding of power and elaborates on its social implications in 13.3-4. He does so by invoking the image of the Christ who 'was crucified in weakness, but lives by the power of God', and relating it to his anticipated encounter with the Corinthians. His specific application of the power in weakness principle of 12.9-10 to his own apostleship in 13.4 further elucidates the conception of power he is arguing for in these chapters. Paul has

the term love to depict the same thing christologically (*II Corinthians*, p. 417).

119. Dunn, *Jesus and the Spirit*, pp. 202, 329.

120. Cf. R. Hammerton-Kelly, 'A Girardian Interpretation of Paul', *Semeia* 33 (1985), p. 76.

121. *Contra* O'Collins, 'Power Made Perfect in Weakness', p. 534.

5. *The Social Significance of the Death of Jesus* 201

so closely identified the 'power of God' with the notion of authority in this context that they are functionally equivalent terms, as is evidenced in 13.10 where he uses ἐξουσία to express the same idea. This idea of power as ruling authority is derived from Christ, who in his resurrection power rules over his people.[122] However, Paul also emphasizes that he is at the same time the Christ who 'was crucified in weakness', and on the basis of the indivisibility of Christ's power and weakness he asserts that though he is weak in Christ (ἀσθενοῦμεν ἐν αὐτω) he will nevertheless exercise the power of God if necessary when he arrives in Corinth (ζήσομεν σὺν αὐτῷ ἐκ δυνάμεως θεοῦ).[123] The reference here to the dialectical relationship between the weakness of the crucifixion and the power of the resurrection functions as a paradigm of authentic power, but it is clear that for Paul this power takes the form of authority.[124]

In his attempt to alter the way power was conceived in the community and to set forth a different vision of authority Paul again employs irony. He introduces the paradoxical notion of power modelled on the crucifixion–resurrection paradigm by alluding to the Corinthians' demand for proof that Christ is speaking in him (13.3). But since he has no intention of offering the kind of proof they solicit, his rehearsal of what they require of him is little more than a pretext for calling them to account for *their* behaviour. Paul will give the Corinthians proof of Christ's power, but in a form they do not expect.[125] He intends to demonstrate the power of God by resorting to the authority which the Lord has given him for 'building up' the community, but on this occasion he is afraid that he may have to use it for disciplinary purposes (καθαίρεσις, 10.8; 13.10). It is noteworthy that the christological paradigm in 13.4 is situated between two of the three verses in which Paul expresses his desire to build up the Corinthians (12.19; 13.10), and that his attention is focused exclusively on their conduct in this section (12.11–13.14). Paul gives no sign of being insecure about his apostolic authority, for it is grounded in the commission he received from the Lord himself (cf. Gal. 1.11-24). This authority is

---

122. Tannehill, *Dying and Rising with Christ*, p. 99.
123. The future ζήσομεν refers to Paul's impending visit. So Furnish, *II Corinthians*, p. 571; Martin, *2 Corinthians*, p. 577; Bultmann, *The Second Letter to the Corinthians*, p. 244; and Schütz, *The Anatomy of Apostolic Authority*, p. 215.
124. Cf. Meeks, *The First Urban Christians*, p. 138.
125. Plummer, *Second Epistle of St Paul to the Corinthians*, p. 374.

something he takes for granted whether others acknowledge it or not, and hence he makes no effort to defend it. As has been maintained throughout, his primary concern in chs. 10–13 is with the Corinthians' obedience to Christ (cf. 10.6). Instead of yielding to the test to which the Corinthians have subjected him, he turns the tables on them and contends that they are the ones who are being tested (13.5).

Although Paul's own apostolic authority is not a matter for debate as far as he is concerned, questions about the nature and mode of authority in the church are an important part of his dispute with the Corinthians. I have argued that the conflict was caused mainly by the opponents' emphasis on the outward display of power in accordance with Greco-Roman cultural values, and that Paul's objective was to reform this perception of power and thereby persuade them to modify their behaviour.[126] The question of authority is integral to his endeavour because, as Schütz has shown, authority is defined as the interpretation of power.[127] Moreover, authority is a social relation and a quality pertaining to communications.[128] Holmberg succinctly explains the social dimension as follows:

> In an authority relation there is something in the ruler's person or behaviour that effects willing compliance on the part of the subordinate. He is constrained to submit to the other, not by external means, but out of the conviction that it is right to do so, that it is indeed his duty.[129]

With regard to the quality of communication he remarks that 'authority rests upon the ability to issue communications capable of reasoned elaboration', which, following Friedrich, he understands to be 'the reasoning which relates actions to opinions and beliefs, and opinions and beliefs to values'.[130] If, with Meeks, this letter is thought of as 'an attempt to exert authority as an interpretive enterprise',[131] then what is being interpreted with special reference to Paul's apostleship are the values and attendant actions which are consistent with obedience to the Christ who 'was crucified in weakness, but lives by the power of God'

---

126. Cf. Meeks, *The First Urban Christians*; Holmberg, *Paul and Power*, p. 83.
127. Schütz, *Paul and the Anatomy of Apostolic Authority*, p. 14.
128. Holmberg, *Paul and Power*, pp. 129-30.
129. Holmberg, *Paul and Power*, p. 131.
130. Holmberg, *Paul and Power*, p. 131.
131. Meeks, *The First Urban Christians*, p. 122; cf. Holmberg, *Paul and Power*, p. 189.

(13.4). Fundamental beliefs about the death and resurrection of Christ which he could assume the Corinthians shared with him form the basis of his appeal for them to exhibit a lifestyle that is congruous with those beliefs.[132]

While it is true that Paul's personal authority is contingent upon his ability to get the community to respond out of conviction to the interpretation of the gospel he embodies, for him their perception of his apostleship was a concern of secondary importance to their behavioural compliance with the christological pattern that integrates weakness and power.[133] Nevertheless, questions pertaining to the values and conduct appropriate to the gospel are necessarily focused on personal representations of that gospel because, as has already been observed, values and power are socially defined and the definitions are always embodied. The alternative values and concomitant notions of power typified by Paul and his opponents find expression in their respective social interpretations of power, that is, their particular views of authority and how it should be exercised. And the manner in which they exert their authority has a direct bearing on the social structure of the community, including the character of interpersonal relations. Schütz and Holmberg designate the authority of both Paul and the rival apostles as charismatic, but they are careful to distinguish between the types of charismatic authority represented.[134] Using different approaches they have both dealt with the topic in more depth than I can hope to here, however, a synopsis of Schütz's analysis will help to clarify the social implications of what has the appearance of a very personal contest for authority in the community.

According to Schütz, the opponents best fit Weber's understanding of charismatic authority, which he sums up with this phrase from

---

132. Meeks, *The First Urban Christians*, p. 136. Holmberg also emphasizes the importance of shared beliefs: 'Different apostles or missionaries within the same tradition may go different ways in the continuous process of institutionalization. But the starting point is always the common fund of invariable, institutionalized fundamental elements or patterns ("the Gospel")' (*Paul and Power*, p. 186).

133. Holmberg asserts that 'when the subordinate discovers, suddenly or gradually, that the opinions, beliefs and values to which the ruler appeals have no social validity the ruler's authority ceases to exist' (*Paul and Power*, p. 133). This means that the extent to which Paul's apostolic authority is at issue is proportionate to the degree to which the Corinthians' accept the beliefs and values he represents.

134. Schütz, *The Anatomy of Apostolic Authority*, pp. 252-80; Holmberg, *Paul and Power*, pp. 186-91, 155-58.

Economy and Society: 'Charisma is self-determined and sets its own limits'.[135] By this he simply means that 'no criteria can be established outside the framework of the charismatic personality itself'.[136] This principle recalls Paul's criticism of the rival apostles in 10.12, and Schütz's description of the proof of this kind of charismatic authority is very similar to my account of the situation in Corinth:

> Proof is apparently the sign of the gift, but we notice that it is virtually equated with success, i.e., the fruit of the power the gift betokens. If there is no success, there is, logically speaking, no charismatic gift. But success is itself equated with acceptance of the charismatic's claim to authority. In all of this, the charisma itself is of no account.[137]

In his attempt to classify Paul, Schütz follows E. Shils understanding of charismatic authority, which goes 'beyond the charismatic personality to the charismatic property itself, inherently separable from the personality'.[138] To put it concisely, Paul is different from his opponents in that he regards all Christians as having *charismata*, and his own charismatic authority 'depends not on hoarding charismatic qualities but facilitating their dispersal throughout the institution'.[139] Schütz stresses that 'the function of the charismatic is not merely to embody the gift but provide or author its structural interpretation'.[140] In contrast to those within and without the Corinthian community who oppose him, Paul understands power as transcendent and thus separable from his person.[141] For him it serves the purpose of οἰκοδομή, not of enhancing the social reputation of individual believers.

There is, then, a real contest over apostolic authority reflected in chs. 10–13, but its significance lies in the implications the respective types of authority, as interpretations of power, had for the manifestation of power in the community. How the exercise of authority

---

135. Schütz, *The Anatomy of Apostolic Authority*, p. 266, citing *Economy and Society*, III, p. 1112.
136. Schütz, *The Anatomy of Apostolic Authority*, pp. 268-69.
137. Schütz, *The Anatomy of Apostolic Authority*, p. 268.
138. Schütz, *The Anatomy of Apostolic Authority*, p. 274.
139. Schütz, *The Anatomy of Apostolic Authority*, p. 276.
140. Schütz, *The Anatomy of Apostolic Authority*, p. 277.
141. Schütz, *The Anatomy of Apostolic Authority*, p. 277. Holmberg agrees that Paul thinks of charisma more as Shils does, and that his opponents have a more Weberian view, but he complains that this does not explain why authority relations between Paul and the Corinthians deteriorated (*Paul and Power*, p. 190 n. 92).

influenced the life of the community would depend upon how conduct was related to the pivotal theological symbols (e.g. death and resurrection), and theological symbols to values in any given interpretation of power. Paul has explained his apostolic ministry in terms of the dialectic of Christ's death and resurrection, which means that the power of God is brought to fulfillment in weakness (12.9-10). Although his weakness denotes social shame and inferiority, he endorses it because in the weakness of the crucifixion Christ gives himself for others, and this is decisive for Paul, who in his weakness thinks of apostleship as διακονία. Furthermore, his weakness and the weakness of other Christians gives rise to the interdependence which is characteristic of genuine community. Paul's objective is οἰκοδομη, and in pursuing it he is guided by a vision of community that bears the stamp of the crucified *and* risen Lord. This vision is concisely described in 2 Cor. 1.3-7 where both his suffering and the Corinthians' is seen to bring about mutual comfort (cf. 1 Cor. 12–14). It is exemplified in his own apostolic existence, and even though he makes no explicit reference to imitation in this context, it is evident from 1 Cor. 4.16 that Paul expects the Corinthians to pattern their lives after his.[142] To do so would effect the kind of social interaction which in 1 Cor. 12.12-27 he depicts as 'members' of 'the body of Christ' living in harmony with each other because despite diversities of gifts, status and so on. 'the members have the same care for one another' (v. 25). This is the opposite of the discord, or mimetic rivalry, caused by the individualistic interpretation of power espoused by the opposition (12.20).

In conformity with the community he envisages, God's power is conceived of as something which is shared; precisely because it is manifested in weakness. But because the ideal of community which predicates the simultaneous display of power and weakness has been contravened, resulting in the situation described in 12.20, Paul intends to exercise his unique authority as an apostle over the Corinthians.[143] With reference to the fact that Christ 'was crucified in weakness, but

142. On the imitation of Paul and Christ see Schütz, *The Anatomy of Apostolic Authority*, pp. 226-32.
143. Schütz, in affirming Paul's restricted view of authority and his attempt to educe from others an awareness of shared power, asserts that 'when others perceive this power correctly and act accordingly, they share the same power with Paul and are themselves authoritative. When they misperceive, he exercises power over them' (*The Anatomy of Apostolic Authority*, p. 204).

lives by the power of God', he asserts that although he is weak, he will nevertheless show that he does indeed live by the power of God in his role as apostle of the community (13.4). Paul's willingness to be authoritarian if necessary does not, on the surface anyway, appear to be any different from the very notion of power that is the focus of his critique of the rival apostles', but there are some important differences between their respective uses of authority. In contrast to his depiction of the interlopers' relationship with the Corinthians as men who 'enslave' (καταδουλόω), 'exploit' (κατεσθίω), and 'take advantage of' (λαμβάνω) them, Paul typically respects the freedom of the community and is reluctant to impose the norms he recommends as rules.[144] Nevertheless, Paul does regard himself as the 'father' of the community (1 Cor. 4.15) and he is willing to resort to his paternal authority when the community deviates from the gospel. As a 'father' to the Corinthians his ultimate concern is with their obedience and he will command it if necessary.

The authoritarianism masked by his role as 'father' does, however, involve him in a paradox that cannot be resolved. On the one hand, the reason Paul may have to use the authority/power of God in his dealings with the Corinthians (13.4) is the existence of an elitism which has undermined the unity and harmony of the community (cf. 12.20). On the other hand, while his main concern is that the church be a place in which people exhibit mutual concern and respect for one another, he can ensure this only by appealing to his own superior status in the community. As Petersen puts it, Paul opposes 'the hierarchical structure of the church in which, in his mind, he plays a superior superordinate role'.[145] But the parent–child metaphoric complex also discloses something about his conception of authority and how he believes it to be different from that of his opponents. Most important, the father–child metaphors emphasize that in his superordinate role he is motivated by love, and as far as he is concerned this distinguishes him from outsiders who would also make claims to

---

144. Cf. Meeks, *The First Urban Christians*, pp. 138-39; M. MacDonald, *The Pauline Churches* (SNTSMS, 60; Cambridge: Cambridge University Press, 1988), pp. 51-52.

145. Petersen, *Rediscovering Paul*, p. 160. This discussion of the question of Paul's authority owes much to Petersen's analysis of social structures and relations in Paul's letters. See especially his discussion of Paul's roles (pp. 124-58).

apostolic authority (cf. 2 Cor. 5.12-14). Hence when Paul raises the sceptre of power in 13.4 he would undoubtedly have said that it was only with the best interest of the community as a whole in view. More specifically, the real focus of the christological reference is the interpersonal problems reflected in 12.20, as is indicated by the admonition to self-examination which immediately follows it in 13.5: 'to see whether you are holding to your faith'.

Paul's injunction in 13.5 may seem to contradict his concession in 13.3 to the Corinthians' claim that Christ was powerful among them, but he acknowledges their claim only with respect to his own understanding of power. Although the Corinthians think of power in terms of pneumatic endowment witnessed by external manifestations, Paul is referring to the indwelling of Christ in the community as 'critical' power.[146] This connotation is suggested by the question which follows the two imperatives (πειράζετε and δοκιμάζετε) in v. 5: 'do you not realize that Jesus Christ is in you?—unless you fail to meet the test'. Paul is willing to identify the Corinthians as powerful only according to their faith.[147] Hence he has assented to their claims in a manner contrary to their expectations in order to transform their definition of power. His recapitulation of the Corinthian profession that Christ is powerful among them (13.3) and his appropriation of the christological paradigm to his own apostleship (13.4) are carefully articulated so as to distinguish between Christ's power as the possession of individuals and that power as Christ himself at work in the community (13.5). Furnish correctly observes that for Paul 'believers do not rule with Christ's power (the point of the irony in 1 Cor. 4.8-13) but are to be ruled by it (cf. 2 Cor. 5.14); and so he writes here of Christ being powerful *toward* or *among* (not "in") them'.[148] By asserting that God's power is a consequence of participation in Christ, and that it is manifested jointly with weakness, Paul has, as Schütz puts it, turned the Corinthians' scale of values upside down.[149] This understanding of power is normative for all believers and provides a necessary corrective to a conception of divine power that is associated with the

---

146. Bultmann, *The Second Letter to the Corinthians*, p. 242.
147. Furnish, *II Corinthians*, pp. 579-80.
148. Furnish, *II Corinthians*, p. 576; cf. Bultmann, *The Second Letter to the Corinthians*, p. 242.
149. Schütz, *The Anatomy of Apostolic Authority*, p. 217.

idea that the believer is powerful. It is in the light of this perspective that the Corinthians are to examine and test themselves.[150]

The Cross as a Symbol for Social Change

In his reply to the opposition Paul has used the criticisms of his apostleship to mediate a set of values which were constitutive of an ethos that was distinct from that of the established social order.[151] The charges against him reflected the importance of honour and status to opponents from within and without the Corinthian community, and he saw this as a threat to the unique Christian ethos that he was seeking to establish and maintain. Honour and status were the main components of the Greco-Roman social system, and as such they were in conflict with the Christian community as Paul was trying to construct it in Corinth. Not only were these values the basis of the opponents' attempt to undermine his apostolic authority because he was 'weak' in terms of the cultural conventions associated with them; they were also the cause of social discord among the Corinthians themselves. Despite Paul's apparent preoccupation with his competition, the stated aim of his argument is to 'build up' the community (12.19; cf. 10.8; 13.10). He sets out to do this by taking the personal affront to himself as a vehicle for conducting a head-on assault on the values of the cultivated elite in Greco-Roman society, to which the opponents had appealed as the criteria of apostolic, and thus Christian, existence.[152]

According to Malina, 'a social system is a system of symbols, i.e., meanings, values, and feelings about these meanings and values are attached to, embodied in and by persons, things, events'.[153] Values are the highest level of the normative structure of a social system.[154] In endorsing the weakness for which he has been criticized, Paul is rejecting the secular values which were esteemed by certain Corinthian believers of high social standing, and which were the source of the 'quarreling, jealousy, anger, selfishness, slander, gossip, conceit and

---

150. Dunn, *Jesus and the Spirit*, p. 329.

151. L. Keck defines ethos as 'a Gestaltic term, gathering up into itself the practices and habits, assumptions, problems, values and hopes of a community's style' ('On the Ethos of Early Christianity', pp. 440-41).

152. Cf. Judge, 'Cultural Conformity and Innovation in Paul', p. 5.

153. Malina, *The New Testament World*, p. 21.

154. H. Johnson, 'Ideology', in the *International Encyclopedia of the Social Sciences*, VII, p. 78.

5. *The Social Significance of the Death of Jesus* 209

disorder' that he feared he might find when he arrived for his third visit (12.20). More than that, and in a more positive vein, Paul's weakness demonstrated the preeminent Christian value of love—the value which for him is expressed in διακονία. Judge goes so far as to say that 'Paul spelled out a structural model of social relations', yet he points out that he does not analyse human affairs in institutional terms but rather attacks the problems at a personal level.[155] He describes what Paul has done at this personal level as 'the deliberate abandonment of status so as to open the way to a new spirit of human cooperation through mutual service', but on the structural level his example presents a challenge to the prevailing status system.[156]

On the personal level the cross of Christ functions as a symbol of identity. In this regard it serves to legitimate Paul's weakness by showing its correspondence to the reality mediated by the symbol, but more than that the symbol itself actually impels him to reject Greco-Roman social values and to personify the values which he has inferred from the reality symbolized in Christ's death.[157] But since what he personifies is a set of *values*, the character of his apostleship is relevant to the social structure of the community. Although Paul has formulated the theme of power in weakness with reference to his own apostleship, its primary significance pertains to the values which he expects to form the social structure of the community. That this is his predominant concern is indicated in the first place by the social connotations of the terms weakness and power, and in the second place by the prominent emphasis on οἰκοδομή (10.8; 12.19; 13.10). Judge asserts that Paul deliberately used this terminology of building because it was 'a graphic and innovatory formulation of how people were to manage their relations with each other'.[158] He notes that the word οἰκοδομή was a solecism by Attic standards, but it was widely used as the ordinary term for the process of construction on a building site.[159] Judge attributes the extensive metaphorical development of this concept to Paul's own inspiration and remarks that

---

155. Judge, 'Cultural Conformity and Innovation in Paul', p. 5.
156. Judge, 'Cultural Conformity and Innovation in Paul', pp. 5-6.
157. Symbolic anthropologists contend that all social behaviour is a response to symbols (cf. Vernon, 'The Symbolic Interactionist Approach to the Sociology of Religion', pp. 135-39).
158. Judge, 'Cultural Conformity and Innovation in Paul', p. 23.
159. Judge, 'Cultural Conformity and Innovation in Paul', p. 23.

it is the great encounters in the church at Corinth which stimulate his reflection on constructive as opposed to destructive relations. The constructive spirit is that of love, by which each contributes to the others' good, as distinct from the 'puffed up' spirit which pulls down the building (10.8; 13.10).[160]

Paul's consistent orientation to this idea of οἰκοδομη throughout chs. 10–13 suggests that his reply to his critics served the aim of facilitating constructive relations in the community, and the way that he has constructed his argument supports this.[161]

Paul's strategy in this polemical section of 2 Corinthians can best be explained if we understand his thematization of weakness and power as a type of symbolic inversion and the cross as a symbol of reversal. Barbara Babcock defines symbolic inversion as

> any act of expressive behaviour which inverts, contradicts, abrogates, or in some fashion presents an alternative to commonly held cultural codes, values, and norms be they linguistic, literary or artistic, religious, or social and political.[162]

Moreover, Babcock asserts that 'symbolic inversion is central to the literary notions of irony, parody, and paradox'.[163] I have shown that these three literary notions pervade chs. 10–13, and that paradox is not just a literary device but is intrinsic to the dialectic of power and weakness which is grounded in the death and resurrection of Christ (12.9-10; 13.4; cf. 1 Cor. 2.8). Paul emphasizes the weakness symbolized in Christ's death more than the power of his resurrection because it negates worldly standards of evaluation, that is Greco-Roman values, and epitomizes the transcendent value of love. In the cross of Christ, which in 1 Cor. 1.25 Paul refers to as 'the weakness of God', God has 'chosen what is weak in the world to shame the strong' (1 Cor. 1.27); in other words, God has reversely valued the social hierarchy of Greco-Roman society. Paul's own apostleship bears witness to this fact, but his task is to convince the Corinthians

---

160. Judge, 'Cultural Conformity and Innovation in Paul', pp. 23-24; cf. also P. Vielhauer, 'Oikodome: Das Bild vom Bau in der christilichen Literatur vom Neuen Testament bis Clemens Alexandrinus', in G. Klein (ed.), *Oikodome: Aufsätze zum Neuen Testament* (Munich: Kaiser Verlag, 1979), p. 73.

161. Vielhauer says that the purpose and content of apostolic authority is οἰκοδομη ('Oikodome', p. 73).

162. Babcock, *The Reversible World*, p. 14.

163. Babcock, *The Reversible World*, p. 16.

that the values he embodies are more representative of what God has done in Christ than are those of his opponents. In order to do this he parodies the boasting of the rival apostles and thus demonstrates the foolishness of their criteria of apostleship. Most effective, however, is his use of irony to convey a meaning directly opposite to that intended by their claims.[164] The symbolic inversion culminates in the paradox of 12.9-10, which, in accordance with Babcock's understanding of paradox as a challenge to some orthodoxy, is 'an oblique criticism of absolute judgement or absolute convention'.[165]

As an apostle whose distinguishing mark was weakness, Paul was living out the social implications of Christ's crucifixion, and in this sense the cross can be viewed as a symbol which has the potential to bring about social change. Jonathan Z. Smith contends that 'social change is preeminently symbol or symbolic change', and that 'society or culture is preeminently the construction of significance and order through symbolic activity'.[166] Paul's rejection of Greco-Roman cultural conventions, the abandonment of the status which he had, especially as a Roman citizen, and the intentional debasement which was endemic to his idea of διακονία were all symbolic actions which represented an alternative set of values and social order to that of the larger society. These symbolic actions were legitimated by the Christ who 'was crucified in weakness' (13.4). For Paul the cross of Christ was a symbol of reversal turning the prevailing notions of weakness and power, and honour and shame upside down. As such it was, as Stephen Barton observes, 'a potent symbol for community formation' providing 'a basis for individual and communal identity which was quite at odds with contemporary social classification'.[167] Paul interpreted his own weakness in terms of the weakness of the crucifixion with a view to implementing in the Corinthian community the values symbolized in this event and embodied in his own apostleship.

---

164. Following R. Lanham's definition of irony (cited by Spencer, 'The Wise Fool [and the Foolish Wise]', p. 349).

165. Babcock, *The Reversible World*, p. 17. She asserts that 'the paradox is always involved in dialectic'.

166. J.Z. Smith, 'The Influence of Symbols upon Social Change: A Place on Which to Stand', *Worship* 44 (1970), pp. 471-72.

167. S. Barton, 'Paul and the Cross: A Sociological Approach', *Theology* 85 (1982), p. 17.

Epilogue

CHRIST CRUCIFIED AND THE CORINTHIAN COMMUNITY

In 1 Cor. 2.2 Paul reminds the Corinthians that the exclusive content of his original message to them was 'Jesus Christ and him crucified'. Although it appears that he had to remind them of the gospel they initially embraced because they had either forgotten or deviated from it, what he has to say about the death of Jesus in Romans and especially Galatians suggests that the problems and concerns addressed in the Corinthian correspondence may have had their origin in this gospel. In both Romans and Galatians the death of Christ symbolizes a disjunction that has occurred between the powers which enslave, whether they be the law, sin, or death itself, and new life in the Spirit which is characterized by freedom (cf. Rom. 6.6-11; Gal. 3.13-15; 4.8-9, 31; 5.1). In those two letters freedom and Spirit are symbols which connote an experience which is effected by the believer's having died with Christ.[1]

If in his early preaching in Corinth Paul presented a version of 'Jesus Christ and him crucified' which emphasized freedom in the context of a social world in which there was no room for individual freedom because, as Koester puts it, 'the astrological view of the world delivers every human being into the hands of fate',[2] it is not difficult to imagine why the Corinthians found his gospel so compelling. This astrological cosmology provided the legitimation for a hierarchical society in which the powers and relationships of the social structure of

---

1. In an unpublished paper presented to the Pauline section of SBL in 1988 C. Cosgrove argued that in Galatians the life of the Spirit flows from the cross (cf. Gal. 3.14-15) because for Paul the cross is the beginning of the new creation (Gal. 6.14-15) ('Resurrection in Galatians'). See also his *The Cross and the Spirit: A Study in the Argument and Theology of Galatians* (Macon, GA: Mercer University Press, 1988).

2. Koester, *Introduction to the New Testament*, I, p. 159.

human life were rigidly determined.³ But according to Paul, the preordained cosmic order and the concomitant social order had been subverted by the death of God's Son inasmuch as not only Christ but the world itself was crucified (cf. Gal. 6.14), and this meant that distinctions of status, rank, ethnicity and even sexuality had been relativized (cf. Gal. 3.28; 1 Cor. 12.13).⁴ To participate in Christ's death through baptism was to be set free from the social codes and conventions that restricted the individual's opportunities and relationships in Greco-Roman society.

In reading Paul's letters to the Corinthians we get a glimpse of how the freedom of the gospel and new life in the Spirit found concrete expression in the life of the community. Although the letters mainly disclose the ethical and interpersonal problems that resulted from what Paul perceived to be abuses of this freedom, that should not obscure the fact that such problems could only exist because the Corinthian Christians transcended cultural and religious constraints in a way that was probably unparalleled in the Greco-Roman world. Nonetheless, unrestrained individual freedom usually incites the kind of competition of (self-) interests which can lead to social disorder and even chaos, and all of the problems Paul addresses in the Corinthian correspondence are symptomatic of this deeper problem of disunity which he seeks to resolve.

The great irony of the Corinthian situation is that while their participation in the death and resurrection of Christ liberated them from restrictive cultural norms and values, some of those same cultural norms and values were spiritualized and became a vehicle through which individual freedom was exhibited. I have tried to explain this phenomenon in terms of primary and secondary socialization, and though Paul could not have used this interpretive category to describe the problems he was confronting, his own analysis suggests that he did perceive the 'world's' norms and values to be a fundamental cause of the disintegration of the community into elitist splinter-groups. Whatever other concerns Paul had in the two extant letters to Corinth, his primary objective in both is to restore the unity which for him was requisite of a gospel which subverted all religious, ethnic and social

3. Koester, *Introduction to the New Testament*, I, p. 159.
4. The elimination of the distinction between male and female in Gal. 3.28 is conspicuously absent in 1 Cor. 12.13 because of the concerns Paul has about sexuality in the community.

boundaries. But his commitment to that gospel also required that he do so without compromising the freedom which it also promoted.

Paul attempts to achieve this aim by extending the meaning of the death of Jesus, the event which is the very basis of the freedom which appears to be the preeminent value in the community. Although the references and allusions to the death of Jesus in 1 and 2 Corinthians have different nuances, when considered in terms of their function or performance two connotations in particular are consistently evidenced throughout. In the first place, Paul appeals to the symbol of the crucified messiah to deconstruct those secular norms and values which are in conflict with his ideal of an egalitarian community. As far as Paul was concerned, the grace of God in Christ undermines all attempts to establish one's self or one's own ways as superior. By emphasizing the weakness and foolishness of the cross, which included his own embodiment of that weakness and foolishness, he critiques the cultural values of power and wisdom which some in Corinth prized. This is the negative function of his theology of the cross as it is set out in 1 and 2 Corinthians.

But Paul's references to the death of Jesus also serve the constructive purpose of building up the community. If the Corinthians had attained new heights of personal freedom by virtue of their baptism into the death and resurrection of Christ, now the communal context of that freedom needed to be elucidated. Hence Paul invokes the symbol of Christ's death to interpret the nature of individual freedom in Christ vis-à-vis other members of the community. Christ's death is a death for others, and as Paul says in 2 Cor. 5.15 'he died for all that (ἵνα) those who live might live no longer for themselves'. From Paul's perspective that was precisely the problem—freedom in Christ had become a pretext for self-indulgence—and he seeks to correct it by showing that the death of Christ symbolizes the other-regarding behaviour which he himself exemplified and the Corinthians should imitate. In the Corinthian correspondence the death of Christ is first and foremost a symbol of Christian community in the sense that it represents the self-giving love which for Paul is essential to true community.

BIBLIOGRAPHY

Babcock, B.A., *The Reversible World* (Ithaca, NY: Cornell University Press, 1978).
Banks, R., *Paul's Idea of Community* (Grand Rapids: Eerdmans, 1980).
Barbour, R., 'Wisdom and the Cross in I Cor 1 and 2', in C. Andersen and G. Klein (eds.), *Theologia Crucis—Signum Crucis* (Tübingen: Mohr, 1979), pp. 57-71.
Barre, M.L., 'Paul as Eschatological Person: A New Look at 2 Cor. 11.29', *CBQ* 37 (1975), pp. 500-26.
Barrett, C.K., 'Christianity at Corinth', reprinted in *Essays on Paul* (Philadelphia: Westminster Press, 1982).
—*The First Epistle to the Corinthians* (New York: Harper & Row, 1968).
—*The Second Epistle to the Corinthians* (New York: Harper & Row, 1973).
—'Paul's Opponents in 2 Corinthians', reprinted in *Essays on Paul*, pp. 60-86.
Bartchy, S., *Mallon Chresai: First-Century Slavery and the Interpretation of 1 Corinthians 7.21* (SBLDS, 11; Missoula, MT: Scholars Press, 1973).
Barton, S., 'Paul and the Cross: A Sociological Approach', *Theology* 85 (1982), pp. 13-19.
Beker, J.C., *Paul the Apostle* (Philadelphia: Fortress Press, 1980).
—'The Faithfulness of God and the Priority of Israel in Paul's Letter to the Romans', *HTR* 79 (1986), pp. 10-16.
Berger, P., and T. Luckmann, *The Social Construction of Reality* (New York: Penguin Books, 1967).
Bertram, G., 'μωρός', *TDNT*, IV, pp. 832-47.
Best, E., 'The Power and the Wisdom of God', in L. De Lorenzi (ed.), *Paolo a Una Chiesa Divisa (1 Co 1–4)* (Rome: Abbazia di S. Paolo, 1980).
Betz, H.D., *Der Apostel Paulus und die sokratische Tradition: Eine exegetische Untersuchung zu seiner 'Apologie' 2 Korinther 10–13* (BHT, 45; Tübingen: Mohr, 1972).
—'The Problem of Rhetoric and Theology according to the Apostle Paul', in A. Vanhoye (ed.), *L'Apôtre Paul: Personalité, style et conception du ministère* (Leuven: Leuven University Press, 1986).
Beyer, H., 'διακονέω', *TDNT*, II, pp. 81-86.
Black, D., *Paul, Apostle of Weakness: Astheeneia and its Cognates in the Pauline Literature* (American University Studies Series, 7; Theology and Religion, 3; New York: Peter Lang, 1984).
Black, M., *Models and Metaphors: Studies in Language and Philosophy* (Ithaca, NY: Cornell University Press, 1962).
Boers, H., 'Interpreting Paul: Demythologizing in Reverse', in P. Opitz and G. Sebba (eds.), *The Philosophy of Order: Essays on History, Consciousness and Politics* (Festschrift Eric Voegelin; Stuttgart: Ernst Klett, 1981), pp. 153-72.

Bruce, F.F., *I & II Corinthians* (London: Marshall, Morgan & Scott, 1971).
Bultmann, R., 'αἰσχύνω', *TDNT*, I, pp. 189-91.
—*The Second Letter to the Corinthians* (trans. R. Harrisville; Minneapolis: Augsburg, 1985).
—*Theology of the New Testament* (New York: Charles Scribner's Sons, 1955).
Carrez, M., 'Le "Nous" en 2 Corinthiens', *NTS* 26 (1980), pp. 474-86.
Castelli, E., *Imitating Paul: A Discourse of Power* (Louisville: Westminster/John Knox Press, 1991).
Conzelmann, H., *1 Corinthians* (Philadelphia: Fortress Press, 1975).
—'χάρις', *TDNT*, IX, pp. 372-402.
Cosgrove, C., *The Cross and the Spirit: A Study in the Argument and Theology of Galatians* (Macon, GA: Mercer University Press, 1988).
—'Resurrection in Galatians' (unpublished paper presented at SBL, 1988).
Countryman, W., *Dirt Greed and Sex: Sexual Ethics in the New Testament and their Implications for Today* (Philadelphia: Fortress Press, 1988).
Culpepper, A., *The Johannine School* (SBLDS; Missoula, MT: Scholars Press, 1975).
Dahl, N., 'Paul and the Church at Corinth according to I Corinthians 1.10–4.21', in *Studies in Paul* (Minneapolis: Augsburg, 1977).
—'Rudolph Bultmann's *Theology of the New Testament*', in *The Crucified Messiah and Other Essays* (Minneapolis: Augsburg, 1974), pp. 90-128.
Davies, W.D., *Paul and Rabbinic Judaism* (Philadelphia: Fortress Press, 1948).
Davis, J., *Wisdom and Spirit: An Investigation of I Corinthians 1.18–3.20 against the Background of Jewish Sapiential Traditions in the Greco-Roman Period* (Lanham, MD: University Press of America, 1984).
Deidun, T.J., *New Covenant Morality in Paul* (Rome: Bibilical Institute Press, 1981).
Delling, G., 'Der Tod Jesu in der Verkündigung des Paulus', in W. Eltester (ed.), *Apophoreta* (Festschrift E. Haenchen; Berlin: Töpelmann, 1964), pp. 85-96.
—'πλεονέκτης', *TDNT*, VI, pp. 266-74.
Douglas, M., *Natural Symbols* (New York: Penguin Books, 1973).
—'Social Preconditions of Enthusiasm and Heterodoxy', in R. Spencer (ed.), *Forms of Symbolic Action: Proceedings of the 1969 Annual Spring Meeting of the American Ethnological Society* (Seattle: University of Washington Press, 1969).
Dungan, D., *The Sayings of Jesus in the Churches of Paul* (Philadelphia: Fortress Press, 1971).
Dunn, J., *Jesus and the Spirit* (Philadelphia: Westminster Press, 1975).
—'Paul's Understanding of the Death of Jesus', in R. Banks (ed.), *Reconciliation and Hope* (Grand Rapids: Eerdmans, 1974), pp. 137-41.
Elliott, J., *A Home for the Homeless* (London: SCM Press, 1982).
Ellis, E., 'Christ Crucified', in *Prophecy and Hermeneutic in Early Christianity* (Grand Rapids: Eerdmans, 1980), pp. 72-79.
Esler, P., *Community and Gospel in Luke–Acts* (Cambridge: Cambridge University Press, 1987).
Fee, G., *The First Epistle to the Corinthians* (Grand Rapids: Eerdmans, 1987).
Fisher, N.R.E., '*Hybris* and Dishonour: I', *Greece and Rome* 23 (1976).
Fitzgerald, J.T., *Cracks in an Earthen Vessel: An Examination of the Catalogues of Hardship in the Corinthian Correspondence* (SBLDS, 99; Atlanta: Scholars Press, 1988).
Forbes, C., 'Comparison, Self-Praise and Irony: Paul's Boasting and the Conventions of Hellenistic Rhetoric' *NTS* 32 (1986), pp. 1-30.

—' "Strength" and "Weakness" as Terminology of Status in St Paul: The Historical and Literary Roots of a Metaphor, with Special Reference to 1 and 2 Corinthians' (BA thesis, Macquarie University, 1978).
Funk, R., *Language, Hermeneutic and Word of God* (New York: Harper & Row, 1966).
—'The Hermeneutical Problem and Historical Criticism', in J. Cobb and J. Robinson (eds.), *New Frontiers in Theology*. II. *The New Hermeneutic* (New York: Harper & Row, 1963), pp. 164-97.
Furnish, V., *II Corinthians* (New York: Doubleday, 1984).
—*The Love Command in the New Testament* (Nashville: Abingdon Press, 1972).
—*Theology and Ethics in Paul* (Nashville: Abingdon Press, 1968).
Gadamer, H., *Truth and Method* (New York: Continuum, 1975).
Geertz, C., *The Interpretation of Cultures* (New York: Basic Books, 1973).
Georgi, D., *Die Gegner des Paulus im 2 Korintherbrief. Studien zur religiösen Propaganda in der Spätantike* (Neukirchen: Neukirchener Verlag, 1964).
Güttgemanns, G., *Der leidende Apostel und sein Herr: Studien zur paulinischen Christologie* (Göttingen: Vandenhoeck & Ruprecht, 1966).
Hahn, F., ' "Siehe jetzt ist der Tag des Heils": Neuschöpfung und Versöhnung nach 2. Korinther 5,14–6,2', *EvT* 33.
Hainz, J., *Ekklesia: Strukturen paulinischer Gemeinde-Theologie und Gemeinde-Ordnung* (Regensburg: Verlag Friedrich Pustet, 1972).
Hammerton-Kelly, R., 'A Girardian Interpretation of Paul', *Semeia* 33 (1985), pp. 65-82.
Hasler, V., 'Das Evangelium des Paulus in Korinth. Erwägungen zur Hermeneutik'. *NTS* 30 (1984).
Hauerwas, S., 'Casuistry as a Narrative Art', *Int* 37 (1983), pp. 377-88.
Hays, R., 'Crucified with Christ: A Synthesis of 1 and 2 Thessalonians, Philemon, Philippians, and Galatians' (SBLSP; Atlanta: Scholars Press, 1988).
Hengel, M., *Crucifixion* (Philadelphia: Fortress Press, 1977).
—*The Atonement: The Origins of the Doctrine in the New Testament* (Philadelphia: Fortress Press, 1981).
Héring, J., *The Second Epistle of St Paul to the Corinthians* (trans. A.W. Heathcote and P.J. Allcock; London: Epworth, 1967).
Hickling, C., 'Is II Corinthians a Source for Early Church History?', *ZNW* 66 (1975), pp. 284-87.
Hock, R., *The Social Context of Paul's Ministry: Tentmaking and Apostleship* (Philadelphia: Fortress Press, 1980).
Holladay, C., *Theios Aner in Hellenistic Judaism: A Critique of the Use of this Category in New Testament Christology* (SBLDS, 40; Missoula: Scholars Press, 1977).
Holmberg, B., *Paul and Power: The Structure of Authority in the Primitive Church as Reflected in the Pauline Epistles* (Philadelphia: Fortress Press, 1978).
Hooker, M., ' "Beyond the Things which are Written": An Examination of I Cor. IV.6'. *NTS* 10 (1963–64), pp. 295-309.
—'Interchange in Christ', *JTS* 22 (1971), pp. 349-61.
Horsley, R., 'Pneumatikos vs. Psychikos Distinctions of Spiritual Status Among the Corinthians', *HTR* 69 (1976), pp. 269-88.
—'Wisdom of Word and Words of Wisdom', *CBQ* 39 (1977), pp. 224-39.
Hughes, P.E., *Paul's Second Epistle to the Corinthians* (Grand Rapids: Eerdmans, 1962).
Humphries, R., 'Paul's Rhetoric of Argumentation in I Corinthians 1-4' (PhD dissertation, Berkley, The Graduate Theological Union, 1979).

Hurd, J.C., *The Origin of I Corinthians* (New York: Seabury, 1965).
Jervell, J., 'Der schwache Charismatiker', in J. Friedrich, W. Pöhlmann and P. Stuhlmacher (eds.), *Rechtfertigung* (Festschrift Käsemann; Tübingen: Mohr; Göttingen: Vandenhoeck & Ruprecht, 1976).
Jewett, R., *Paul's Anthropological Terms* (Leiden: Brill, 1971).
—'The Redaction of 1 Corinthians and the Trajectory of the Pauline School'. *JAAR* 44/4 (1978), pp. 398-444.
Johnson, H., 'Ideology', in *The International Encyclopedia of the Social Sciences*, VII (New York: Macmillan, 1968–73), pp. 66-85.
Judge, E.A., 'Cultural Conformity and Innovation in Paul: Some Clues from Contemporary Documents', *TynBul* 35 (1984).
—'The Early Christians as a Scholastic Community', *JRH* 1 (1960), pp. 4-15, 125-37.
—'Paul's Boasting in Relation to Contemporary Professional Practice', *Australian Biblical Review* (Oct., 1968), pp. 37-50.
—'The Social Identity of the First Christians: A Question of Method in Religious History', *JRH* 11 (1980), pp. 201-17.
—'St Paul as a Radical Critic of Society', *Interchange* 16 (1974), pp. 191-203.
Käsemann, E., 'Die Legitimät des Apostels. Eine Untersuchung zu II Korinther 10–13', *ZNW* 41 (1942), pp. 33-71.
—*New Testament Questions of Today* (Philadelphia: Fortress Press, 1969).
—'The Saving Significance of the Death of Jesus', in *Perspectives on Paul* (Philadelphia: Fortress Press, 1971), pp. 32-59.
Keck, L., 'On the Ethos of Early Christians', *JAAR* 42 (1974), pp. 435-52.
Kertelge, K., 'Das Verständnis des Todes Jesu bei Paulus', in *idem* (ed.), *Der Tod Jesu. Deutungen im Neuen Testament* (Freiburg/Basel/Vienna, 1976), pp. 114-36.
Koester, H., *Introduction to the New Testament* (2 vols.; Philadelphia: Fortress Press, 1982).
Kuhn, H., 'Jesus als Gekreuzigter in der frühchristlichen Verkündigung bis zur Mitte des 2. Jahrunderts', *ZTK* 72 (1975).
Kümmel, G.W., *Introduction to the New Testament* (trans. H.C. Kee; Nashville and New York: Abingdon Press, 1975).
Lambrecht, J., 'The Nekrosis of Jesus: Ministry and Suffering in 2 Cor.4, 7-15', in Vanhoye (ed.), *L'Apôtre Paul*.
—'Transformation in 2 Cor. 3,18', *Bib* 64 (1983), pp. 243-54.
Lietzmann, H., *An die Korinther I/II* (HNT, 9; Tübingen: Mohr, 1969).
Lim, T., 'Not in Persuasive Words of Wisdom, but in the Demonstration of the Spirit and Power', *NovT* 29 (1987).
Lindbeck, G., *The Nature of Doctrine* (London: SPCK, 1984).
Luck, U., 'σωφρονέω', *TDNT*, VII, pp. 1097-1104.
Lüdemann, G., *Paulus, der Heidenapostel, Band II. Antipaulinismus im frühen Christentum* (Göttingen: Vandenhoeck & Ruprecht, 1983).
Luz, U., 'Theologia Crucis als Mitte der Theologie im Neuen Testament', *EvT* 34, (1974), pp. 116-41.
MacDonald, M.Y., *The Pauline Churches: A Socio-historical Study of Institutionalization in the Pauline and Deutero-Pauline Writings* (SNTSMS, 60; Cambridge: Cambridge University Press, 1988).
MacDowell, D.M., '*Hybris* in Athens', *Greece and Rome* 23 (1976), pp. 14-31.

MacIntyre, A., *After Virtue: A Study in Moral Theory* (Notre Dame, IN: University of Notre Dame Press, 1981).
MacMullen, R., *Roman Social Relations* (New Haven: Yale University Press, 1974).
Malherbe, A., 'Antisthenes and Odysseus, and Paul at War', *HTR* 76 (1983), pp. 143-73.
—'Exhortation in First Thessalonians', *NovT* 25.3 (1983), pp. 238-56.
Malina, B., *The New Testament World: Insights from Cultural Anthropology* (Atlanta: John Knox, 1981).
Marshall, P., *Enmity in Corinth: Social Conventions in Paul's Relations with the Corinthians* (Tübingen: Mohr, 1987).
—'*Hybrists* Not Gnostics in Corinth' (SBLSP; Atlanta: Scholars Press, 1984), pp. 275-87.
Martin, R., *2 Corinthians* (Waco, TX: Word Books, 1986).
Martyn, J.L., 'Epistemology at the Turn of the Ages: 2 Corinthians 5.16', in W. Farmer, C.F.D. Moule and R.R. Niebuhr (eds.), *Christian History and Interpretation* (Cambridge: Cambridge University Press, 1967), pp. 269-87.
McWilson, R., 'Gnosis at Corinth', in M.D. Hooker and S.G. Wilson (ed.), *Paul and Paulinism* (Festschrift Barrett; London: SPCK, 1982).
Meeks, W., *The First Urban Christians* (New Haven: Yale University Press, 1983).
—*The Moral World of the First Christians* (Philadelphia: Westminster Press, 1986).
—' "Since then you Would Need to Go out of the World": Group Boundaries in Pauline Christianity', in T.J. Ryan (ed.), *Critical History and Biblical Faith: New Testament Perspectives* (The Annual Publication of the College Theology Society; Villanova, PA: The College Theology Society, 1979), pp. 4-29.
Minear, P., 'Christ and the Congregation: 1 Corinthians 5-6', *RevExp* 80 (1983), pp. 341-50.
Mott, S., 'The Power of Giving and Receiving: Reciprocity in Hellenistic Benevolence', in G.F. Hawthorne (ed.), *Current Issues in Biblical and Patristic Interpretation* (Festschrift Tenney; Grand Rapids: Eerdmans, 1975).
Moule, C.F.D., *An Idiom-Book of New Testament Greek* (Cambridge: Cambridge University Press, 1953).
Munck, J., 'The Church without Factions: Studies in I Corinthians 1-4', reprinted in *Paul and the Salvation of Mankind* (London: SCM Press, 1959), pp. 135-67.
Murphy-O'Connor, J., 'Freedom or the Ghetto (1 Cor. VIII, 1-13; , 23-XI, 1)', *RB* (1978).
Newton, M., *The Concept of Purity at Qumran and in the Letters of Paul* (SNTSMS, 53; Cambridge: Cambridge University Press, 1985).
Neyrey, J., 'Body Language in 1 Corinthians: The Use of Anthropological Models for Understanding Paul and his Opponents', *Semeia* 35 (1986), pp. 129-70.
O'Collins, G., 'Power Made Perfect in Weakness: 2 Cor 12.9-10', *CBQ* 33 (1971), pp. 528-37.
Olson, S., 'Epistolary Uses of Expressions of Self-Confidence', *JBL* 103/4 (1984), pp. 585-97.
Painter, J., 'Paul and the πνευματικόι at Corinth', in M.D. Hooker and S.G. Wilson (eds.), *Paul and Paulinism* (Festschrift Barrett; London: SPCK, 1982).
Patte, D., *Paul's Faith and the Power of the Gospel* (Philadelphia: Fortress Press, 1983).
Pearson, B., *The Pneumatikos-Psychikos Terminology in I Corinthians* (SBLDS, 12; Missoula, MT: Scholars Press, 1973).

Petersen, N., *Rediscovering Paul: Philemon and the Sociology of Paul's Narrative World* (Philadelphia: Fortress Press, 1985).

Plank, K., *Paul and The Irony of Affliction* (SBLSS; Atlanta: Scholars Press, 1987).

Plummer, A., *A Critical and Exegetical Commentary on the Second Epistle to the Corinthians* (Edinburgh: T. & T. Clark, 1915).

Pogoloff, S., *LOGOS AND SOPHIA: The Rhetorical Situation of 1 Corinthians* (SBLDS, 134; Atlanta: Scholars Press, 1992).

Richardson, P., 'Judgement in Sexual Matters in 1 Cor.6.1-11', *NovT* 15.1 (1983), pp. 37-58.

Ricoeur, P., 'The Metaphorical Process', *Semeia* 4 (1975), pp. 75-106.

Rissi, M., *Studien zum zweiten Korintherbrief. Der Alte Bund—Der Predigt—Der Tod* (Zurich: Zwngli Verlag, 1969).

Robertson, A., and A. Plummer, *A Critical and Exegetical Commentary on the First Epistle of St Paul to the Corinthians* (ICC; Edinburgh: T. & T. Clark, 1914).

Robinson, J.A.T., *The Body: A Study in Pauline Theology* (London: SCM Press, 1952).

Robinson, W.C., 'Word and Power (I Corinthians 1.17-2.5)', in J. McDowell (ed.), *Soli Deo Gloria. New Testament Studies in Honor of William Childs Robinson* (Richmond, VA: John Knox, 1968), pp. 68-82.

Roetzel, C., *Judgement in the Community* (Leiden: Brill, 1972).

Ruef, J., *Paul's First Letter to Corinth* (Philadelphia: Westminster Press, 1971).

Sanders, B., 'Imitating Paul: I Cor 4.16', *HTR* 74 (1981), pp. 553-63.

Sanders, E.P., *Paul and Palestinian Judaism* (Philadelphia: Fortress Press, 1977).

Sänger, D., 'Die δυνατόι im I Kor 1.26', *ZNW* 76 (1985), pp. 285-91.

Sasse, 'κόσμος', *TDNT*, III, pp. 867-98.

Schoeps, H.J., *Paul: The Theology of the Apostle in the Light of Jewish Religious History* (Philadelphia: Westminster Press, 1961).

Schrage, W., 'Leid, Kreuz und Eschaton: Die Peristasenkataloge als Merkmale paulinischer theologia crucis und Eschatologie', *EvT* 34 (1974), pp. 141-75.

Schutz, A., and T. Luckman, *The Structures of the Life World* (Evanston, IL: Northwestern University Press, 1973).

Schütz, J., *Paul and the Anatomy of Apostolic Authority* (SNTSMS, 26; Cambridge: Cambridge University Press, 1975).

Schweitzer, A., *The Mysticism of Paul the Apostle* (New York: Seabury Press, 1968).

Scroggs, R., 'Paul: SOFOS and PNEUMATIKOS', *NTS* 14 (1967), pp. 33-55.

Segal, R., Review of *The Meaning of Aphrodite*, *RSR* 10 (1984).

Smith, D., 'Social Obligation in the Context of Communal Meals: A Study of the Christian Meal in 1 Corinthians in Comparison with Greco-Roman Communal Meals' (unpublished PhD Thesis, Harvard University, 1980).

Smith, J.Z., 'The Influence of Symbols upon Social Change: A Place on which to Stand', *Worship* 44 (1970), pp. 457-74.

Smith, W.H., 'The Function of 2 Corinthians 3.7–4.6 in its Epistolary Context' (PhD dissertation, Southern Baptist Theological Seminary, 1983).

Spencer, A.B., 'The Wise Fool (and the Foolish Wise): A Study of Irony in Paul', *NovT* 23 (1981), pp. 349-60.

Spittler, R., 'The Limits of Ecstasy: an Exegesis of 2 Corinthians 12.1-10', in G.F. Hawthorne (ed.), *Current Issues in Biblical and Patristic Interpretation* (Festschrift Tenney; Grand Rapids: Eerdmans, 1975), pp. 259-66.

Stuhlmacher, P., 'Achtzehn Thesen zur paulinische Kreuztheologie', in J. Friedrich, W. Pöhlmann and P. Stuhlmacher (eds.), *Rechtfertigung* (Festschrift Käsemann; Tübingen: Mohr, 1976).
—'Erwägungen zum ontologischen Charakter der *kainé ktisis* bei Paulus', *EvT* 27 (1967), pp. 1-35.
Tannehill, R., *Dying and Rising with Christ* (Berlin: Töpelmann, 1967).
Theissen, G., *Psychologische Aspekte paulinischer Theologie* (Göttingen: Vandenhoeck & Ruprecht, 1983).
—*The Social Setting of Pauline Christianity* (Philadelphia: Fortress Press, 1982).
Thiselton, A., 'Realized Eschatology at Corinth', *NTS* 24 (1978).
—*The Two Horizons* (Grand Rapids: Eerdmans, 1980).
Vernon, G., 'The Symbolic Interactionist Approach to the Sociology of Religion', in J. Matthes (ed.), *International Yearbook for the Sociology of Religion. Sociology of Religion: Theoretical Perspectives (I)* (Cologne und Opladen: Westdeutscher Verlag, 1966).
Vielhauer, P., 'Oikodome: Das Bild vom Bau in der christlichen Literatur vom Neuen Testament bis Clemens Alexandrinus', in G. Klein (ed.), *Oikodome: Aufsätze zum Neuen Testament* (Munich: Kaiser Verlag, 1979), pp. 1-168.
Wanamaker, C.A., 'Christ as Divine Agent in Paul', *SJT* 39 (1986), pp. 517-28.
Watson, F., *Paul, Judaism and the Gentiles* (SNTSMS, 56; Cambridge: Cambridge University Press, 1986).
Weder, H., *Das Kreuz Jesu bei Paulus* (Göttingen: Vandenhoeck & Ruprecht, 1981).
Weiss, J., *Der erste Korintherbrief* (Göttingen: Vandenhoeck & Ruprecht, 1897).
Welborn, L.L., 'On the Discord in Corinth: 1 Corinthians 1–4 and Ancient Politics', *JBL* 106 (1987), pp. 83-113.
Whiteley, D.E.H., *The Theology of St Paul* (Oxford: Basil Blackwell, 1964).
Wilckens, U., 'Das Kreuz Christi als die Tiefe der Weisheit Gottes zu I Kor 2.1-16', in L. De Lorenzi (ed.), *Paolo a Una Chiesa Divisa* (Rome: Abbazia di S. Paolo, 1980).
—*Weisheit und Torheit. Eine exegetisch-religionsgeschichtliche Studie zu I Kor 1 und 2* (BHT, 26; Tübingen: Mohr, 1959).
—'Zu I Kor 2.1-16', in C. Andersen and G. Klein (eds.), *Theologia crucis—Signum crucis* (Festschrift Dinkler; Tübingen: Mohr, 1979), pp. 501-37.
Wilder, A., *Jesus' Parables and the War of Myths* (Philadelphia: Fortress Press, 1982).
Williams, R., 'Values', in the *International Encyclopedia of the Social Sciences* (New York: Macmillan, 1968–73), pp. 283-91.
Willis, W., 'Apostolic Apologia? The Form and Function of 1 Corinthians 9', *JSNT* 24 (1985), pp. 33-48.
—*Idol Meat in Corinth, The Pauline Argument in 1 Corinthians 8 and 10* (SBLDS, 68; Chico, CA: Scholars Press, 1985).
Windisch, H., *Der zweite Korintherbrief* (Göttingen: Vandenhoeck & Ruprecht, 1924).
Wuellner, W., 'Greek Rhetoric and Pauline Argumentation', in W. Schoedel and R. Wilken (eds.), *Early Christian Literature and the Classical Intellectual Tradition* (Paris: Editions Beauchesne, 1979).
—'Paul as Pastor: The Function of Rhetorical Questions in First Corinthians', in Vanhoye (ed.), *L'Apôtre Paul*, pp. 46-77.

INDEXES

INDEX OF REFERENCES

OLD TESTAMENT

Exodus		*Jeremiah*		*Acts*	
12.6	110	9.22-23	74	18.1-3	166
12.14-20	110	9.22	58	18.24-28	50
				18.24	54
Isaiah					
29.14	69				

NEW TESTAMENT

Romans		11.29	122, 123	1–2	51, 53, 54, 77
1–14	125	12–14	124		
1.16-32	13	12	124, 125	1	48, 55, 79
1.16	65	12.3	80	1.2	60, 91, 102
1.18-31	124	12.6	199	1.4-5	199
1.26-29	125	12.23	124	1.4	199
3.21-29	122	12.25	124	1.9	61, 102
3.24-25	12	13	125	1.10–4.21	38, 42, 59, 61, 75, 81, 86, 172, 174
4.16	124	14	125		
5.8	145	15.2	118		
6.1-11	61, 182	15.3	118		
6.3-11	60	16	163	1.10-17	183, 200
6.6-11	212			1.10	37, 39, 59, 68, 81, 102
6.9	145	*1 Corinthians*			
8.3	15	1–4	37-39, 41, 45, 47, 48, 50, 57-59, 61, 62, 64, 68, 72, 75, 76, 83, 85-87, 93, 99, 103, 108, 109, 114, 182	1.11-12	38
8.34-35	145			1.11	39, 85, 102
10.17	123			1.12	38, 39, 45, 47-50
11.1	124				
11.17-34	124			1.13	60
11.21	123			1.14-17	60
11.22	123, 124			1.17–2.5	41, 54
11.23-26	124			1.17-25	56
11.24	124, 125			1.17	37, 41, 53, 54, 61, 65, 76, 77, 168, 172
11.26	122				
11.27	122, 123	1–3	69, 79		

Index of References

1.18–2.16	51	2.1-16	39, 50, 74	3.6-9	56
1.18–2.5	66	2.1-5	40, 53, 74	3.6	50
1.18-31	21, 58, 78, 99, 122	2.1-4	37, 65, 66, 75, 78, 84, 168, 174	3.10-15 3.10-14 3.10-11	37 61 69
1.18-29	76			3.10	50, 63, 106, 199
1.18-25	34, 38, 40, 59, 64, 68-75, 77, 78, 81-83, 93, 107, 114, 194	2.1-2 2.1 2.2	59, 69 41, 53, 54, 75, 77, 102, 172 62, 74, 84, 212	3.16-23 3.16-17 3.16 3.17	93 92, 93, 109 92, 94, 105 102
1.18	49, 61, 65, 66, 69, 71, 72	2.3-5 2.3-4 2.4-5	200 53, 74 77	3.19-20 3.19 3.21-22	79 64, 93 57
1.19–2.5	66	2.4	41, 53, 54, 65, 75, 77,	3.21	57, 58, 76, 78
1.19-25	67		133, 172	3.22	50
1.19-21	67, 69				
1.19	69	2.5	53, 75, 76, 78	4 4.1-21	48 40
1.20-24	66				
1.20-21	53	2.6-16	42, 55, 56, 63	4.1-16 4.1	48 194
1.20	40, 64				
1.21-24	55	2.6-10	38	4.3	41, 172
1.21	63, 64, 67, 72	2.6 2.7	40, 64 55	4.6-13 4.6-10	81 47, 48
1.22	52, 67	2.8	71, 187, 210	4.6-7	78
1.23-24	69, 71, 84	2.12	63, 64	4.6	50, 54, 57,
1.23	69	2.13-16	55		60, 79, 80,
1.24	66	2.14–3.4	174		84, 102,
1.25	71, 72, 78, 210	2.14 2.15	63, 64 63	4.7	116, 173 47, 57, 58, 81, 173
1.26-31	65, 72	3–4	51	4.8-13	43, 83, 207
1.26-29	72	3	52	4.8-10	42, 98
1.26-28	69, 82, 173	3.1-4	41, 66, 73	4.8	44, 45, 57,
1.26	40, 43, 45, 47, 48, 62-64, 72, 73, 76, 78, 96, 98, 100, 102	3.1-3 3.1 3.2 3.3-15	63, 80 40, 67, 102, 172 41, 172 48	4.9-13	62, 81, 173 81-84, 113, 114, 166, 173
1.27-29	72	3.3-4	50	4.9	81, 82
1.27-28	72-74, 78	3.3	40, 41, 60, 67, 77, 78	4.10-12 4.10	76 42, 43, 45,
1.27	64, 72, 76, 102, 210	3.4-23	49		48, 57, 62, 66, 82, 172,
1.28	72	3.4	40, 41, 48, 50, 52		173
1.29-31	76, 78				
1.29	57, 74	3.5–4.5	79	4.11-13	42, 43, 83,
1.30	65, 102	3.5-15	40, 50, 77		172
1.31	57, 58, 74	3.5	41, 50, 52, 79, 194	4.11-12 4.11	42, 82 174
2	55				

1 Corinthians (cont.)		6.1-6	82, 99, 114	8.11-12	116	
4.12-13	82, 114	6.1-2	102	8.11	85, 106, 116	
4.12	42, 174	6.1	90, 113	8.12-14	174	
4.13	42, 81	6.2	105, 113	8.12	117, 118	
4.14-21	84	6.3	105	9	83, 117, 118, 167	
4.14	81, 83	6.5-8	102			
4.15-17	83	6.6	90	9.1-2	150	
4.15	84, 206	6.7-8	112	9.3-18	166, 167, 174	
4.16-17	60, 81	6.7	83, 113, 114			
4.16	59, 79, 81, 84, 114, 205	6.8	113	9.13	105	
		6.9-11	99, 112-14	9.24	105	
4.17	59, 84	6.9-10	113	10–11	90	
4.18-19	109, 173	6.9	90, 105	10	115	
4.18	57, 76	6.10	113	10.1-22	115	
4.19-20	77, 109	6.11	60, 91, 113	10.1	102	
4.19	57	6.12-20	112, 113	10.11	92	
4.21	41, 84	6.12	95, 98, 107, 109	10.16	118	
5–14	85-89, 93, 96-98, 100, 101, 103, 104, 107-109			10.17	119, 120	
		6.13-14	105	10.23–11.1	82	
		6.14	108	10.23	95, 98, 107, 109	
		6.15	105			
		6.16	105	10.25-27	100	
5–10	120	6.19	92, 105	10.27	90	
5–7	90, 113	7.1-16	95, 96	10.33–11.1	118	
5–6	96, 109	7.12-16	100	11–14	118	
5	40, 109	7.12-15	90	11.2-16	118	
5.1-12	109	7.12	102	11.17-34	95, 97, 118, 120	
5.1-2	107, 174	7.14	102			
5.1	90, 99	7.15	102	11.17-22	183	
5.2	57, 60, 109, 173	7.17-24	100	11.20	118	
		7.17	102	11.21	119	
5.4	109	7.23-24	105	11.22	119	
5.6-7	110	7.24	102	11.23-26	102, 120, 121	
5.6	24, 57, 105, 109	7.29	102			
		7.34	102	11.23-25	120	
5.7	85, 105, 110, 111	8–11	98, 101	11.24	121	
		8–10	97, 114, 115	11.26	85, 106	
5.8	111	8	90, 115, 118	11.27-29	120	
5.9-13	112	8.1-13	60, 82, 115	11.29	121	
5.9-11	112	8.1	57, 95, 107, 115, 116, 173, 174	11.33	102	
5.9-10	91, 100			12–14	90, 95, 101, 120, 205	
5.10	112					
5.11	102	8.4	106, 115	12	94, 106, 120, 121	
5.12	90, 99	8.7-12	115			
5.13	90	8.7	115	12.1	102	
6	109	8.9	95, 115, 118	12.2	90	
6.1-11	112-14	8.10	115	12.12-27	102, 205	
6.1-8	95	8.11-13	102, 117	12.12-26	98	

Index of References

12.13	91, 102, 106, 122, 213	2.14–3.6	126, 164	4.11	131, 132, 137	
		2.14	133			
		2.17	133	4.12	131, 132, 141, 142, 166	
12.20	205	3.1-6	186			
12.25	205	3.1	143			
12.26	180	3.2	150	4.13-18	188	
13.4	57, 60, 173	3.4	129, 134	4.13	134	
14	94, 106, 120, 121	3.5	133, 134	4.14–5.10	134	
		3.7–4.6	186, 187	4.15	142, 143, 199	
14.2	95	3.7-18	186, 188			
14.5	96	3.7-11	154	4.16-18	188	
14.6	102	3.10-11	187	4.16	132	
14.12	96	3.10	187	4.17	188	
14.20	102	3.12	134	4.40	131	
14.22-24	90	3.18	132, 187	5.1-10	154	
14.26	96, 102	4	131	5.1-4	141	
14.33	102	4.1-16	130	5.3-7	145	
14.39	102	4.1-15	126	5.5	132	
15	107, 108	4.1	134	5.6	134	
15.3	19, 85, 145	4.2	150	5.8	134	
15.5	145	4.3-4	187	5.11-15	147, 151	
15.10	199	4.4	187	5.11-13	149	
15.27	15	4.5	195	5.11-12	126	
16.1	102	4.6	129, 130, 187	5.11	134, 143	
16.13-14	68			5.12-14	207	
16.15	102	4.7–5.19	126, 160	5.12-13	127, 133, 143	
16.17	39	4.7-18	127			
		4.7-14	139	5.12	127, 142-44, 149, 154, 186, 196	
		4.7-12	129, 130, 132, 136, 137, 139, 143, 149, 158, 187, 192			
2 Corinthians				5.13-14	149	
1–9	126, 135, 160			5.13	143, 145, 149, 150, 154	
1–7	160, 164, 189, 190					
1.3-7	180, 195, 205	4.7	130, 140	5.14-17	126	
1.8-10	130	4.8-12	130, 182	5.14-15	84, 112, 125, 142-44, 147, 149, 151-55, 189, 193, 199	
1.9	134	4.8-11	195			
1.12-14	160	4.8-10	194			
1.12	134, 199	4.8-9	130, 135, 137	5.14	142, 143, 145, 148, 149, 153, 155, 158, 207	
1.14	143					
1.15	134	4.8	130			
1.22	132	4.10-11	130, 135, 138, 141, 142			
1.24	150, 195			5.15	142, 143, 145, 148, 149, 153, 154, 157, 214	
2.1-5	127					
2.3	134	4.10	76, 126, 130-32, 136, 137, 140			
2.12-13	130					
2.14–7.4	134					
2.14–6.13	134					

2 Corinthians (cont.)		10.4-6	160	11.11	167
5.16-21	151	10.4-5	161	11.16	176, 177,
5.16-19	150, 151	10.4	160-62, 182		179
5.16-17	145, 151,	10.5-6	161, 182	11.17	177
	188	10.5	161, 162	11.18-21	179
5.16	151, 153-58	10.6	162, 184,	11.18	127
5.17	132, 148,		192, 202	11.19-20	177
	151-58	10.7	196	11.20	195
6.1	199	10.8	134, 160,	11.21-33	179
6.2	132, 154,		161, 180,	11.21	165, 179,
	155		182, 192,		180, 182
6.3-13	134		196, 200,	11.22-28	179
6.3-10	127		201, 209,	11.22	150, 168,
6.4-10	126, 130,		210		179
	194, 195	10.10	127, 161,	11.23-33	194
6.9	199		162, 164,	11.23-29	197
6.16	92		165, 174,	11.23-28	180, 194
7–15	131		181, 182,	11.23	179, 193,
7.4	134		184, 196,		194, 196
7.5-7	130		198	11.24-29	194
7.6-13	135	10.12-18	150	11.28-29	196
8	199	10.12-13	176, 177	11.29-30	182
8.1	199	10.12	150, 176,	11.29	165, 180,
8.2	167		191, 204		194
8.9	199	10.13	176	11.30	165, 179,
9.3	143	10.15	176		195
9.4	167	10.16	176	12.1-10	168, 174,
9.8	199	11.1–12.10	162, 169,		178, 184,
9.12	167		176		197
9.14	167, 199	11.1-33	177	12.2	178
9.15-18	167	11.1-4	182	12.4	178
10–13	56, 126,	11.1	177	12.5	165, 182
	135, 160,	11.2-4	184	12.7-9	178
	163-65, 167,	11.2	180, 196	12.7	197
	168, 170-72,	11.3-11	167	12.9-10	76, 178,
	174, 175,	11.3-4	161		182, 183,
	180, 182,	11.3	162, 196,		193, 197-
	190, 191,		197		200, 205,
	193, 202,	11.4	127, 162,		210, 211
	204, 210		197	12.9	165, 179,
10–12	167, 175,	11.5	134, 168		197, 199,
	177	11.6	165, 174,		200
10.1-2	161		184	12.10	165, 174,
10.1	162, 164,	11.7	127, 166,		194
	165, 181,		167, 174	12.11–13.14	201
	184, 196	11.9	167	12.11-12	198
10.2	160	11.10-11	180, 196	12.11	176, 177
10.3	161	11.10	127	12.12	127, 133,

	154, 168,	13.4	140, 141,	3.13-15	212
	174, 178,		181-84, 188,	3.14-15	212
	184		191, 193,	3.28	91, 122, 213
12.13	127, 167,		200, 201,	4.8-9	212
	174		203, 206,	4.31	212
12.14-15	180, 196		207, 210,	5.1	212
12.14	167		211	5.11	70
12.15	167, 195	13.5-10	126	5.24	21
12.19-21	126	13.5-7	184	6.14-15	212
12.19	160, 163,	13.5-6	192	6.14	14, 21, 182,
	180, 192,	13.5	163, 182,		213
	196, 200,		202, 207		
	201, 208,	13.6	134	*Philippians*	
	209	13.9	165, 182	2.6-11	181
12.20-21	163, 182,	13.10	160, 161,	2.7	15
	196, 197,		180, 182,	3.10	182
	200		192, 196,	4.15	167
12.20	163, 183-85,		200, 201,		
	192, 196,		208-10	*Colossians*	
	197, 200,	13.13	199	4.5	90
	206, 207,				
	209	*Galatians*		*1 Thessalonians*	
13.3-4	127, 165,	1.4	15	4.12	90
	200	1.11-24	201		
13.3	165, 174,	2.20	145, 182,		
	183, 184,		199		
	186, 197,	2.21	199		
	201, 207	3.1	14		

CLASSICAL AUTHORS

Aristotle		326D	79, 80	2.8.6	46
Pol.				16.1-4	46
5.1.6	47	Plutarch			
5.2.3-4	46	*Mor.*		Xenophon	
5.3.3	46	631 CDF	46	*Cry.*	
5.6.4-5	46	634 DEF	46	7.2.18	46
Plato		*Rhet.*			
Prt.		2.8.2-3	46		
320C–28D	80				

INDEX OF AUTHORS

Babcock, B.A. 71, 210, 211
Banks, R. 121
Barbour, R. 55
Barre, M.L. 180
Barrett, C.K. 38, 44, 50, 53, 54, 56,
    61, 63, 66, 72, 75, 77, 79, 109,
    110, 124, 130-33, 137, 148, 150,
    151, 163, 164, 170, 181, 184, 196,
    199
Bartchy, S. 173
Barton, S. 211
Beker, J.C. 27, 69, 129, 141
Berger, P. 29-35, 61, 62, 64, 67, 92,
    98, 99, 101, 103, 104, 128, 129,
    135, 137, 143, 145, 147, 148, 151-
    53, 188, 190, 191
Bernstein, B. 62
Bertram, G. 70, 71
Best, E. 61
Betz, H.D. 56, 98, 165, 177-79, 184
Beyer, H. 195
Black, D. 43
Black, M. 132
Blount, B. 14
Boers, H. 30, 34
Bruce, F.F. 71, 73, 131
Bultmann, R. 11, 21, 22, 24, 64, 67,
    73, 126, 127, 130, 131, 142, 144,
    145, 148, 149, 155, 181, 196, 201,
    207

Carrez, M. 130
Castelli, E. 84
Collange, J.F. 133
Conzelmann, H. 38, 52, 60, 63, 67,
    69, 74, 76, 95, 111, 199
Cosgrove, C. 212

Countryman, W. 113
Cousar, C. 20
Culpepper, A. 52

Dahl, N. 22, 38, 40-42, 44, 49, 50, 59,
    75, 86, 172
Davies, W.D. 12, 13
Davis, J. 38, 52
Deidun, T. 92, 105
Delling, G. 22, 23, 113
Douglas, M. 31, 62, 89, 90, 95-97,
    138
Dungan, D. 167
Dunn, J. 15, 16, 18, 19, 132, 144,
    146, 199, 200, 208

Elliott, J. 34, 35
Ellis, E. 58, 69, 169, 170
Esler, P. 35

Fee, G. 68, 79, 109-11, 113, 115, 120,
    123
Fisher, N.R.E. 46, 47
Fitzgerald, J.T. 43, 79-81, 83, 160,
    165, 172
Forbes, C. 43, 46, 165, 174-77, 179,
    180, 194-96
Foucault, M. 84
Funk, R. 17, 28, 37
Furnish, V. 87, 102, 104, 126, 130,
    131, 133-35, 142-46, 148-50, 156,
    157, 164, 168, 181, 182, 187, 195,
    196, 199, 201, 207

Gadamer, H.-G. 24-26
Geertz, C. 30-32, 104, 106, 117, 122,
    138, 152, 153

Index of Authors

Georgi, D. 14, 133, 171, 194
Güttgemanns, G. 131, 198

Hahn, F. 146, 157
Hainz, J. 161, 171
Hammerton-Kelly, R. 200
Hasler, V. 62, 84
Hauerwas, S. 103
Hays, R. 15, 29
Hengel, M. 18-20, 70, 145, 146, 194
Héring, J. 131, 133
Hickling, C.J.A. 127, 190
Hock, R. 82, 166
Holladay, C. 171
Holmberg, B. 165, 202-204
Hooker, M. 16, 79
Horsley, R. 40, 50, 51, 55
Hughes, P.E. 130
Humphries, R. 61, 62, 65, 68, 78
Hurd, J.C. 38, 39, 50, 85, 109

Jervell, J. 165, 198
Jewett, R. 68, 85
Johnson, H. 208
Judge, E.A. 60, 76, 78, 166-69, 173, 177, 193, 208-10

Käsemann, E. 21, 22, 44, 69, 93, 135, 144, 154, 170, 191
Keck, L. 31, 33, 208
Kertelge, K. 23, 144, 145
Koester, H. 26, 212, 213
Kosmala, H. 124
Kuhn, H.W. 23
Kümmel, G.W. 66, 85, 181

Lambrecht, J. 131, 132, 141, 187
Lanham, R. 211
Lategan, B. 20
Levinson, J. 17
Lietzmann, H. 66, 71, 130, 133, 161, 165, 181
Lim, T. 75
Lindbeck, G. 137
Louw, J. 13
Luck, U. 143
Luckmann, T. 29-35, 61, 62, 64, 67, 92, 98, 99, 101, 103, 104, 128, 129, 135, 137, 145, 147, 148, 151-53, 188, 190, 191
Lüdemann, G. 174, 175
Luther, M. 17, 21
Luz, U. 23

MacDonald, M. 206
MacDowell, D.M. 45, 46
MacIntyre, A. 87, 88, 103
MacMullen, R. 167
Malherbe, A. 87, 104, 161, 162
Malina, B. 42, 170, 189, 208
Marshall, P. 35, 42, 45, 46, 53, 54, 58, 74, 80-83, 164, 165, 167-70, 173-77, 179, 196
Martin, R. 130, 131, 181, 184, 201
Martyn, J.L. 156-59
Meeks, W. 35, 60, 61, 88-91, 96-98, 100, 102, 103, 107, 115, 118, 121, 122, 140, 169, 173, 184, 201-203, 206
Minear, P. 109
Mott, S.C. 167
Moule, C.F.D. 141, 151
Munck, J. 39, 49, 58
Murphy-O'Connor, J. 117

Newton, M. 90, 92, 93, 110
Neyrey, J. 90, 93, 95, 96
Nida, E. 13
Nock, A.D. 44, 104
North, H. 58

O'Collins, G. 193, 198-200
Olbrechts-Tyteca, L. 68
Olson, S. 134, 135

Patte, D. 88
Pearson, B. 38, 55
Perelman, C. 68
Petersen, N. 34, 104, 124, 206
Plank, K. 43, 83
Plummer, A. 54, 55, 59, 67, 79, 130, 131, 133, 144, 181, 201
Pogoloff, S. 45, 77

Richardson, P. 112, 113
Ricoeur, P. 30, 131, 132, 136

Rissi, M. 133, 140, 141
Robertson, A. 54, 55, 59
Robinson, J.A.T. 196
Robinson, W.C., Jr 41, 69
Roetzel, C. 109, 110
Ruef, J. 109

Sanders, B. 80, 83, 84
Sanders, E.P. 10, 11, 16, 146
Sänger, D. 48
Schoeps, H.J. 11
Schrage, W. 139
Schutz, A. 147
Schütz, J. 61, 65, 72, 73, 154, 157, 165, 192, 194, 195, 197, 201-205, 207
Schweitzer, A. 9, 10
Scroggs, R. 51
Shils, E. 204
Smith, D. 118-20, 124
Smith, J.Z. 211
Smith, W.H., Jr 186, 187
Spencer, A.B. 179, 211
Spittler, R. 178, 179
Stendahl, K. 17
Stowers, S. 12, 15

Stuhlmacher, P. 23, 156, 157

Tannehill, R. 10, 111, 125, 134, 136, 139, 153, 201
Theissen, G. 35, 43, 48, 57, 72, 115, 119, 121, 122, 127, 135, 150, 164, 165, 173
Thiselton, A. 26, 27, 41, 44

Vernon, G. 31, 209
Vielhauer, P. 210

Wanamaker, C.A. 82
Watson, F. 54
Weber, M. 106, 203, 204
Weder, H. 71, 72
Weiss, J. 117
Welborn, L.L. 38, 47, 57
Wilckens, U. 38, 50, 51, 74
Wilder, A. 152
Williams, R.M. 49, 185, 186
Williams, S. 19, 189
Willis, W. 115-17
Windisch, H. 144, 161
Wuellner, W. 68, 69, 105, 107